Y0-BUY-044

Community Service

Community Service

ENCOUNTER WITH STRANGERS

Howard B. Radest

HN
90
.V64
R33
1993
West

PRAEGER

Westport, Connecticut
London

Library of Congress Cataloging-in-Publication Data

Radest, Howard B.
    Community service : encounter with strangers / Howard B. Radest.
      p.   cm.
    Includes bibliographical references and index.
    ISBN 0–275–94186–8 (alk. paper)
    1. Voluntarism—United States. 2. Social service—United States.
    3. National service—United States. I. Title.
    HN90.V64R33 1993
    361.3′7—dc20   93–17116

British Library Cataloguing in Publication Data is available.

Copyright © 1993 by Howard B. Radest

All rights reserved. No portion of this book may be
reproduced, by any process or technique, without the
express written consent of the publisher.

Library of Congress Catalog Card Number: 93–17116
ISBN: 0–275–94186–8

First published in 1993

Praeger Publishers, 88 Post Road West, Westport, CT 06881
An imprint of Greenwood Publishing Group, Inc.

Printed in the United States of America

The paper used in this book complies with the
Permanent Paper Standard issued by the National
Information Standards Organization (Z39.48–1984).

10 9 8 7 6 5 4 3 2 1

COPYRIGHT ACKNOWLEDGMENTS

The author and publisher gratefully acknowledge permission to reprint the following copyrighted material:

Combining Service and Learning: A Resource Book for Community and Public Service, Volumes I and II, 1990, published by the National Society for Internships and Experiential Education, 3509 Haworth Drive, Suite 207, Raleigh, NC 27609–7229, 919–787–3263.

Robert Bellah, et al., *Habits of the Heart: Individualism and Commitment in American Life.* Copyright © 1985 The Regents of the University of California.

Nel Noddings, *Caring: A Feminine Approach to Ethics and Moral Education.* Copyright © 1984 The Regents of the University of California.

Wilson McWilliams, *Idea of Fraternity in America.* Copyright © 1973 The Regents of the University of California.

For Jes and Nora and Robert
and
For Karen and Michael

I would like to thank the University Seminars at Columbia University for assistance in the preparation of the manuscript for publication. The ideas presented have benefitted from discussions in the University Seminar on Moral Education.

Contents

Preface

This book is the work of many and the responsibility of one. Family, colleagues, students and friends have taught me the realities of altruism and the puzzles of service. Above all, they have taught me to listen to the unspoken dialogue, the questions people are afraid to ask, the doubts they are hesitant to voice, the answers they are embarrassed to give. Listening to it is even more necessary when everyone agrees that it's a good thing to be doing good things. Reflection, criticism and skepticism then have a certain urgency. That is my sense of things not because I am a cynic but because human experience is never unalloyed, never without its ambiguities.

The organization of this book is an effort to uncover the unspoken dialogue. I open in Chapters 1 and 2 with the politics of the National and Community Service Act of 1990 and with my experience as a teacher and school administrator. The puzzles of community service begin to appear. Focusing them is what I call "Rachel's dilemma." She knows she is doing a good thing but she cannot say what it is she is really doing—and she is not alone. Then, in Chapters 3 and 4, I review the present scene and its roots in the settlement house, the New Deal, and the Peace Corps. As this project advances, two terms emerge that expose the ambiguities of the subject, need and service. Both seem self-evident; both stir up a number of questions. Need and service are the themes of Chapters 5 and 6. Putting things together in Chapters 7, 8 and 9, I connect community service with developmental psychology, with schooling, and with democracy. Finally, in Chapter 10, I suggest the moral and political preconditions for a community service worth supporting.

My thinking on community service was shaped by my colleagues for twelve years in the Ethics Department of The Ethical Culture-Fieldston Schools. I am grateful for the creativity and the critical skill of Lori Gold, Mal Goodman, Harold Kelvin, Alejandro Nivon, Elizabeth Saenger, and Judith Stecher. I am particularly indebted to Angela Vassos who headed the Service-Ethics program at Fieldston and who helped many other schools develop their own projects. One of my students, Rachel Hochhauser, played a special role in stimulating my reflections although she may be surprised to learn how important her efforts were to me. My colleagues in the University Seminar on Moral Education at Columbia University were a continuing reminder of the virtues of critical inquiry and critical intelligence. Aaron Warner, director of the University Seminars and an old and dear friend, arranged for a grant that facilitated the preparation of the manuscript. My colleague at the University of South Carolina-Beaufort, Gordon Haist, offered invaluable comments, suggestions and criticisms. I am grateful for the assistance of the National Society for Experiental Education (formerly the National Society for Internships and Experiental Education). "Barb" Baker of its staff was invaluable in suggesting materials to me and in researching their extensive library on community service. Naturally, none of these people are responsible for my interpretation of the possibilities and problems of community service.

A personal word of thanks for the support of my family. Robert, Nora and Jes, and Michael and Karen may not realize how much their models of loving connection have served my reflections. Finally, my wife, Rita, has—as usual—read my words with critical affection, always supportive yet never without suggestive ideas.

Community Service

Chapter One

A Preliminary Conversation

PUZZLES

I support community service. There are questions to be asked however, and I want to talk about them in preliminary fashion. I am struck by a certain lack of clarity about the aims of community service and the assumptions on which it rests. Unfortunately, so much of the argument about community service concerns its details that thought seems only afterthought and so much is caught in partisanship—political, psychological and educational—that the philosophic import of community service is scarcely addressed. Our thinking becomes only tactical. While I am surely not indifferent to the latter—I began my own encounter with community service as a practitioner—practice turns out to be problematic.

We congratulate ourselves on helping people in need, point with pride at the initiatives of young people, and agree that the economic benefits of service far exceed the costs. We applaud community service as a moral remedy for moral ill, as a promise of loyalty for social disarray and of educational effectiveness for school failure. These promises, however, suffer from the same ills as other examples of moralism and sentimentality. So, as we shall see, I cannot offer a simple statement of my theme—and this because of the nature of community service and not, I hope, because of confusions in my thinking.

At first glance, there seems little that is problematic in the notion of community service and therefore little that should excite philosophic attention. To be sure, as public debate about proposed projects or laws or finances illustrates, there are practical problems, differences of emphasis, and many ideological controversies.[1] But despite these quarrels, community service seems both a good in itself and good for praiseworthy purposes. To serve others and not just oneself is, after all, a virtue, like courage and magnanimity and truthfulness, or so it would seem to most of us.

We take it for granted that we need a remedy for the so-called selfishness of the young who are regarded ambivalently as the precious future and the annoying present. Since service is supposed to teach responsibility, it is, in a sense, seen as a cure for youthfulness itself. Community service thus appears both as a children's crusade and a form of punishment. Indeed, we reveal ourselves when a criminal is sentenced to perform "community service." Finally, we agree that a democratic society needs active citizens and community service teaches active citizenship. Our intuitive response to community service then rests on the expectation that it will meet at least three distinct but related needs: social solidarity, moral growth, and effective citizenship. At the same time, we suppress its ambiguities and our own ambivalence as well. Already, then, what appears as a *prima facie* good raises a number of issues of relationship, that is, between self-expression and selfishness, between old and young, between society and its members.

A look at the term "community service" is suggestive of some of the things we will have to explore. Service needs a context which begins to appear in a sentence like "I serve you," or "We serve them," or whatever. This asks for clarification of the status of the "doer" as well as of the "done-to" and of the relationship between them. When "community" modifies "service," further thought is then needed about how that changes the service to be done. In our industrial culture with its separation of public, private, and intimate, it is possible to distinguish more clearly than in other cultures the service of parent to child or of friend to friend from that service that is intended by "community service." This suggests that community service entails a notion of impersonality, a departure from intimacy. At the same time, impersonality may so shape the relationship as to make it insulting to the one being done to and uninteresting to the doer. Finally, a service done impersonally may well be ineffective.

Functions and roles call attention to the fact that the sentence I have introduced needs a phrase like "by doing this rather than that and in this way rather than that," that is, by announcing what is to be done by the doer to/ with/ on behalf of the done-to and further why that counts as community service. Indeed, service must also be modified by a moral adjective. Some service is worthy of approval and some is not. Moreover, what looks like the "same" act may be worthy or unworthy depending upon how it is chosen and by whom, how it is done and by whom, and so forth. Finally, the justification for being a doer of service is often put in terms of some larger goal—ideological, religious, political, moral—as in "I serve you by doing this because it is commanded of me," or "because it is the right thing to do," or "because it is expected of a citizen." Similarly, the "done-to" may choose to accept or reject a service on some ground or other. And the proposed service itself is chosen with some criterion in mind that helps us decide what counts as a suitable and worthy response.

Despite the fact that community service is taken as a good, the story of community service in the United States reveals that little is done about it except under conditions of crisis. The "crisis" may be widely felt because of a common reading of a situation, for example, the alleged immorality of the young, or because of a common experience like war or pestilence. Or the "crisis" may reflect the views of some group or party, as in the "crisis of faith" which fundamentalists attribute to the secularization of society or as in the AIDS "crisis" first announced by the gay community. The implication of such crises is the blindness of the general population. A successful strategy then transforms an interest-group campaign into a public interest whether or not the situation warrants it on independent grounds. By contrast, a simple discovery of needs will not do. We must add some "charge" to an event in order to convert it into crisis.

By interpreting community service as a response to crisis, we are able to justify the expenditure of extra-usual energies. We are able to use a language of mobilization.[2] Military symbolism is not incidental. Hidden behind it is a desire for power. The motivations for instituting community service then includes implicit political premises. It is not sufficient for me to undertake a merely personal response or for some group to act quietly and privately. The community must be organized.

"Community" thus appears in two ways. It is a description of the arena—understood as a troubled arena from the point of view of the "doer"—within which service is to take place. At the same time, it is a description of the agent who may legitimately serve in time of crisis. That agent, at least in the United States, is often, as DeTocqueville noted, an "association."

> As soon as several of the inhabitants of the United States have taken up an opinion or a feeling which they wish to promote in the world, they look out for mutual assistance and as soon as they have found each other out, they combine. From that moment they are no longer isolated men, but a power seen from afar, whose actions serve for an example and whose language is listened to. The first time I heard in the United States that a hundred thousand men had bound themselves publicly to abstain from spirituous liquors, it appeared to me more like a joke than a serious engagement; and I did not at once perceive why these temperate citizens

could not content themselves with drinking water by their own firesides. I at last understood that these hundred thousand Americans, alarmed by the progress of drunkenness around them, had made up their minds to patronize temperance.[3]

Even those who take a *laissez-faire* approach to community service embed action in collectives. But, for them, the rallying cry is the "volunteer." Consequently a unique institution has developed with its own mores, goals, legitimacies and powers; that is, voluntary non-profit organizations have evolved into a "third sector" alongside the "private" and the "governmental" sectors.

As a response to crisis, community service is distorted, its promise overblown, and its complexities hidden by anxiety and faddism. Not the least of the consequences of a "crisis mentality" is the suppression of ambiguity and the simplification of reality into exclusive choices. The dangers of manipulation already present in the relationship of doer and done-to increase as crisis calls forth a psychology of "crusades" and "wars." We must have our enemies. We find them in those who do not agree that our crisis is everyone's crisis.

The present is reminiscent. As happens periodically, we believe ourselves to be in crisis and that we are living in time of moral decay.

America faces mounting problems. As the nation approaches the 21st century, citizens must tackle an enormous national debt, respond to the many people who live in poverty, and lessen the environmental damage that threatens the future of our air and our atmosphere. We may, however, be faced with an even bigger problem: the loss of civic participation to meet these challenges. Despite technological expertise that narrows geographical barriers, citizens have become more and more alienated from each other at a time when we need each other most.[4]

We are convinced that the needs of sociability and citizenship are not being met as, it is believed, they once upon a time were. Our presumed failure transforms ordinary discussion into high drama. We are, if the prevalent rhetoric is to be believed, living in a country that has lost its way morally, socially, economically and politically. Community service, then, finds its place in our consciousness, our language and our policies as a response to crisis and in a context of nostalgia for lost connections.

ONCE AGAIN—COMMUNITY SERVICE

Philanthropy has played a significant role in the American story. Ethnic self-help societies, children's aid, the relief of the poor, charitable giving appeared early in our history. With the development of a large middle class, however—particularly after World War II—the habit of giving money or service became a reality for millions of people. Campaigns for this or that worthy cause now appear daily; the media broadcast such appeals everywhere. And Americans respond. Typically, in 1988,

> Seventy-five percent of all families give an average of $790 a year to the causes of their choice, 20 million give 5 percent or more of their income to charity, and 23 million volunteer five or more hours a week. Contributions to voluntary organizations exceeded $100 billion in 1988 and 80 million people volunteered a total of 14.9 billion hours, which is worth at least another $150 billion.
> . . . One half of what is contributed comes from families with incomes under $30,000.[5]

It is little wonder, given the size of things, that even for those who do not feel nostalgia for the small town, the need to deal with manageable dimensions appears. As public relations campaigners know, getting people to give demands an identifiable focus like a sick child or a villainous illness. Because the problems resist personal solution, however, giving becomes a way of hiring service done. At the same time, the habit of giving is channeled into socially acceptable projects. Health—more particularly disease—is a ready and noncontroversial claimant for attention except where, as with AIDS, it raises sexual anxieties in a country still shaped by puritanism. Youth-serving agencies and church-related activities are major beneficiaries. The sheer number and frequency of appeals, however, deadens awareness of their human content so that "causes" gain support because of effective public manipulation and not necessarily on the ground of a rational assessment of priorities. The moral value of our benevolent impulses is mixed.

With thoughts in mind about the ambivalence of good things, I approach the current interest in "community service." And it is a current interest. There had been an evident lull between the "peace corps" idealism of the Kennedy years and the egoist moralism of the Reagan presidency. If the former conveyed a mood of global confidence and optimism, the latter revealed a cramped judgment about the essential weakness of those in "need." The 1980s called forth a reaction to the organized selfishness emanating from Washington and the corresponding self-seeking pervading the rest of the country. Interest in community service began to pick up. It is false, of course, to believe that the 1970s were passive. Volunteer organizations and fund-raising campaigns went right on doing their work. But, the young were not targeted for community service. Those few schools and colleges that had a habit of service continued it; those that didn't simply had another agenda. Independent schools, for example, had a long tradition of including community service in their programs. For some this was simply *noblesse oblige*, for others—as with the Friends schools and the Ethical Culture-Fieldston Schools—service represented a mixture of social idealism and pedagogy.

But things were changing. As a sign of renewed interest, the National Association of Independent Schools conducted a study of the subject in the mid–1980s. One of the first issues identified was the question of making it a "requirement" or leaving it "voluntary" for the students. Lee M. Levison noted,

> Among the nine schools visited (as in-depth case studies in NAIS research), students in required service programs were found to support required community service unequivocally. Asked if they would advocate changing from a required to a voluntary program, the common refrain was "Keep it mandatory. It is too easy not to do it." Many students echoed that sentiment: "If it was voluntary, I would not have done it." "If you don't require it, students would never do it. They would just pass it over." . . .
>
> Students in voluntary programs feel quite differently. "In a required program not everybody will be interested and they won't put everything into it. You should have people who want to do it." Required service "detracts from the voluntary nature of the program. It takes the heart out of it." . . . Required service, according to one student, "is stupid because you can't force someone to volunteer." Part of volunteering is the spirit of giving, which such students see as essential for *really* helping people. Making someone serve turns service into a job.[6]

By 1987, however, the Carnegie Foundation for the Advancement of Teaching was calling for a new "Carnegie Unit" so that a community service requirement would be added to those like English, mathematics, science, languages, and history that should be completed in order to earn a high school diploma.[7] In explaining its reasons, the text cited David W. Hornbeck, superintendent of schools in Maryland,

> The state "should make clear we believe helping to meet the needs of others is a fundamental component of being an effective adult."
>
> It has been demonstrated that students engaged in community service acquire a responsible attitude toward others, gain "feelings of self-esteem and personal adequacy," and usually have a better record of attendance and behavior than they otherwise would.
>
> Students learn important job skills. "Thus, while constituting a secondary objective of the service requirement, implementing elements of the work ethic could be taught effectively."
>
> Community service helps fill the human need for belonging. "It has been shown that contributing to society in a meaningful way leads to a feeling of belonging."[8]

The Carnegie Foundation noted the relationship of service and democracy, of altruism and career development, and of enriching studies with both curricular and co-curricular activities. Above all, it deplored the development of a nation of "takers" and a "me-me" generation.

In 1988, at one of the many conferences that began to appear on community service, Governor Rudy Perpich of Minnesota said,

> On my visits to schools around the state, I went to Marshall High School in Duluth where community service is a requirement and where most of that service is one-on-one mentoring. I could see in that program a certain chemistry and joy among the students. I could see that this mentoring program was clearly very successful. I saw that here is a way to achieve two things in one program—doing a better job with at-risk youth in schools and getting many more students interested in teaching as a career. So I have become an advocate of community service programs.[9]

With some seventy-five people in attendance, the conference was described by its organizers as a "summit meeting" of leaders who "are creating new opportunities and model programs for young people in community service." A review described programs in California, Massachusetts, Minnesota, Ohio, and Pennsylvania as well as the "Youth Volunteer Corps of Greater Kansas City" and "City Year in Boston."

By the fall of 1988, community service proponents joined in the typically American habit of celebrating a special "day." Organized by the Campus Outreach Opportunity League and Youth Service America, "A Day in the Life of Youth Service" aimed to "document, promote, and celebrate people making a difference."[10] And in its 1988–1989 annual report, Youth Service America—a national coordinating organization for various youth service programs—noted, "a national movement comes of age. For the first time over 600 leaders from all levels of the field convened at YSA's national conference in June 1989 to develop a common action agenda for the future."[11]

In February 1989, the newly elected President, George Bush, echoing his "thousand points of light" speech, asked the Congress for a four-year $100 million appropriation to fund a proposed "YES (Youth Entering Service) to America Foundation." It would seek matching funds from corporations and individuals and would encourage youth service initiatives as a way of dealing with the problems of the inner city.[12] In the *Phi Delta Kappan* (publication of the national honor society of education school graduates), Anne C. Lewis wrote,

> Congress is betting on a turnaround among young people—from the "me" generation to the "me too" generation. And so are a good many other people, including President Bush, Admiral James Watkins, the new secretary of energy; university presidents; youth advocates and workers; and

most of all young people themselves.... At least four bills have strong
support in Congress, either because they are sponsored by congressional
leaders or because they have the support of a growing number of organizations that are concerned with youth service.[13]

Later that year, the National Association of State Boards of Education
adopted a policy statement which read, "State boards should encourage
every school to develop community service programs as an integral part
of the elementary and secondary learning process. There is now docu-
mentation that participating in structured community service provides
significant benefits to both young people and their communities."[14]

In the fall of 1990, after the usual compromises, the National Community Services Act was passed by the Congress and signed by the
president. Presenting the "Conference Report," Senator Kennedy said,

> This legislation is a call to action for the nation ... It is also a hopeful sign
> that in spite of a divided government that plagues Congress and the
> Administration ... we have not lost the ability to work together on ques-
> tions that deeply affect our future ...
>
> This measure will remind Americans of all ages of the responsibilities
> of citizenship, but its most important result may well be its effect on young
> citizens in the earliest grades. No age is too young to begin meeting the
> needs of the community.[15]

Joining Senator Kennedy in supporting the legislation, President Bush
said,

> I am particularly pleased that S 1430 includes provisions for the initial
> funding of a private, nonprofit foundation that will promote the ethic of
> community service, disseminate information about successful local activ-
> ities to other communities across the Nation, and stimulate the develop-
> ment of new leaders and their community service initiatives. Government
> cannot rebuild a family or reclaim a sense of neighborhood, and no bu-
> reaucratic program will ever solve the pressing human problems that can
> be addressed by a vast galaxy of people working voluntarily in their own
> backyards. The Points of Light Foundation will help that galaxy to grow
> and flourish in the years ahead.[16]

Community service like volunteerism denotes activities as varied as
cleaning a vacant lot or reading to a bedridden patient. It may be undertaken by schools or governments or churches, by youth organizations
like Boy Scouts or Girl Scouts or service clubs like Elks and Rotary and
Lions. To be sure, there are partisans of each of these, even efforts to
establish one or another type as the model for all the others. Community
service, however, lacks clear boundaries and new claimants for inclusion

appear as human inventiveness finds yet another project, starts yet another organization.

Two comprehensive claimants for attention are "national service," which is marked by a language of civics, and "service learning," which is marked by a language of pedagogy. "National service" is modeled on a military notion of good citizenship. "Service learning" arises as a progressive criticism of the abstractness of classroom education. The former addresses an issue of political ideology; the latter an issue of educational ideology. Together, they help establish the terms of our discussion. As we shall see, however, these two—and many others— are not easily kept apart nor should they necessarily be. What I want to find out is if and how these myriad activities justify concluding that community service is good for good purposes.

CONSENSUS?

In the present "crisis," a rare and unexpected consensus seems to have emerged, although I am sure it is temporary. Community service stirs the interest and support of those on the "right" and those on the "left," from William F. Buckley to Ted Kennedy.[17] Support for the 1990 legislation ranged widely over the political spectrum. To achieve it, the bill includes just about any usable idea anyone had—from a reprise of the Civilian Conservation Corps to the "Points of Light" Foundation, from encouraging volunteerism to providing stipends for work done, and from encouraging action by the respective states to national pro- grams on the one hand and localities on the other. Of course, there are dissenting voices. The "left" interprets community service as mere mid- dle-class do-gooding and, more seriously, as an excuse for ignoring systemic social problems and for abdicating our collective social respon- sibilities. Thus, in addition to the expected partisan skepticism about President Bush's "points of light," community service is also taken as simply one more reflection of a politics of greed. It masks indifference to human need while seeming to respond to it. It is, at best, a form of therapy for the "doer" and a mere "band-aid" for the "done-to." Con- servative critics tend to view community service as an invitation to one more governmental "boondoggle." For example, Doug Bandow of the Cato Institute in Washington, D.C., wrote,

Today, policymakers of both parties are pushing a variety of national service proposals. Although the sponsor's motives are worthier than Bel- lamy's [Edward Bellamy, author of *Looking Backward* in the late nineteenth century]—none seems enthused by the sort of totalitarianism he favored— even their "kinder, gentler" forms of national service would create more problems than they would solve. . . .

Despite the best efforts of President Bush and of policymakers and philosophers with varying perspectives, government-sponsored national service, if elective, would likely duplicate private efforts, stifle existing organizations, and waste money. If mandatory, it would subvert the compassionate impulses that animate true volunteerism and violate the principles of what is supposed to be a free society. What we need is more individual service, not a program of government service.[18]

Despite consensus, I think it clear enough that not everyone is speaking the same language. There are real disagreements about the nature of human nature and human motivation embedded in the various proposals. Some see people as essentially benevolent. After obstacles are removed, people simply need to be pointed in the "right" direction and given a bit of encouragement. Few examine the reason why the obstacles exist and many perpetuate the myth of Leviathan by attributing these obstacles to some nonhuman ogre like "the government" or "the corporation." Others see people as self-centered. They need to be forced to do what is good for them and more particularly for others.

Ironically, it is not easy to predict which of the narratives of human motivation—which have little to do with the results of psychological inquiry—will appeal to the various protagonists. For example, consider those who identify themselves with an economics and politics of self-interest or a religion of sin, that is, the neighborhood of conservative and right wing political religionists. Unexpectedly, they are to be found singing the praises of community service. Self-interest suddenly gives way to a benevolent, even optimistic, picture of human nature, a picture once said to be drawn by "unrealistic" liberals. One of several alternative American mythologies is invoked, the nostalgic picture of rural and small-town neighbors helping each other in times of trouble. Apparently, where service is concerned—unlike faith, politics or economics—proponents of community service on the right are prepared to trust in the willingness of people to help others where needed. Their views seem incoherent. More cynically, the ideology of the volunteer justifies destroying governmental social programs without appearing indifferent to human needs.

The situation on the center and left is no more edifying. The proponents of national service adopt a military model with its inversion of liberal values. The notion of the free citizen is surrendered to imposition of authority for the sake of a good result. Another American mythology is invoked, the legitimacy of authority in times of emergency as in the military draft. Variations on mandated national service are advanced in order to evade authoritarianism and insure "voluntary" response. Payments are proposed—direct as in stipends, indirect as in providing scholarships—particularly for "at-risk" and "inner-city" young people. The more ambitious of these payment schemes is a modified copy of World War II's GI Bill of Rights.

Yet a third narrative is relied upon: the myth of the commonwealth. In a democratic society, burdens must be shared by a diverse population; thus the need to use payment to insure that community service will not simply be an exercise for middle-class youngsters who can afford it. Implicit in this is the universalization of middle-class values. In a variation on the "melting pot" ideal, payment for service promises to reduce annoying diversities by providing the wherewithal—money, schooling, recognition—for everyone to become middle class. There are valid arguments for volunteering and for mandating service, for paying or not paying. What is interesting, however, is that community service seems to evoke a crossover of premises and this suggests that the premises have been scarcely explored. Consensus, in other words, implies a certain blindness—not unexpected in "crisis"—but it cannot be sustained. It is thereby a risky strategy.

The consensus begins to fall apart once the generality of "community service" is replaced by specific models. It is not surprising that the military model should be attractive. National service appeals to the egalitarian in us. It evokes the lost art of duty, and has potency for a rousing imagery in a country jaded by aesthetic triviality and political indifference. It reminds us of the glories of the past and stirs us by promising that we will once again hear the music of loyalties too easily forgotten. In a sense, a hidden motivation for a genuinely universal national service is finally to lay the ghost of resistance to the Vietnam war to rest. Moreover, national service has administrative appeal. It lends itself to bureaucratic convenience, quantification, and measurement of costs and benefits. It invites a rhetoric of common commitments to meeting common needs.

A military model is not the only universalist model available. The strongest of the alternatives, a spiritual model as it were, is derived from a theology of stewardship on the one hand and a secular notion of human solidarity on the other. More pluralistic and less administratively conceived, such a model offers the benefits and suffers the confusions of ideological blurriness. In its weaker forms, a spiritual model of community service turns into volunteerism and sooner or later invites the superficialities of mere doing. In its stronger form, it moves toward fundamentalism.

A pedagogical model is also part of the conversation about community service. In its strong form, community service inheres in the curriculum. Less committed is that form of community service which is located in the school but is not really of the school. It is offered as an enrichment program or as an "extra-curricular" activity as in the many service projects undertaken by students in free time and after school. This pedagogical model, then, is shaped by its different locations as well as by the intensity of its commitments and depth of its practice.

In its weakest form, community service is reduced to volunteerism and is found in the many cause-oriented agencies which, except for some coordination and common fund raising through "united funds," stand alone and often compete with each other. Given the personal dedication of the volunteer, it is the "cause"—usually identified with a particular health or welfare need—that shapes the service. To be sure, none of these models is neatly separated from the other. Traces of pedagogy are found in the military model, of spirituality in pedagogy, and so on. Nevertheless, each highlights a special sense of what counts as community service. In a way, the military model serves the cause of duty and country, the spiritual model serves the soul, the pedagogical model serves the learner and the volunteer model serves the activist.

One item of consensus, however, pervades just about all models and all proposals. Community service is peculiarly the province of the young. This permits excursions into near bribery and authoritarianism.

> [T]he long held assumption that various institutions will, without too much deliberate effort, acculturate youth to society's expectations for volunteering and community service is changing too.
>
> The good news about youth community service is that advocacy for it is growing, . . .
>
> Too few young people, however, are answering the call; . . .
>
> Consequently, concern and attention to the issue of the status of service in the youth culture and ways to encourage a renewal and new approaches to it are emerging from many corners and several levels. Foundations, Congress, the states, cities, national groups, and colleges/universities are in the forefront. Media attention, when it is directed at youth service, finds heartwarming anecdotal evidence that the younger generation is as much "we" as "me."[19]

We adults agree that it is young people who are peculiarly in need, peculiarly eligible, and peculiarly able. They are available in large organized groups through schools and colleges. Hence the logistics of program development are manageable. Their life careers do not yet call for them to support families and pay the bills. They have the time. They are mobile and malleable. In any event, they are accustomed to being told what to do by teachers, counselors, and parents. Finally, the young are more "idealistic" than their elders or, at least, it is easier to believe this of them.

By focusing on the young, community service also responds to a gap in our culture. It has been a secular "rite of passage," for example, most noticeably in the Peace Corps. In calling for sacrifice and service, and in promising to help the young grow up to adult responsibilities, we are following the patterns of such rites in all cultures without knowing it. Too pedestrian and prosaic, however, we have not done much to attach celebration and ceremony to service, to deal with its aesthetics. The best we can do, apparently, is to bury community service in moralistic rhetoric and public relations gimmickry. One example—and by no means an unworthy activity—is "StarServe." Given our affinity for anagrams, "StarServe" stands for "students taking action and responsibility in service." It was introduced to "educators and school administrators" in an elaborate brochure that began,

> There's a movement in this country that's growing stronger every day. It's the movement President Bush calls "Points of Light," whereby every individual and every institution in America plays a direct and consequential role in solving critical social problems through community service. The President has challenged young people to lead this movement by making community service a central part of their lives. Responding to the President's call, a group of leaders in education, business, community service, entertainment, and the media have undertaken a collaborative effort to encourage the growth of community service among young people.[20]

Included in the kit that "StarServe" circulates are a letter from the president, examples of programs underway, resource guides, and program suggestions. Included as well is a multi-colored poster and a "message from the Stars" addressed to the "students of America" and signed by luminaries in popular music, television and athletics.

Justifications of community service routinely and even ritualistically include the promise of preparation for membership in adult society and, in particular, for citizenship in American democracy. Among many examples,

> It is appropriate that higher education take a lead role in crafting legislation supporting national service, for this issue lies at the heart of our institutional missions.
>
> The underlying educational foundation of our universities—indeed, of schooling at all levels—is the preparation of young women and men for responsible citizenship in a pluralistic, democratic society. There is evidence that we are in the early stages of a shift among young people from a "me" to a "we" generation.[21]

Earlier, William James caught the spirit of community service as a rite of passage,

> There is nothing to make one indignant in the mere fact that life is hard. ... But, that so many men, by mere accident of birth and opportunity, should have a life of *nothing else* but toil and pain and hardness and inferiority imposed upon them ... while others ... no more deserving

never get any taste of this campaigning life at all—*this* is capable of arousing indignation in reflective minds. . . . If now . . . there were, instead of military conscription a conscription of the whole youthful population to form for a certain number of years a part of the army enlisted against *Nature*, the injustice would tend to be evened out and numerous other goods to the commonwealth would follow. The military ideals of hardihood and discipline would be wrought into the growing fibre of the people; no one would remain blind, as the luxurious classes now are blind, to man's real relations to the globe . . . and to the permanently sour and hard foundations of his higher life. . . . They would have paid the blood tax.[22]

Although they are not frequently consulted, there are initiatives undertaken by young people themselves who report their experience, often, in glowing terms of hope and achievement. Less happily, adults are once again exercising their power. I wonder, for example, why adults are somehow less in need of the benefits of community service. Yet, adults are not the subject of community service campaigns and presidential messages. Adults, instead, are free to volunteer or to give money or to do nothing. The current "crisis," we seem to be saying, rests with and among the young and not among the rest of us. The adult task is to see it done; the young person's task is to do it.

A strong smell of disdain for the young hides within the rhetoric of community service. As Diane Hedin, director of community relations for the Pillsbury Company writes,

the argument for expanding service opportunities as remedial education for selfish and unconcerned teenagers is troublesome . . .

This line of analysis argues that the changing values of young people themselves are primarily the source of the problem. But it is equally plausible that youth mirror the dominant values of the larger society. . . . Blaming young people for not being more altruistic and other-centered than their adult models is unfair; indeed, it is a variation on the theme of blaming the victim.

It also seems particularly unfair for educators to blame adolescents for being self-centered in view of the nature of educational institutions which are designed primarily to help some young people achieve at the expense of others. There is competition for a limited number of academic social prizes—being in the top 10 percent of the class, acceptance at top universities, merit scholarships, homecoming king or queen, and so on.[23]

SERVICE AND PARADOX

With these introductory remarks, I have tried to open up some of the problems of community service. In a sense, community service is as old as the association of human beings in groups whose members depend upon each other. At the same time it is very modern. Not least of its novelty is the possibility of refusing service in the name of freedom or of paying for someone else to do it, options absent in tribal and traditional communities. Community service then becomes problematic in its modernism, not so much in the doing as in the meaning.

I would not want to close this introduction, however, without again making clear my sense of the value and values of community service. I am not ambivalent about the practice of doing good for others and thereby for myself. Nor am I indifferent to the energies that can be released by confidence in our ability to make a difference in the doing. That calls for critical exploration too of what "doing" is all about. All of this, as I hope I have illustrated, is caught up in the notion of community service. There is much that we do not know about it and much that is less than honest in our arguments about it.

Because of my roots, schooling is a centering activity for me. But that, of course, leads right back to our culture and to the young. Summing it up, Janice Earle wrote for the National Association of State Boards of Education,

> Many are concerned about how youth fare in today's world. Many are concerned about the disaffection of our students . . . high truancy, high dropout rates . . . high rates of unwed teen pregnancy, substance abuse that seems to occur at ever younger ages, and a suicide rate that's on the rise . . .
>
> Those concerned with preparing students to be members of an educated citizenry identify community service as containing rich opportunities for students to learn how public systems work and the value of participating, along with the knowledge that participation can make a difference.
>
> Still others feel that youth service offers students an excellent opportunity to explore various career options while providing services to others who need help . . .
>
> Finally, those who listen to the voices of young people themselves hear their pleas for commitment and connection.[24]

Taking schooling seriously means taking democracy seriously even if that relationship is problematic too. I know that community service is not simply a matter of schooling apart from the history and polity within which it appears. My interest moves in two directions. In politics and in schools habits of participation must be matched by experiences of effectiveness. If participation is empty of consequences, its habits never get established. So, it is not enough to address community service without, at the same time, addressing issues of the community within which service happens. Community service is not just a matter of doer and done-to and, indeed, reducing service to such an exchange of subjectivities probably insures its failure.

Finally, community service stirs reflection on the lost third of the democratic trinity. We are well supplied with partisans of freedom and partisans of equality and we are well supplied with instances of the struggle between them. We are missing the middle term, "fraternity" or better in today's more enlightened world, "community." So community service has a place in the heart of democratic theory and is not just a pedagogical, political or psychological tool. In what follows, then, I must look at community service within a democratic polity and as a feature of progressive education. Community service is a way of retaking the lost community under new conditions. But first, let me retrace my personal excursion into this theme.

NOTES

1. Periodically, columnists discover community service. Thus, in a recent *Wall Street Journal* (August 4, 1992), David Laband criticizes Maryland's community service requirement for high school graduation, "Unpaid Child Labor, Compliments of Maryland."

2. The *locus classicus* of a "crisis" view of community service to which most refer is William James' *The Moral Equivalent of War* (New York: American Association for International Conciliation, 1910). James has in mind the unity brought about by patriotism in the face of an enemy as well as the selfless motivation allegedly evoked in times of war.

3. Alex De Tocqueville, *Democracy In America*, ed. Andrew Hacker, trans. Henry Reeve (New York: Washington Square Press, 1976), pp. 184–185.

4. Suzanne W. Morse, "Executive Summary," *Renewing Civic Capacity: Preparing College Students for Service and Citizenship*," ASHE-ERIC Higher Education Report No. 8 (Washington, D.C.: School of Education and Human Development, The George Washington University, 1989), p. iii.

5. "Already, 1,000 Points of Light," *The New York Times*, January 25, 1989, p. A23.

6. Jane C. Kendall and Associates, *Combining Service and Learning: A Resource Book for Community and Public Service* (Raleigh, N.C.: National Society for Internships and Experiental Education, 1990) Volume I, pp. 546–547 passim.

7. Charles H. Harrison, *Student Service (The New Carnegie Unit)* (Princeton, N.J.: Carnegie Foundation for the Advancement of Teaching, 1987).

8. Ibid., p. 10.

9. *A Report of the Youth Service America and Brown University Youth Service Leadership Conference* (Providence, R.I.: February 25/26, 1988), p. 5.

10. Louisa B. Meacham, Carolyn S. Mecker, and Judith Chayes Neiman, *A Guide to a Day in the Life Of Youth Service* (Washington, D.C.: Youth Service America and Campus Outreach Opportunity League, 1988).

11. *Annual Report* (Washington, D.C.: Youth Service America, 1989), p. 19.

12. William Montague, "Bush Asks Congress for $100-Million to Spur Youth Service," *The Chronical of Philanthropy* 18 (February 21, 1989), p. 1. I am not surprised that another new president has also called for community service. As of June 1993, however, it is much too early to see how Mr. Clinton's ideas will work out.

13. Anne C. Lewis, "The Time for Youth Service Has Come," *Phi Delta Kappan* 70, 8 (April 1989), p. 580.

14. Jane C. Kendall and Associates, ed., "Policy Statement, The National Association of State Boards of Education" (October 1989), reprinted in *Combining Service and Learning: A Resource Book for Community and Public Service*, (Raleigh, N.C.: National Society for Internships and Experiental Education, 1990), vol. I, p. 460.

15. Statement of Senator Edward M. Kennedy on the "Conference Report on the National and Community Service Act of 1990," Washington, D.C., October 12, 1990.

16. Statement by the president, November 15, 1990. By 1992, however, neither "points of light" nor "community service" played much of a role in the presidential election campaign.

17. See, by way of example, William F. Buckley, Jr., *Gratitude (Reflections On What We Owe to Our Country)* (New York: Random House, 1990).

18. Doug Bandow, "National Service: 'Idea Whose Time Will Never Come,' " *Education Week* 9, 36 (May 30, 1990), p. 32.

19. Anne C. Lewis, "Executive Summary," *Facts and Faith: A Status Report on Youth Service* (Washington, D.C.: The William T. Grant Foundation Commission on Work, Family and Citizenship, 1988), p. v.

20. "StarServe, A Points of Light Initiative," a partnership of the Kraft General Foods Foundation, the Love Foundation and The United Way of America. The StarServe trademark is copyrighted by The Love Foundation for American Music, Entertainment, and Art, 1990.

21. Gresham Riley, "The Value of National-Service Programs," *Education Week* 9, 40 (August 1, 1990), p. 47.

22. William James, *op. cit.*, p. 17.

23. Diane Hedin, "The Power of Community Service," *School Youth Service Network* 1, 2 (Spring 1989).

24. Janice Earle, "Helping Youth to Serve: Issues for State Policy Makers," *The State Board Connection, Issues In Brief* 9, 9 (September 1989) (Alexandria, Va.: National Association of State Boards of Education), p. 1.

Chapter Two

From Classroom to Community

ORIGINAL INTENTIONS

When I began, my goal was to work out a sequel to my discussion of teaching ethics,[1] and the assumption that it could not be confined within the walls of the classroom. The student needed to touch moral problems as lived. I was appalled by the ability of teachers and students to explore profound moral truths separate from simple decencies of conduct. We all needed to confront actual moral situations and to make moral judgments and moral decisions in contexts that were not comfortable and familiar.

Ethics poses its intellectual difficulties to be sure. But it is not enough to talk a good ethics game—my students, like my philosophic peers, were good at interesting talk. Concern for introducing a certain ethical realism to students was by no means new. It was shared by the many fellow wanderers that I met in seminars and conferences on moral education. It was a deeply felt problem for my colleagues in the Ethical Culture-Fieldston Schools. As one of them noted,

Underlying all this is the maddening discrepancy between what students say and how they act. How can they, after twelve years of an ethical education, so full of noble sentiments and good causes, be such slobs in the cafeteria, so rude to adults, so mean to each other? How can students, after spending an hour sanctimoniously proclaiming equal rights for homosexuals and the self-worth of every individual, use the taunt "faggot" five steps from the classroom door? How, after denouncing cliques and scapegoating in class, do they fall so readily into that very behavior? It may seem like a tag-line from a Woody Allen movie, but I have actually had a student cheat on the final examination in his ethics course.[2]

To be sure, our alumni did tell us that Fieldston's ethics classes, which they had resisted as students, remained among the significant influences on their lives after leaving school. As reported in answering the question, "What have been your community service activities and interests as an adult?"

> The replies . . . consisted, almost exclusively, of listings of organization by name. Their summaries, therefore, comprise similar—though not identical listings. . . . The nature of the replies here was such as to preclude conclusions beyond the fact that the alumni of these Ethical Culture Schools, as represented by this sample, are active in numerous and varied community services and activities in localities across the country.[3]

While the 1962 study has, unfortunately, not been repeated, annual questionnaires revealed the continuing activist and participant character of many alumni. Anecdotal records corroborated the finding. No doubt, a similar picture would emerge from other schools guided by moral idealism and a tradition of social reform.

Effective moral education, however, is not merely the concern of the school. For example, I recall many a conversation with Lawrence Kohlberg and his colleagues as they developed their ideas of the "just community."[4] They too were caught in the puzzles involved in connecting moral conduct with moral cognition. All of us were struggling with a perennial problem of ethics. In fact, more than 2,000 years ago, it was addressed by Aristotle,

> Virtue, then, being of two kinds, intellectual and moral, intellectual virtue in the main owes both its birth and its growth to teaching . . . while moral virtue comes about as a result of habit.
> [E].g. men become builders by building and lyre-players by playing the lyre; so too we become just by doing just acts, temperate by doing temperate acts, brave by doing brave acts.[5]

I was moved by what seemed obvious, the Aristotelian idea: ethics is as ethics does. But it wasn't quite that easy as I well knew and as, I suspect, Aristotle knew too. So, at the same time, I lived with a troubled conscience. The failure of students—and their teachers—to act morally challenged the truthfulness of the claim to be doing moral education and yet that was a claim that I and others were making. In looking for a remedy, I turned to community service. Because it was accessible and institutionally manageable, it seemed an obvious place in which to locate moral action and in which to test moral education. It offered the chance to make a visible difference in moral situations. Above all, it seemed a ready way to deal with the troubled conscience of the moral educator.

Even at this early stage, however, community service raised a number of questions of perspective. As a teacher, I wanted to explore community service because it looked very promising for an effective moral pedagogy. I had toyed with the alternative images of community service as an ethics "laboratory." Unfortunately, this presumed a methodological rigor that was not available in ethics although I was quite tempted by the public relations possibilities of community service as an ethics laboratory. But, it had to be more than a rhetorical device or else I would be adding to the burden of an uneasy conscience. Of course, ethics lends itself to inquiry and has its empirical content. But in ethics, inquiry lacks the structural strictness required by a laboratory model.

I realized that the fascinations of investigation were not really at the center of the moral enterprise. Certainly, I wanted to know better and to know more, but always in the service of practice, an insight which led Kant to distinguish "pure reason" from "pure practical reason." Moreover, I was skeptical about distancing myself enough to achieve what a laboratory at its best achieves. Indeed, it was just the problem of distancing that had led me, in the first place, to explore community service. All too often, the "distance" of the classroom turned into abstraction and moral irrelevance. So, reluctantly, I surrendered the laboratory metaphor.

Field study seemed a more promising way of understanding the place of community service in moral education. Students would be in position to explore the moral situation, to experience its pains and rewards, and to enrich their moral experience. Community service was a way of making tangible differences in the lives of people. So learning would be informed by the experience of achievement and of failure. And this in turn was yet another kind of learning. In short, community service was a *praxis*, neither entirely *theoria* nor entirely *techne*. With community service, moral education could complete itself much as an art completes itself.

I saw community service as means of improving moral education that otherwise ran the danger of intellectual and moral arrogance. But, I was not yet paying enough attention to what this would look like from a student's perspective. I was modifying curriculum. But, the student wanted to act and not just to know. I was still taking the position of the other. Yes, I was looking for the formation of habits of action and not simply of habits of inquiry. Students, by contrast, were more directly caught up in a moral reality. I realized that my motivation placed me in a limbo between classroom and world. It lacked the very *engagement* I wanted for students. And yet, *engagement* is in the character of ethics and the peculiar talent of the young. Not entirely caught in the patterns, routines, and demands of the social life of adults, they are accessible to experience in ways that an adult must struggle—often unsuccessfully—to achieve. Finally, then, community service needed to catch my own moral passions and not just my passions as a teacher if it was not to become just another classroom "enrichment."

I was comforted by the fact that community service had already played a role in my own moral education and in the moral education of students. I knew that community service was not a new idea. Indeed, it had, from the outset, been part of the life of the schools I worked most closely with. Thus, one of my predecessors as head of the Ethics Department, Algernon D. Black, commented,

> Community service—helping in a settlement house or camp, caring for children in a day nursery, first-hand experience in an election campaign—makes students more aware of the needs and character of our society than any textbook could do. This awareness is reinforced when a school makes its own resources and facilities available to the community—as we do through the Fieldston School Art Center and the Fieldston Day Camp. A student's ability to function in the wider community takes on increased importance with Fieldston's work-service requirement for graduation.[6]

By looking at my own experience and at students' experiences, I might find ways of grasping the interaction of effective pedagogy and of personal commitment which were caught up in my subject. That, at least, was where my search for community service began to take me.

GOOD PEOPLE

I reflected on my own career. It was a reminder and a caution. I had been the leader of an Ethical Culture Society, and had come to know the pains and rewards of the "helping" relationship. I had been a volunteer, had done my share of envelope-stuffing and board memberships and all the many tasks in between. I had served on the committees and boards of a county and state health and welfare council, a coordinating body for voluntary and tax-supported community serving agencies. For several years, I had served on the county hospital and on the county mental health boards as well. When not engaged in these volunteer and "policy" roles, I was directly at work with people in need of counseling or jobs or housing.

I was struck by how much of my experience was shaped by professional staffs who were often trapped into behaving as functionaries and, above all, how uncritical the experience was for all of us. To be sure, there were problems to be solved—usually those of budgets and personnel. Only occasionally would we debate our mission and its priorities. More often, our concerns had to do with money and public relations. I recalled endless attention to operational matters, often tedious, never resolved, always recurring. Seldom, however, did we address the meaning of what we were doing; it was enough, apparently, to be doing good things. I was, in short, a good volunteer.

Looking back, I realized how busy it all was—for me, for the many others who were similarly engaged. I realized, too, how easy it was to encourage others to be as busy. There was always so much that needed doing. Problems came fast and often and even if I had been inclined to stop and reflect, they couldn't wait. So, it was all too easy to get lost in the doing and all too easy to let others shape it or, which was as likely, to let programs grow like Topsy. Indeed, as I looked backward, I realized that those who were supposed to be responsible for reflection were as caught up in practice as I was. At the same time, I realized that I did not regret the experience. Clearly it had its satisfactions. Satisfaction, I reminded myself, however, could bring its own dangers, particularly the dangers of benevolent arrogance.

I was led from thinking about my experience to multiply rather than resolve questions about the connections between community service and moral education. I understood that mere exposure like mere activity would not do. Nor was it possible by means of a division of labor to assign action to some and thinking to others. Or, to put this another way, I had to keep the idea of the classroom as vivid as the idea of service. I knew how tempting it was to conclude from the ethics classroom's limitations that it could be replaced altogether by community service. Finally, I had to avoid thinking of community service as "experience" and classroom as something else.

I reflected on my years as director of an "independent"—that is, private—school. It was easy enough to understand the "privileged" status of most of my students and their families and therefore the consequent dangers of moral indifference on the one hand and self-righteousness on the other. As a teacher in the Friends Academy in Locust Valley, New York put it,

> Students in independent schools often have very little sense of living in a community let alone the notion of serving this community. . . . Most of our students come from families that have the financial resources to buy needed services and therefore seldom experience the need for community cooperation to provide service . . . the world they experience seems to require money and lots of it for services to be rendered.
>
> Community service can also help students learn first hand about human tragedy and the truth that we do not completely control our lives. On a recent workcamp serving the homeless, a student was shocked to find a Bryn Mawr graduate homeless. Previously, her world view said if you

worked hard enough and got into a good college, like Bryn Mawr, you
were set for life. . . . Now she was confronted first hand with the truth,
no doubt presented in her history and literature courses, that life has a
tragic dimension that can frustrate our best efforts.[7]

I was tempted to think that the privileged status of private school students somehow presented a unique opportunity for community service.
But the thought of privilege also took a different turn. I realized that
anyone doing community service was inevitably going to be in some
kind of privileged position, if for no other reason than the fact that he
or she was able to be a doer. Privilege, in other words, was a structural
problem. So, for example,

> Rubber soles padded soundlessly along a hallway of Coler Memorial Hos-
> pital recently as Yaninth Maldonado guided an elderly man in a wheelchair
> to a nearby day room. With each step, Ms. Maldonado, a teenage mother
> with an eighth-grade education moved closer to her own goal: attaining
> a college diploma.
>   Ms. Maldanado, a soft-spoken 18-year-old, joined the City Volunteer
> Corps of New York shortly before Christmas last year. She turned to the
> group, the largest urban full-time youth service organization in the United
> States, hoping that its offerings of public service projects, class-room work
> and college assistance programs would speed her on her chosen way.[8]

The source of privilege might vary, but the pattern of relationship did
not. And this, in turn, alerted me to the way that diversity of position,
a certain inequality, is unavoidable. That called for an acknowledgment
of the politics of authority embedded in community service.

   Of course, I talked with friends and colleagues and students. Like me,
most of them saw immediate connections between moral education and
community service and agreed that "it was a good idea," even "a natural." The doing itself seemed to present few difficulties. After all, the
needs were clear enough and the responses they called for—reading to
a patient, helping out in a nursing home, tutoring a child, planting a
tree, raising money—were not particularly complicated. So typical was
this agreement, that I wondered if my growing sense of the complexities
of service was not just a result of my philosophic habits. After all, I was
professionally expected to find difficulties where no one else did—as
with epistemological problems of perception that no one but philosophers raise or with common moral ideas like honesty that no one but
philosophers find problematic. At the same time, I couldn't ignore the
questions raised by my own experience or by my exploration of the
literature or by reports of the experience of others.

   Teachers tended to applaud the idea and then complain that there
was simply no place in an already over-crowded—and rapidly more

crowded—curriculum. Parents and students worried about the risk to college admissions of undertaking community service in place of more academic and so more "worthy" activities. In this, there was a certain realism. Like businesspeople who proclaim the virtues of the liberal arts but who hire MBAs and engineers and accountants, colleges proclaim the importance of co-curricular and nontraditional studies but college admission relies on grade point averages and SAT scores.

> College preparation, the goal of many independent schools, is closely related to college acceptance. But in "A Memo to Secondary Schools, Students and Parents," Stanford University admission director Fred Hargadon notes that "community service" courses can have strong negative effects on university admissions committees. Certain questions may come to the mind of the admission officer: Did this premed applicant take hospital service because he was reluctant to take Advanced Placement biology? Is this student's grade point average high because she is stronger in service courses than in academic subjects?[9]

Community service raised a number of institutional questions. For all its *prima facie* value, it had to compete with other claimants for money and time. But that, as I thought about it, told us about the aims of education in our culture. I wondered: Is a competently performed and well supervised hospital service project less rigorous or demanding than a competently performed and well supervised AP (advanced placement) biology course or is it just different? And if different, in what sense is the latter a more worthy contributor to a student's education than the former? The conversation may have begun with a question of time or money; it raised a question of the nature of schooling itself.

> All too often, however, success in school involves trivial forms of learning. . . . As Newmann states: "To be engaged in learning, the student must be involved in authentic work . . . that has value and meaning beyond the instructional context." Students become engaged from an internal commitment to address a concern. . . . Students are involved in efforts which have and are perceived to have an obvious impact on others. Realizing this, students are motivated to learn what is required to ensure that the impact is positive. For some students, this psychological investment in learning is novel. Formerly motivated (if at all) by grades on tests, they discover a deeper value in their education.[10]

Finally, many of the adults I talked with had either heard or heard of John Kennedy's inaugural challenge, "Ask not what your country can do for you but what you can do for your country." And most of them, sadly and no doubt with no small mixture of wishful thinking, wondered what had happened to us. They talked about community service in an almost mythic context. Community service was not simply a pedagogy and not simply doing good things, but it seemed, a symbolic retaking of lost ground.

PREJUDICES

If my experience plays its role in this essay, so too do my prejudices. The political particulars are not relevant here, I think, but the implications of these for my attitudes toward and expectations of community service are. I am a liberal, a progressive and a Humanist. So, I am confident that, once known, problems can be solved and that once we know that, problems will be solved. To be sure, this near-visceral optimism is chastened by encounters with indifference where I do not expect it and bad consequences where "good" ideas predict none.

Of course, I am a critic and a skeptic—what Humanist is not this strange mixture of optimistic faith and realistic doubt? At the same time—a difference of generations again—I still keep my confidence in America as the "city on the hill." I do not share the peculiar despair of cynicism that seems so attractive to so many these days, particularly those whose reference point is the late 1960s and beyond. So, I doubt our traditional rhetoric and am tuned in to it.

Invariably, politicians and teachers invoke the American dream and John Kennedy and, over and over again, William James. For example, the Senate Report on the National and Community Service Act of 1990 began,

> Service to others is an ideal that has served America well throughout history. John Winthrop, the first elected governor of the Massachusetts Bay Colony, captured this idea in words that ring true even three-and-a-half centuries later. "We must delight in each other," Winthrop told the colonists, "make others' conditions our own, rejoice together, mourn together, labor and suffer together, always having before our eyes our community." ... In this spirit, volunteers have served the nation in times of crisis—in war, depression, or natural disaster. In quieter times, they have served the community, helping a neighbor in need or a stranger in trouble. It is understood that the rights of citizenship carry with them the responsibilities of looking out for the good of the community.[11]

To be sure, I can easily poke holes in this reliance on the spirit of neighborliness now that neighborhoods are nearly vanished. Yet I can't help but believe in it too. Along with what, I suspect, is this generationally rooted confidence in the American experiment, I have an essential faith in the powers of schooling, the liberal's faith. The two, America and the school, are connected in our history and in our myth, and in me.

No doubt, these echoes of yesterday tell me that I am out of fashion, a strangely shaped radical traditionalist. Indeed, the fact that the advocates of community share this paradoxical description may account for the strange alliances that form around proposals for national service, for service-learning, and the like. To be sure then, I am not alone in my mixed state but I sometimes wonder if others realize the presence of this strange combination.

This radical traditionalism appears in interpretations of community service as civic responsibility, which echoes too with a lost classicism. At the same time, its democratic affirmation suggests the broader ideological range conveyed by a radical traditionalist language. Thus,

> I contend that there has been a decline in the vitality and clarity of civic education in the United States. . . . The main thrust of my analysis is that the decline in civic education after 1945 was fashioned to a considerable extent by "intellectuals" and teachers more concerned with immediate political issues than with an educational format for understanding the long-term trends in the American "experience." Civic education limited to inculcation of traditional patriotism or conventional nationalist ideology is obviously inadequate for an advanced industrial society and a highly interdependent world. I find the words *national* and *patriotic* limiting, and offer the term *civic consciousness*. It refers to positive and meaningful attachments a person develops to the nation-state.[12]

To be sure, all kinds of groups connect service with community. A band of terrorists, a street gang, a criminal conspiracy no doubt expect their members to serve their collective ends. There is in these less felicitous instances as well as in somewhat happier ones like tribes and clans, a demand to fit in, to earn by means of service the right to occupy roles already well established and historically rooted. Traditional service is then both a repetition and an initiation. The radicalism, however, is missing and with it the sense of development and criticism. At the same time, the notion of community roots radicalism in history and story, sets boundaries and legitimacies. Capturing a typically American—and typically Enlightenment—sense of what the marriage once meant, Douglas Sloan writes,

> The full significance and centrality of moral philosophy in the nineteenth-century college curriculum can only be understood in light of the assumption held by American leaders and most ordinary citizens that no nation could survive, let alone prosper, without some common social and moral values. Americans looked primarily to education for the creation of these common values. This faith in the power of education to build a sense of national community and purpose has been deeply ingrained in American thought. Jefferson was convinced that an enlightened citizenry is

essential to a democratic society. . . . The same faith in the unifying purposes of education is expressed in Horace Mann's idea that the common
school would be "the balance-wheel of the social machinery."[13]

Sadly, I realize the modernity of our lost connections—to our past, to
each other. Vietnam and Watergate have taught us the lessons of a
democratic society that betrays itself. So, I can recite the litany of our
failures. But deep down these events feel to me like contingent intrusions
in what is still a reliable and valued undertaking. More to the point,
however, the modern situation tempts me to see community service as
a form of remediation, even of redemption. At the same time, I understand the oppressive possibilities of our tradition. The "melting pot"
casts its shadow even as I announce my loyalty to democracy and the
common school. That cautions me that community service can all too
easily presume a homogeneity of needs and competences. It could turn
into a not so evident re-incarnation of "melting pot" ideologies.

To my catalogue of prejudices I add a commitment to rationality. I am
less than sanguine about the current affection for intuition as a vehicle
of reliable knowledge, less than convinced of the merits of current fads
like "new thought," a "new ethnicity," "multi-culturalism" and "post-
modernism." All of this—my left-liberalism, my faith in democratic
schooling, and my confidence in rationality—appears in my approach
to community service. For example, I do not think that community
service can become only an exercise in interpersonal relations. Alternatively, were I following an apolitical, even positivist, interpretation of
schooling, community service would be only another instrument for
teaching basic skills toward the ends of any community whatsoever. In
short, my prejudices point me toward a normative social psychology
and pedagogy.

Finally, I am alert to an overriding personal prejudice, my sense of
the promises and possibilities of the young. I need to guard myself
against a romanticism about children and youngsters. Turning again to
"remembrances of things past," a good deal of my life has been spent
with the young—at summer camps, in classrooms, in young people's
groups and, on occasion, on the streets. Most of the time, these have
been good experiences, even joyous ones. I have known and worked
with young people across the divide of class and caste, although in
recent times that has been more and more difficult to do. I have seen
young people reclaim a dying farm, build a house, help a family in
trouble, raise money for a cause, petition a government agency, demonstrate against a war, organize a political campaign. I have seen them
sustaining each other, teaching each other. I have seen foolishness too
and needlessly inflicted pain and, rarely, viciousness and violence. My

experience is the obverse of the headlines which seem, hopelessly, to announce a lost generation of addicts and criminals and egos run wild.

Thinking about what I've just said, I sometimes wonder if I am not merely romantic but naive—or perhaps just lucky. Apparently, however, I am not alone.

A 1980 survey, for example, found that roughly 92% of 14 to 20 year olds wanted to participate in improving their communities. The findings of a 1985 Gallup poll suggest that Americans act on this desire: about 89 million people, nearly one-half of all Americans 14 years or older, volunteered, including 52% of teenagers. Pollster Louis Harris corroborates the Gallup findings in a 1985 survey, concluding that the "youth population has been misnamed the self-centered generation. There is a strong desire to serve others. The problem we face in America today is not a lack of willingness to serve or to help others but to find the appropriate outlet." With 2.9 million Americans turning 18 each year, and 25 percent of them estimated to desire placement in civilian service, the need to develop well thought-out opportunities is clear.[14]

This measure of the powerful idealism and energy of the young is corroborated by anecdotal accounts. I think of a group of young high school students in an ethics class. Joining with their parents, they would spend the early part of an evening once a week preparing sandwiches and the latter part of the evening and through the night working in soup kitchens and among the homeless on the streets distributing the sandwiches. I have listened to teen-agers describe their experiences as tutors to the blind, readers to the old, legs for the handicapped. I have watched tears come to the eyes of their adult listeners. More than once, I have asked why the old were reticent to serve and heard embarrassed anxious messages of fearfulness. And I have heard the recurring defense that time would not permit.

My prejudice for the young is not just directed to adolescents. There was the first grade class who made New York's Central Park their project.

So begins the first grade ethics class on a sunny November day as Rebecca Elfant (their teacher) leads her eager students into the field. . . . The field work is an impact study and the target area, Central Park. It doesn't matter a bit . . . that her 6- and 7-year-olds . . . record their findings with pictures instead of words. . . . What she cares about is how much can be discovered first-hand . . . about the impact of the park on people and of people on the park. . . . Huge litter collages were a product of a study on garbage. "I don't think the children really ever thought about what litter does until I asked them to look for it and collect it. They saw how dangerous litter is to the animals and to people—broken glass, and those little zip-lock things that birds' legs get caught in, or the 6-pack plastics that trap the fish and seagulls.[15]

The collages were exhibited in the school halls for the enlightenment and to the dismay of many of the adults who could not ignore some of the objects on display.

Not every attempt is a success and not every young person—let alone his or her parents and teachers—responds to the demands of community service. But I see young people as more rather than less likely to respond and I see adults as less rather than more likely to respond. At the same time, I'm not recommending a children's crusade nor am I blind to the volatility of the young. They can be simultaneously cruel and generous, self-seeking and altruistic, thoughtless and sensitive.

> *Turning Points,* a report issued by the Carnegie Council on Adolescent Development, estimates that by age 15, millions of young people risk reaching adulthood unable to assume the responsibilities of informed, active citizenship in a pluralistic society. It also states, "Early adolescence offers a superb opportunity to learn values, skills, and a sense of social responsibility."
> Adolescents are very sensitive to the way they are perceived and treated. . . . While much of their self-focusing is healthy, sometimes it can become obsessive and hypercritical. Community service provides an opportunity for adolescents to focus on others. . . . And the more they help others, the more positively adolescents view themselves.[16]

So much, then, for where I stand, a radical who is loyal to Americanism, a rationalist who is romantic about the young.

RACHEL'S DILEMMA

Nothing focused my difficulties with community service so much as the difficulties of one of my students. Rachel was a bright, personable, sensitive and articulate high school senior. She had completed her community service project for graduation and she had become an advocate of community service to her fellow students, to the parent body, and to the faculty. As a graduating senior, she was eligible for "independent study" and we agreed that her project would be a research paper on community service. Her question eventually became my question— what, really, does community service mean and to whom and why?

We met each week to talk about her work. She collected articles, wrote to Washington for information on legislation, gathered notes about her own experience. It seemed straightforward enough if not particularly imaginative or exciting. I suggested that she talk with her fellow students, both those, like her, who were excited about the subject and others who had met a requirement and then moved on. Invariably, she came back with glowing reports of good experiences. At the same time, she seemed to find it more and more difficult to articulate the point of the disparate information she had gathered. When I pressed her, she resisted and then confessed frustration. She knew it was a good thing she had done and her peers agreed with her. But she could not say what it was except in superficial descriptive ways. And each time she tried, she would pull back as if to say that that wasn't it at all. Finally, she wrote,

> For the past six months I have been looking to discover the magic behind community service ... there is undoubtedly, at least in my mind, something magical about community service. There is something inexplicable and indescribable in the way it can make a person feel. . . . The term, magic, is also ironic in a sense. Just as magic is elusive, so seems to be people's understanding of their own ... motivations for community service. In speaking with people, both very active and not so active people, I have not obtained a single definitive reason for the motivation behind community service, nor have I discovered a person who can state exactly what service has done for him or her personally.
>
> After I realized how elusive the concept of community service was, I sat down for a long time to try to reason out these ideas for myself. I discovered that although I could come up with one concrete benefit of my own experience, a deeper valuing of education and a more distinct sense of purpose, I still felt as though the question remained unanswered. . . . Here again, the magic interfered. . . . Even more surprising was the realization that ... people felt that there was no need to question their community service; service was simply to be done and not examined. . . . For most people community service is a feeling. . . . It is simply a part of them and the benefits, which not one person with whom I spoke questioned ... just melt into the fabric of the personality.[17]

Rachel's dilemma—she knew community service was good for her and others, and yet she didn't know how or why it was good—became mine as well. As I listened to her well organized but dead-ended attempts to understand and tried to find leading questions that might get her out of the trap, I realized that I was not much better off than she was.

In other words, if community service was an answer, what was the question? My earliest guess, as I have said, emerged from the needs of moral education. That raised questions of practice and pedagogy but that wasn't sufficient. Another guess—less personal than cultural—was the need for some "rite of passage" in a secular culture. Yet another was the ambivalence of the old toward the young, the compulsion to idealize and to punish. Another had to do with lost connections and the urgency of finding ways of reconstruction. And so it went for a while—recanvassing the territory I have passed over in the openings of this essay.

I reviewed the debate stimulated by the proposal of a National Community Service Act, hoping it might offer clues of meaning. And, as before, I found plenty of debate but not much meaning—at least not much that could satisfy Rachel's dilemma or mine. Symptomatic of our recourse to the market place, many of its supporters saw service as a way of providing cheap labor to meet social needs. Community service was only an instrument for want of a more enlightened or more affluent economy.

> The plan (for national service) adroitly pairs the social goal of serving the needy with the individualist theme of self reliance. Most of the social ills that have worsened during the Reagan years require labor intensive remedies whose principal obstacle is cost. A service corps could provide home care to keep many old people out of nursing homes. It could help staff halfway houses for the mentally ill. Its volunteers might teach adult illiterates to read. This could help staff high-quality day-care centers, neighborhood recreation programs, and an expanded conservation corps...
>
> In effect, the volunteer corps would provide a pool of well-educated labor at below-market wages—but in a socially defensible manner.[18]

Others argued that the work had to be paid for or else it would discriminate against those who could not afford to do it, while still others replied that to pay for it was a form of bribery.[19] I recalled that Rachel had mused about the paradox of requiring volunteer work, but her concern was more moral than economic. But, what was striking in nearly all of the rhetoric was the assumption that everyone knew what they were talking about—and Rachel, in her honesty, did not!

Inevitably, some saw in community service a "mask for the welfare state," and this became an excuse for political attack. For example,

> "The Promise of National Service" [editorial, December 10] describes national service glowingly, as a panacea for disaffected youth and a host of other social problems. Beware the plan that sounds too good to be true; strip away the altruism and behold a monster.
>
> National service programs promise to turn alienated and troublesome young people into useful citizens. At the risk of sounding cynical, I doubt the success rate would be high, not to mention cost-effective. But more frightening and insidious is the message—that social programs would succeed where families have failed.[20]

Less caught up in the need to make points in a political battle, Nel Noddings' comments on "caring" seemed to me to join the issue.

> But there is a genuine crisis in our society and schools that is receiving far too little attention—a crisis in caring.
>
> In schools, the crisis manifests itself in two ways: students often feel that no one cares for them, and they are not learning how to be carers themselves. . . .

At the same time when the traditional structures of caring have deteriorated, schools must become places where teachers and students live
together, talk with each other, take delight in each other's company. My
guess is that when schools focus on what really matters in life, the cognitive
ends we now pursue so painfully and artificially will be achieved somewhat
more naturally.[21]

In short, perhaps I was getting closer to some resolution of Rachel's
dilemma by recognizing that "community service" was not simply a
conjunction of terms. The idea of a "crisis in caring" somehow seemed
to ring true to me as well. Perhaps, then, this might lead to a possible
content for Rachel's "magic." There is, these days, a growing literature
of community,[22] pushed, no doubt, by the problematic nature of community itself in our world. As it were, community service is a *praxis* that
both presumes and creates community in the act. It alerts us, however,
to the evanescence and, paradoxically, the persistence of community
and asks us to reflect on whether or not community can be had again
and if so how and where.

It would not do to be fooled by all the action around us. Rachel's
articulate inarticulateness was a warning. Of course, I shall review the
action and tell the story of how we got to it. The politics and the pedagogy
hold their fascinations as well. But, like the ghost at the banquet, the
doubtful and the problematic lurk behind the good things we do and
the good feelings we report and the good energies that are released.

It would trouble me to close this description of my move from classroom to community on so dour a note. I am mindful, however, that, as
Maxine Greene warned,

There is a heightened interest in what is variously called "choice" today,
in school-based management, parental involvement, collaboration, and
local control. Few of us, picturing ourselves in such contexts, have thought
about what it might actually mean to bridge the gulfs and address ourselves
to the felt concerns of persons who are different, now increasingly involved. We conceal our own life-stories. We avoid dialogue by speaking
through "professional" categories when we are not concentrating on issues
of management or specific pragmatic problems. Despite our recognition
of the damage done by racist exclusion, tracking, and humiliation in the
schools, we are still likely to make members of minority groups "other,"
and to objectify them by doing so. We look at them through the lenses of
altruism often, and that may be another way of distancing. . . . When required, we assign; we arrange.[23]

The move from classroom to community then has its existential complexities and these are deeply rooted in what we have become politically
too. To these difficulties, we add concerns about what it is to be human

and to live in the world we actually have. Community service then cannot be simply located institutionally or simply circumscribed by policy. It needs its narrative roots.

NOTES

1. See Howard B. Radest, *Can We Teach Ethics*, (New York: Praeger, 1989), and, in particular, Chapter 7, pp. 121–143.

2. Mal Goodman, "Some Random Thoughts On Teaching Ethics," *The ECS Professional Newsletter* 2, 2 (Winter 1986), p. 4.

3. Rhetta Arter, *Values and Attitudes: A Study of Alumni of The Ethical Culture Schools* (New York: The Ethical Culture Schools, 1962), pp. 17, 18.

4. Often, these discussions took place between us after meetings of the University Seminar on Moral Education, Columbia University which Kohlberg attended regularly. For a recent essay on the "just community" see William Kolber, Edward Zalaznick, and Beverly Noia, "The Impact of a Just Community Experience on Student Development: Three Views from the Scarsdale Alternative School," *The Kohlberg Legacy for the Helping Professions*, Lisa Kuhmerker, ed., (Birmingham, Ala.: R.E.P. Books, 1991), pp. 123–145.

5. Richard McKeon, ed., "Book II," *Nicomachean Ethics* in *The Basic Works of Aristotle* (New York: Random House, 1941), p. 952.

6. *Values In The Ethical Culture Schools*, Foreword by Algernon D. Black (New York: The Ethical Culture Schools, 1963).

7. Herb Lape, "Community Service—A Focus for the 90's," *NYSAIS Professional Development Exchange* (Milbrook, N.Y.: New York Association for Independent Schools, Fall 1990), p. 1.

8. Michel Marriott, "Youth Service Is New Route to Diplomas and Jobs," *New York Times*, July 18, 1990, B6.

9. Timothy J. Corcoran, "College Preparation and Community Service: A Conflict?," *Independent School* 41, 1 (October 1981), pp. 57–58.

10. Kate McPherson and Mary K. Nebgen, "Setting the Agenda: School Reform and Community Service," 2, 3 (Summer 1991), p. 4. Citation is from "Student Engagement in Academic Work: A Conceptual Model," by F. Newmann, an unpublished paper presented at American Educational Research Association Conference, March 1988.

11. "Background and Need," *Senate Report, on S 1430*, from the resource file on "The National and Community Service Act of 1990," Senate Labor and Human Resources Committee, 1990, p. 44.

12. Morris Janowitz, "The Good Citizen—A Threatened Species?," *University of Chicago Magazine* (Summer 1985), p. 7.

13. Douglas Sloan, "The Teaching of Ethics in the American Undergraduate Curriculum, 1876–1976," pamphlet reproduced from *The Hastings Center Report*, December 1979, p. 21.

14. "III. Background and Need for the Legislation," *House Report on HR 4330*, from materials on "The National Community Service Act of 1990," prepared by the Senate Labor and Human Resources Committee, 1990, p. 48.

15. Janet Hirschfeld, "Big Lessons for Small Kids," *Ethics in Education* (Ontario: Ontario Institute for Studies in Education, 4, March 1985), p. 7.

16. Richard Martinez, "A Case for Community Service for Adolescents," *School Youth Service Network* 3, 1 (Spring 1991), p. 4.

17. From an unpublished essay, Rachel Hochhauser, May 1991.

18. Robert Kuttner, "Give the Young a Better Chance to Serve Their Country," *Business Week*, March 21, 1988. See also the recommendations of "Youth and America's Future: The William T. Grant Commission on Work, Family and Citizenship" (1988), which included,

> Youth service yields substantial economic benefits to the community: in-kind contributions of labor and talent, future social welfare costs saved, and young people prepared for stable work and family life. An estimated 3.5 million full-time volunteers could meet numerous societal needs—among them, a conservative estimate, 500,000 nonprofessional workers in schools, 275,000 caring for severely restricted elderly and handicapped individuals, 225,000 in energy, environmental protection, and urban and rural conservation, 165,000 for services to children, youth, and families, and 200,000 in public safety.

Samuel Halperin, "Pathways to Success: Citizenship Through Service," *Combining Service and Learning*, Jane C. Kendall, ed. (Raleigh, N.C.: National Society for Internships and Experiential Education, 1990), vol. 1, p. 446.

19. For the give and take of this discussion, see as examples, "Don't Make National Youth Service a Ghetto," including letters from George D. Sussman, executive director, Association of Colleges and Universities of the State of New York and from Linda A. Chisholm, president, Association of Episcopal Colleges and Howard A. Berry, director, the Partnerships for Service Learning, *The New York Times*, February 21, 1989; see also, "What a National Service Plan Should Include" with letters from Donald J. Eberly, executive director, Coalition for National Service, John T. Speaks, and Cyril C. Means, Jr., professor of law at New York University, *The New York Times*, May 1, 1989; and see also, "A Quid Pro Quo for Youth," Dave McCurdy, *The New York Times*, June 26, 1989.

20. Brenda W. McClean, "National Service Is a Mask of the Welfare State," letter to the editor, *The New York Times*, January 2, 1987. Ms. McClean is a research assistant at Hoover Institution on War, Revolution, and Peace.

21. Nel Noddings, "Schools Face 'Crisis in Caring,' " *Education Week* 8, 14 (December 7, 1988), p. 24.

22. For example, see Robert N. Bellah et al., *The Good Society* (New York: Knopf, 1991); Jurgen Habermas, *Communication and the Evolution of Society* (Boston: Beacon, 1979); and Richard Rorty, *Contingency, Irony, and Solidarity* (Cambridge, England: Cambridge University Press, 1989).

23. Maxine Greene, "Retrieving the Language of Compassion: The Education Professor in Search of Community," *Teacher's College Record* 92, 4 (Summer 1991), p. 543.

Chapter Three

It's Good to Do Good

THE "THIRD" SECTOR

Once upon a time, before the New Deal and welfare capitalism, the American world was neatly divided into two parts. One was called the "public" sector and was tax supported. Here were to be found an expanding number of activities: the military, the police, sanitation, road building, the postal service, the courts, and diplomacy together with tax collection and law making and a government printing office. After a struggle, public schooling was added although this remained a local matter and was, with some few exceptions like New York's City College, restricted to primary and secondary education. The second part of society was called the "private" or "business" sector, although it was really no less public but far less accountable than the other. All in all, this was a story easily told and easily understood. Everything was in its place and everyone knew his or her place.

The story also told of a rich and complex communal life. Here were to be found families, friendships and ethnicities, churches and temples and synagogues, and all kinds of associations tied to neighborhoods and communities. Of course, nearly all of these communal associations relied on indirect government support like property tax exemptions and on direct government services like police and fire and sanitation. They relied as well on the charitable gifts made possible by the wealth generated in the "private" sector. It was in the associational and communal life that charitable works were located: mission and benevolent aid societies, parochial schools, youth serving groups, old age homes, hospitals, free clinics and all the other inventions of an inventive people. In other words, community as such entailed services. If the social life was characterized by function, the communal life was characterized by connection.

The story was believed even as it became decreasingly believable, and the myth of an American golden age is still celebrated in conservative political rhetoric and the editorial pages of *The Wall Street Journal*. Liberated by this functional division of labor, the market would provide the goods necessary for life's needs and luxuries. The rest of our lives was simply not the affair of the government or the business world. Wealthy individuals provided communal life with financial resources. So a Carnegie built libraries and a Rockefeller endowed universities and everyone was supposed to support his or her churches and relatives. But it became less and less clear whether an institution like a hospital or school was social or communal. For example, the churches originally sponsored some of our most "prestigious" colleges and universities. Today, even those that still retain their communal ties—like Fordham or Notre Dame or Yeshiva—enter the secular market place for teachers, students, and curriculum and, more recently, for members of boards of trustees. Within the business world, other crossovers became necessary as corporate organization required more and more of government particularly as business moved beyond national borders.

Shifting boundary lines blurred the distinctions between government and private activity. Increases in power, and most particularly in the abuse of power, led as well to deliberate interventions by government. Most dramatic and long-lived, of course, was the New Deal but it had been forecast in the various states long before it reached national dimension. New language appeared signalling these blurred social lines like a "level playing field" and "fair trade" and "disclosure" and "safety-net." The transformation of a minimalist government was symbolized by the normalization of multi-million member armed forces and multi-billion dollar budgets after World War II. In short, the narrative was becoming unintelligible.

At the same time, communities were deteriorating and communal activities were being transformed into social functions. The neighborhood with its wealth of personal relations all but vanished. A large and mobile population worked in a new industrial work place and lived in housing developments and planned "communities." Left behind to live in the shell of vanishing communities were the old and the poor. Community-founding and community-supporting associations came to do symbolic rather than real things, resigning more and more of their activities to the social world. Personal connections, in other words, were not so much destroyed as withered away. The extended family became the nuclear family and the one-parent family and the "nontraditional" family. The church and synagogue were finally reduced to meeting needs that were essentially ceremonial. Thus, function replaced connection and regulation replaced relationship. Alongside their symbolic communal activities like the rituals surrounding birth and marriage and death or celebrating holy-days, church and temple adopted the habits and practices of the social world, professionalizing behaviors that had once relied on rooted and implicit relationships. The clergy, by and large, became functionaries and managers.

But the social world was neither ready for nor appropriate to a communal life. While function replaced connection, a good deal was left out and left over so to speak. Nor were we insensitive to this fact although we were mystified by it. Over and over again, we tried to make the functional response more comprehensive and, it was hoped, more adequate. These efforts could not succeed, however. Society was no surrogate for community and this led to further failure for both deteriorating communities and ineffective functionalities.[1] In the effort to rationalize what could not be rationalized and to communalize what could not be communalized, a so-called third sector evolved. In it were to be found those activities of connection once rooted in community but now to be undertaken according to the habits of the social world.

The third sector, however, was only pseudo-social just as it was only pseudo-communal.[2] The inordinate energy devoted to fund raising required the disconnection between, and so the alienation of, those who were to give and those who were to get. The rich ideological and ceremonial pluralism of communal life had to be sacrificed to a strategy of blandness lest offense be given and taken. The functionalism that became a third-sector ideal required that those relationships of community which were existential be ignored. Agency annual reports and social worker time-sheets were filled with efforts—demanded by the "job"—to quantify the unquantifiable. Membership statistics and balanced budgets came to signify the religious institution's achievement. Categories of productivity so widely praised these days filled the talk of educational reform. We spoke of quantities as a replacement for quality, for example, "time-on-task," teaching hours, length of school year, and so forth. We tried to solve our medical problems using the methods of cost/benefit analysis.

I do not mean to demean our efforts to gain some control in our social practices. Schools and health care have become unmanageable. But then, so have mega-corporations as the recent story of America's banks, brokerages and automobile producers illustrates. Nevertheless, in the effort to meet the needs once met by our lost connections, we carry over the functional habits of the social life. But, in some intuitive way, we know that this doesn't make sense. Allowing for the inevitability of partisan rhetoric on all sides, it is this discomfort that nurtures the habit of

glorifying the virtues of family and loyalty and of discounting the virtues
of social functions. So, no one has a good word to say for a "bureaucrat"
and everyone is for "God and motherhood." We argue endlessly the
merits of government "with a heart" or complain of welfare dependency.

These considerations suggest a context for distinguishing community
service from volunteerism. With the latter we try to provide a functional
equivalent to what was once a fact of living in a community; neighbors
helped each other. Community service, then, reflects an inchoate acknowledgment that volunteering, for all its value, is still functional and
that connection cannot be transformed into function. Community service
is an effort to establish connection in a contemporary environment. And
the context suggests, too, that community service will need to avoid the
illusion that we can restore old connections, retell the old story, so to
speak. We try to, of course. So, President Bush could say,

> We know that government can't rebuild a family, or reclaim a sense of
> neighborhood. . . .
> Most Americans understand that the key to constructive change is build-
> ing relationships, not bureaucracies. And they know that those who say,
> "It's government's problem" are really part of the problem themselves. . . .
> Today, more than ever, we need community service to help drop-outs,
> pregnant teens, and drug abusers. The homeless and AIDS victims. The
> hungry and illiterate. Often, they are disadvantaged, and as their com-
> munities disintegrate around them, they become disconnected from so-
> ciety.[3]

Mr. Bush had plenty of company as he seized upon the nostalgic themes
of our lost connections. Thus, in April of 1991, the Points of Light Foundation published "A Declaration of Commitment to Community Service," signed by hundreds of academics, politicians, health and welfare
executives, and business people. They agreed,

> Government's role is crucial, but government alone can never fill the void
> left by disintegrating families, neighborhoods, and lives. Only people
> working in their own communities—through their workplaces, unions,
> schools, places of worship, and other groups to which they belong—can
> do so. . . .
> Service to others is a unique and enduring American tradition. In com-
> munities across the country today, people are finding ways to make a
> difference in the lives of those who need them. But more, much more,
> must be done.[4]

Despite the reference to our "traditions," however, service is absorbed
within the functional assumptions of the market place. Efforts are

made—seldom successfully—to insulate it from the vicissitudes of "politics." Mechanisms like a "service corps" or a "project team" are used. So-called autonomous agencies are given contracts for service. As one study summed it up,

> Following a long tradition of service in American history—the Civilian Conservation Corps under Franklin Roosevelt, the Peace Corps under John Kennedy, VISTA under Lyndon Johnson, ACTION under Richard Nixon, Youth Conservation Corps under Jimmy Carter—the California Conservation Corps started in 1976 under Governor Jerry Brown, became a permanent state agency in 1983 under Governor George Deukmejian. . . .
>
> Other state corps operate in a variety of ways. The Wisconsin Corps has a two-year $4 million budget to support 65 predominantly rural projects and 750 participants. . . . In Maryland, the Department of Natural Resources coordinates and funds twenty-four county programs. The Washington State Service Corps focuses entirely on human service projects. . . .
>
> The City Volunteer Corps of New York City, with an annual $48 million budget from the city, has pioneered volunteer efforts in human service delivery. . . . The New York City model spawned the Youth Volunteer Corps of Greater Kansas City. . . . A recent urban corps effort, Boston's "City Year," has the added feature of adult mentors from the civic and business community who are paired with youth corps participants.[5]

The nonprofit foundation is another invention used to define the boundaries of the third sector. Earlier in our history—as with Carnegie or Rockefeller—the foundation was a vehicle for personal contribution. Schools and universities are yet another vehicle of the third sector. Thus, at Swarthmore College,

> It is hardly a rarity to find students engaged in this form of volunteerism, especially at Swarthmore, where social responsibility is heartily encouraged. What is different . . . is the funding source: a new and probably unique foundation established to promote effective charitable work.
>
> Called simply the Swarthmore Foundation, this philanthropic entity is one program up and running because of gifts to the $75 million campaign for Swarthmore.[6]

Another university effort is "Campus Compact," a coalition of 120 college and university presidents committed to increasing the number of students involved in public service.[7]

It is striking that so much energy is expended to build a third sector in order to avoid direct action by government. Yet, the market place is also suspect as an agency for meeting communal needs. Hidden by the ideological debate on the "privatization of public services" are the echoes of the once-upon-a-time narrative of a world of clear distinctions and communal connections. We can see this clearly by glancing briefly at

other countries, places that do not enjoy a narrative that radically separates society and community. Despite histories of tyranny unknown to
us, they seem not to have the same sense of the dangers of governments.
In Scandinavian countries, the Netherlands, Japan, and Germany, for
example, it is expected that government will respond to communal
needs. Communal associations are tax supported with few of the controls
we seem to find necessary. Citizens participate as a matter of course,
serving as home visitors, volunteer counselors and the like. They are
called "volunteers" but volunteerism—a deliberate, individual, and gra-
tuitous choice—simply makes no sense in the context. To be sure, there
are some community service organizations: Community Service Volunteers in Great Britain, Katamavik in Canada, Zivildienst in Germany.
In my discussions with teachers, social workers, and counselors abroad,
I am struck by the fact that there is little concern with insulating service
from government. There are, of course, struggles over budgets and the
like but little of the principled cynicism built into the American experience.

Yet, we go on trying to meet communal needs without the direct
interventions of government, even preaching the virtues of doing so to
a global audience. We mount fund-raising campaigns where a simple
tax check-off or a budgetary allocation would do the job quickly and
provide more money with less effort. And this reflects our story as much
as it seeks to guard against the leviathan state. We do not let go of the
lost connection—or perhaps it will not let go of us—while a functional
world, despite ritual protestations, really makes no place for it any
longer.

In this context, community service reflects a persistent strain of American populist romanticism. In our affection for what is called the "grass
roots," we exhibit the hope for a communal democracy, another echo
of the lost connection. We claim that virtue is to be found in the people
and yet the people no longer live with each other in diverse but knowable
communities. So, we exhibit a certain piety in the presence of all the
good things done in the name of volunteering. At the same time, all
that energy in the absence of community is often impotent, a re-living
of the myth of Sisyphus. Indeed, it sometimes seems that volunteering
becomes an end in itself and that volunteer agencies become self-serving
institutions.

GETTING INVOLVED

If the meanings of community service are elusive, the action is not.
Just about anywhere we look we will find people getting involved and
hoping to "make a difference." Trying to sum this all up is an unmanageable task and the statistics only touch the least interesting part of the

story. Typically, when adults are "involved," it is called "volunteering,"
a reflection of the freedom we grant each other as adults. For example,
a poster issued by New York City's School Volunteer Program urges
adults, "Be a school volunteer!" And continues, "Volunteer a few hours
. . . feel good all week." A hint of the difference between community
service and volunteering, even for adults, shows up in the description
of an atypical program,

> One non-profit organization which has been trying to make a contribution
> in this area [housing] since 1976 is Habitat for Humanity. . . . A volunteer
> . . . explains the way it works in the United States.
>
> > Habitat for Humanity is not a charitable organization. "We give away
> > nothing except a great opportunity," a Habitat volunteer says. The
> > opportunity is a significant one however; a new home at cost with
> > an interest-free mortgage loan repayable over twenty years. . . .
>
> The organization was begun by a millionaire who decided to give up
> his successful business for philanthropic pursuits. Willard Fuller now lives
> a modest life as the director of Habitat. . . . All their funds are private
> contributions from individual citizens and corporations because the or-
> ganization relies on a staff of 100 full-time volunteers.[8]

It is revealing that in an encyclopedic review of the history of volunteerism in the United States, the service of young people—with the
exception of military service—is hardly noted until World War II.[9] And,
not surprisingly, the literature that is addressed to young people, school
teachers and school administrators refers to community service. For
example,

> StarServe [Students Taking Action and Responsibility in Service], a new
> national program, gets students creatively involved in community service.
> Every school principal and superintendent in the country has received a
> StarServe kit with materials to help teachers and students plan and im-
> plement a community service project. In addition, every United Way and
> volunteer center across the country has the kit and may be available to
> serve as a resource on community service and volunteer placement op-
> portunities.[10]

A newsletter—there are many of them these days—reports, "Youth
Engaged in Service (YES) Ambassadors," a program to send out "seven
distinguished young people" with the mission to "challenge every
young person, age five to twenty-five, to engage in service directed at
meeting important social needs and to stimulate the creation of opportunities and support necessary to make that service meaningful." Another news item refers to an executive order issued by Governor John

Engler on October 3, 1991, establishing a Michigan Community Service Commission.[11] The illustrations could be multiplied indefinitely.

The difference in address is not just a matter of semantics. Adult volunteers may in many instances do the same things that young people performing community service do. Both may visit the sick, help the elderly, tutor a child, clear an urban dump, clean a roadside. But, community service also conveys a transcending purpose which volunteering does not. It endorses the search for the lost connection even while it is ambivalent about the virtues of those to whom it is addressed. Hence, repeated recurrence to the "me" generation in the rhetoric of community service as if young people had invented egoism and self-seeking. And yet, it designates these least powerful members of society as the carriers of hope. Not incidentally, there is in these modes of address a message of condescension. The volunteer, although seldom alone in his or her task, responds as an individual. He or she is the autonomous citizen making a personal choice. In the appeal to volunteers we are directed to the work to be done. The community service participant, on the other hand, is embedded in an environment filled with symbols and references, a gender and class and caste environment, and finally a preparatory environment. Community service is addressed to the participant's needs as much as if not more than to the work to be done. It is addressed, too, to the transcending purposes of the work to be done. In a sense, the present is more significant for the volunteer than the past or the future. But it is the past and the future which help to make sense of community service.

Another difference between volunteering and community service becomes clear when we look at the typical structures of community service. Community service can be organized as school-based or agency-based, as stand-alone or partnered, as peer-specific or intergenerational. In the doing, community service like volunteering may directly serve the needs of persons or indirectly serve the needs of those providing such direct services. It can include working in nonpersonal environments like vacant lots, parks, forests and the like. Unlike volunteering, however, community service is a collective and historic project, a try at connection beyond the doing. The act as such does not define community service.

But, before moving to the larger themes, we need to look at what is being done. Fortunately, for purposes of description, the projects tend to look very much alike. They address a finite number of needs and benefit from a network of communication. I am quick to add that this is neither an accusation nor a complaint. In any event, a sampling can adequately convey the features of community service in the doing.

It is not surprising that schools are a natural location for doing community service. But the choice of the school is not dictated only by practical considerations like manageability. Schools, after all, inhabit what I have called a "middle ground" between family and society.

> Our teachers, like our parents, are interested in our growth. We develop relationships with them—and they with us—in a setting that is supportive as family is supportive. We will, by and large, be protected by them in our errors and encouraged by them to risk the bounds of conduct without paying the ultimate penalties.
>
> To be sure, schooling will have another face, too. Love and distance will compete. The school will look very much like the rest of society, not least of all like the workplace.[12]

Schools are among the very few institutions we have left for making connections.

By way of example, I will again draw upon my experience with the Ethical Culture-Fieldston Schools. Community service is traditional at the schools and began with their establishment in 1878. For the sake of brevity, I rely on numbers as an indicator of activity. Graduates must complete at least 60 hours of supervised service (120 hours if service is performed during vacation). As described by a group of students and their teacher,

> The "community" served may be defined in many ways: The Ethical Culture Schools, Riverdale (the Bronx neighborhood in which Fieldston is located), a Manhattan neighborhood, a home for older adults, a Westchester town, or a hospital.
>
> "Service" means a contribution to the welfare of others and is often unpaid. (Note: a salaried position which otherwise meets these guidelines is acceptable for credit.) Some service jobs are primary, that is, the students provide services directly, often to people in need such as answering correspondence for a blind person or tutoring a child with learning problems. Other service jobs are secondary, that is, the student performs routine tasks such as filing, book sorting, or envelope stuffing to aid the work of a service organization or to give adult professionals more time to do what they are trained to do. Both kinds of services are worthy. . . . Some students may prefer to work directly with people while others may seek a position in the background of an organization.[13]

More than 250 students may be active at any time in one or another of the nearly 200 agencies that cooperate.

A special feature of the community service program is the peer-counseling project. Some thirty to forty high school juniors and seniors are enrolled in a course that helps them learn to serve as discussion group leaders for middle school discussion groups and ethics classes, to provide tutorial services, to assist regular classroom and homeroom teachers, and to orient students entering high school for the first time. The psychological accessibility of adolescent peers is particularly helpful in addressing matters that teen-agers usually refuse to discuss honestly with adults, for example, peer pressures, parent relationships, substance abuse, sexuality.

Younger students participate as well. Inspired by former New York Mayor Edward Koch's call for a "public and private school" partnership, middle school students (ages twelve to fourteen) from Fieldston and a partner public school, Bronx I.S. 121, have joined together in teams to provide tutoring services to even younger children. Most ambitious of efforts with elementary school children is "Helping Hands." Its start was described by a parent,

> As my son and I were walking to school, I noticed the troubled expression on his face when he saw an old man in tattered clothes lying on the local church steps. In struggling to find the right words to explain this situation, my son asked, "Aren't we going to help him?"
>
> . . . a group of concerned parents, teachers, and school administrators came together . . . to explore ways our children, classes and parents could participate in service projects. . . . Specific grades were responsible for planning and implementing social services projects from food and clothing drives for the homeless, working with senior citizen groups, cleaning up Central Park, working with recent immigrants, to hostessing an afternoon of games and fun with children from a local shelter for homeless families.[14]

Other schools throughout the country have worked out their own community service programs. For example, in 1987, The Council for Religion in Independent Schools described "service opportunities in 46 leading schools, grades K–12." Typically, students were expected to do a required number of hours of work each week or each term in order to avoid momentary and sporadic attention. Continuity and consistency were emphasized as was the need to "encourage young people to realize that their education will be sorely lacking if their hearts learn less than their heads."[15] The second report, in 1990, cited thirteen "award winning programs." It included advice on how to initiate a program and a "master list" of over 150 placement opportunities organized under 18 categories.[16]

Community service is not an "independent" school monopoly although the relative lack of "red-tape" makes such programs more likely. Many public schools are engaged in community service. For example, the Bethlehem Area School District (Pennsylvania) has developed a highly organized community service program requiring the completion of sixty hours of "unpaid community service" for high school credit. Characteristically, the program is described in a language that illustrates the bureaucratic necessities that afflict the tax-supported school.[17] Less

formal—probably because located in a primary school—is a program of
the North Canaan Elementary School.

> The brunch/concert given by Kindergarten through Grade 3 to area senior
> citizens last week was the first of many such community activities and
> events the school has planned this year.
>   The young students, some shy and tentative at first, slowly became
> more and more receptive to their elderly guests and by the end of the
> concert, given by the first graders, there seemed to be an air of mutual
> understanding and admiration in the room. . . .
>   . . . other activities outside of school are being planned. Mrs. Lackner
> [the school principal] says she has talked to the 8th graders about vol-
> unteering as candy stripers over at Geer Memorial Health Center and other
> classes are considering forming a group to clean the road to the town's
> landfill. The school is considering a student-run flower garden to beautify
> the front of the school and the 5th grade is planning to send valentines ·
> to area veterans this week.[18]

Another example of public school activity is the Early Adolescent Helper
Program which began in 1982 at three of New York City's intermediate
and junior high schools. Initially a pilot project of the National Commission on Resources for Youth, sponsorship was assumed in 1983 by
The Center for Advanced Study in Education and now serves schools
throughout the country.

> Designed specifically for eleven to fourteen year olds, the Helper Program
> recognizes their unique needs, as well as their capacity to contribute to
> the community. Young Helpers participate in community agencies such
> as child care and senior citizens centers, preparing for their volunteer roles
> in a seminar led by a skilled adult. The seminar also provides an oppor-
> tunity for students to reflect on and learn from the work experience.[19]

Colleges and universities are no strangers to community service although the language of volunteerism appears with increasing frequency.
For example, in 1987 at Stanford, a Public Service Center provided a
clearing house for placements, an internship program, and advisement
on public service career opportunities. At Brown, the campus volunteer
program assisted in placing students in a number of projects in its Providence, Rhode Island, community. At DePauw, students were active as
"Friends of the Elderly" and in the Big Brother/Big Sister Program as
well as in the more ambitious Winter Break project when 125 students
went to South America as a medical and construction crew. Vanderbilt
University at its Center for Health Sciences provided health examinations
for residents in rural and low income communities. At the State University of New York, Albany, more than 800 students were placed in

some 250 community and government agencies. Notre Dame students
were active in the Head Start Program, in nursing homes, tutoring, adult
literacy.[20]

Funded by the W. K. Kellog Foundation, "Into the Streets" is a more
recent project (1991) developed by students themselves from "the ideas
and experiences of many student campus service programs." Its aim is
to encourage student-led campus coalitions that are "multi-cultural and
represent a cross-section of campus life." Participants are asked to make
a commitment for an entire year and to select their projects from a list
of seventeen issue areas like AIDS, Campus Safety, Children and Youth,
Domestic Violence, Environment, Health Care, Homelessness, Race Relations, Substance Abuse. The tone of "Streets" literature reflects a commitment to a "grass-roots" ideology.

> Before deciding if your campus wants to participate, we ask you to meet
> with other student organizations to discuss the program. . . . It is *essential*
> that you reach out to groups that you have not worked with *before* you
> decide. To allow other groups to feel invested from the beginning, please
> deliberately seek out and speak to those who represent a different con-
> stituency than yours, culturally, politically and socially. This is critical! For
> example, if your student organization is predominantly Asian American,
> you should first approach a student organization which represents a dif-
> ferent cultural constituency. If your organization is more conservative, you
> should approach groups which are more progressive (or vice versa). . . . If
> your organization is a Greek letter organization (a fraternity or sorority),
> you should approach first an organization that is not a Greek letter or-
> ganization.[21]

Cities are likely locations of community service. They grew up around
neighborhoods with habits of service embedded in their political reality.
From the bucket of coal or Thanksgiving turkey distributed by the political machine to acquiescent voters to the transformation of volunteer
fire and police departments into professional agencies, the city became
a surrogate, however, inadequate, for the lost community. Typically,
city efforts in community service take shape as partnerships. Among
examples are New York's City Volunteer Corps, Boston's City Year, and
Los Angeles' Youth Community Service. The New York project was
proposed by Mayor Koch in 1984 to recruit, select, and train young
adults for a year of full-time public service. With an annual budget in
excess of $10 million (1987), it offers participants a weekly stipend of
$80 and to those who have completed their year of service the choice of
a $5,000 college scholarship or $2,500 in cash.

> About three-quarters of the volunteers are high school dropouts yet they
> have managed to teach computer classes to children and adults in East

Harlem, tutor grade schoolers, work with battered children, and conduct a telephone survey to assess a neighborhood's health care needs. Last year when eight children died and 75 were injured in falls from apartment windows, the City Volunteer Corps dispatched its workers to inspect apartments for adherence to city safety codes.[22]

Boston's "City Year" was founded by "two 29-year olds...Mike Brown and Alan Khazei," who "want their program to be considered as the prototype for a year of national service that would be available to every high school graduate in the country."[23] Participants sign on for a year and receive a stipend of $100 per week for expenses and a $5,000 scholarship. Unlike New York's program, City Year is much smaller and less ambitious in its immediate goals. Its aims, however, are global. And, unlike New York's program, "City Year" boasts that it uses no government money.

> City Year is like an urban Peace Corps. This year we have 70 corps members, ages 17–22 recruited from more than 30 communities in Greater Boston and around the country...
> City Year is dedicated to becoming a transformative service resource for Greater Boston and a workshop for a powerful idea—voluntary national service. We think that through a shared generational adventure in idealism young people can be challenged to actually transform their community— and eventually, our democracy. That is our hope.[24]

The Los Angeles program, Youth Community Service, is a joint effort of the Constitutional Rights Foundation and the Los Angeles Unified School District. It sponsors more than 1,000 participants in some 23 public high schools. Included are

> ongoing leadership development activities...weekly school meetings to reinforce leadership...community resource volunteers, adult volunteers from a variety of backgrounds and professions...projects including tree-planting, tutoring, graffiti removal, homeless relief, child care, adopt-a-grandparent...(an) elective course...[which] enables teachers and students to work in a concentrated fashion to develop teamwork...reflect on service...and better prepare for projects.[25]

College and university students, like their younger brothers and sisters, are involved. Unlike high schools and elementary schools, however, faculty participation in the universities and colleges is minimal. Some less than kind souls might attribute this to indifference or even to laziness. For myself, I do not doubt that this lack of participation results, in large measure, from the fact that community service is not considered integral to the academic purposes of academic institutions and that volunteering is really seen as an individual act.

At meetings of higher education administrators, there is increased discussion of the need to educate students toward an understanding of social
problems and an awareness of the traditional responsibilities of democratic
citizenship.

With some exceptions, however, faculty have been noticeably absent
from these activities. Little attention has been given to the faculty role in
supporting service efforts on the part of students, and in setting an example
of civic participation and leadership through their own efforts.[26]

For the college campus, unlike the school, student participation is an
academic incidental, only a matter of convenience. After all, that is where
large concentrations of young people are to be found. Although that is
disturbing, it tells us that connections between learning and action are
not made. Community service is not really understood to have educational or developmental significance, let alone political import, except
in the general way that any experience may be said to be educational
or even good for you. The young are learning the lessons of volunteerism, not community service. With "maturity," the lost connection will
be normalized.

SO, IS IT GOOD TO DO GOOD?

There is no doubt that community service is believed to be an appropriate activity of the young who are not yet socialized. They are regarded
as capable of genuine altruism and of amoralism, exhibiting both the
American dream and a so-called moral vacuum. They are idealistic and
self-seeking, empathetic and egoistic, potent and childlike. Little wonder, then, that young people tend to mistrust their elders who communicate this strange mix of messages. The work to be done is
interpreted as both valuable and pointless, worthy of our best energies
and merely an instrument for personal growth. Moreover, a certain adult
anger often attends the talk of community service, anger at so-called
failing schools and failing families or at some other favorite target. Community service becomes one more weapon of attack. A typical editorial
mixes this anger and enthusiasm,

> An elected member of the Palm Beach County School Board, [Sandra]
> Richmond's full-time job is teaching sociology and psychology at Palm
> Beach Community College. Her doctorate focused on her professional
> passion, ethical decision-making.
> She wants to carry her professional interest into schools by linking it to
> community service . . .
> Unfortunately for her, and more unfortunately for children and parents,
> Richmond's plan is being smothered by the county school system's huge
> and unresponsive bureaucracy.

... school bureaucrats batted down her idea. Relying on such impecc-
able data as "an informal survey" and "the general feeling," the bureaucrats told her essentially to crawl back into her niche on the School Board
and keep quiet. . . . Her plan is at best "superfluous," they grumped, prov-
ing the need to learn ethical decision-making isn't confined to the young.[27]

However, neither editorialists nor politicians nor administrators nor
teachers nor parents capture the realities of the young. The adult world,
caught in its own confusions, tends to project its own puzzles onto
them. That, of course, is not a new phenomenon. And young people
have traditionally resisted their elders. That is not new either. Despite
talk of a "silent generation," however, the young are not silent about
serious things nor are they mere echoes of adults. Even those who seem
silent are not unaware of what is happening and not indifferent either.
Often, their silence is only a way of saying that no one—no adult—is
really listening. That adds an ironic note to the notion that it is the young
that need to be trained for citizenship by community service. It is hard
to find a dramatic moment when today's young people began to find
their voices. Perhaps, we might locate it in the angry pain of Vietnam
protest or the commitments of the civil rights movement. I can recall,
however, high school students protesting civil defense drills in the 1950s.
And I can remember what we have come to call youth activism in the
Henry Wallace candidacy during the 1948 presidential election. What is
clear enough, I think, is that young people after World War II were no
longer content to be "seen but not heard." What is also clear is that the
"causes" they embraced were embedded in communities, albeit temporary gathered communities. Typically, these were marked by distinc-
tive languages, costumes, music, art, and myth.
    When we do listen, we realize that the situation as experienced con-
veys little of the ambivalence that later reflection reveals. We hear the
mixed tones of engagement, achievement and frustration. As one articulate high school senior wrote,

As part of my volunteer work at a local battered-women's shelter, I would
attempt to bring some sense of order and calm to frequently chaotic situations . . .
    . . . I was absorbed in the mechanical motions of my task (sorting a large
donation of socks by size). I was rather startled to hear two voices rising
up the steps and turned to see a woman named Judy, who worked at the
shelter full-time, and another woman I had not seen before. . . . Judy said,
"Mona needs something to wear for a court appearance . . ."
    . . . There seemed an endless supply of wilted knit sweaters and gaudy
men's shirts. The stuff was not appealing. . . . I wanted Mona to feel strong
and confident facing her husband in court, and part of this would mean
feeling secure in her appearance . . .

> ... I spotted a cardboard box ... perused the contents, not expecting to find anything much. I touched a soft white piece of fabric and drew it out of the box ... discovered that it was a reasonable-looking white blouse ... inexplicably impressive in its normality.
>
> ... She tried it on ... turning around in a little dance and moving toward the mirror ...
>
> Mona seemed almost to feel stronger, as if protected by her new outfit. It was time for her to leave for court. We all embraced and said good-bye.
> ...
>
> I never saw Mona again.... Together we had met the requirement of the moment, and for this reason I still feel connected to her.[28]

The vignette and the anecdote dominate the literature of community service unlike the numbers so typical of the adult world. The motives of the participants are transparently benevolent. The participants communicate an abiding confidence in each other and in the possibilities of change, or as is typically put, in "making a difference." Listening to an elementary school student, we hear,

> Most students at my school will never need the tangible benefits of community service. Most will never experience the horrors of hunger or homelessness, the pains of abuse, the shame of illiteracy, or the difficulties of a physical or mental handicap. Although our needs may not be relief from these situations, we will all have the need to be helped by another person's kindness, compassion, and love. And every student has the need and the opportunity for the intangible rewards that come from sharing love with another through community service.[29]

At the same time, story-telling provides evidence of a sense of realism, meeting the "requirement of the moment" as the student put it. "Making a difference" does not depend on changing the world in a sudden dramatic fashion although there is the background dream that as more and more are engaged this will in fact happen. What is expected is that "making a difference" at the very least will make a difference in the person doing the service and the person receiving it. The end is cumulative, personalist and personal. Evident in the story is the hope that the experience in school or college will become a habit of later life. The young, in other words, have accepted the adult assignment of community service. For example, at Susquehanna University (Pennsylvania), "service is a way of life." At least half of the student body have lived in one of nine "Project Houses" and have participated in one or more of the university-sponsored service projects by the time they graduate. Apart from doing worthwhile things like serving as "big brothers" and "big sisters" or working in a Senior Center, the point is made over and over again that it is the student who grows and changes, who experiences a "way of life" and who is not "just a volunteer."[30] Similarly,

The experience that has propelled high school senior Robert Nelson to new insights is St. Louis Metro High School's nationally acclaimed community service program. It pushed students out of their safe, familiar surroundings by forcing them to provide a minimum of 240 hours of community service during their four-year high school careers. . . .

Metro High School's public service requirement has existed since the school opened 15 years ago, giving young people like Nelson experiences they'll never forget and will hopefully seek to repeat throughout their adult lives. Metro is a "magnet" public school, open to 240 above-average students. . . . The student body is half black, half white.[31]

The incorporation of community service within the curriculum is frequently proposed. By way of example, a House of Representatives' report on the National Service Act noted,

On January 19, 1990, Committee (on Education and Labor) staff visited P.S. 38, an elementary school located in Brooklyn, N.Y., which employs a service learning curriculum developed by the College for Human Services in New York City. The Committee staff observed fifth and sixth grade classes engaged in service learning and spoke with teachers and the school's principal about the impact of the curriculum on the students. According to Mrs. Millicent Goodman, Principal of P.S. 38:

1. Attendance in classes using the College's system has been higher than overall attendance at P.S. 38.

2. During the fall semester . . . there was no suspension of any student in classes using the College's system.

3. The sixth and fifth grade teachers and I have observed that youngsters have become excited about learning when they must apply their learning outside the classroom.

4. Students learning under the College's system are reading better and improving their arithmetic skills.

5. Teachers are enthusiastic even though working under the College's system involved additional preparation, time and work.[32]

Our samples offer a consistent message of good actions and intentions. However, all these energies tend to hide the puzzles that appear when we do reflect. At that moment, it is insufficient to rely on moral or political common sense. As community service shades off into volunteerism, we realize that it is described and advocated from the position of the doer and not of the done-to. When, however, doer and done-to are said to be equal members of a democratic community, that becomes problematic. It was, to be sure, not problematic at all when inequalities were taken to be the normal way of things and connections were simply inherited. But, the young have come to believe in our egalitarian rhetoric. We arrive where we began, interpreting community service as part of the effort to reconstruct the vanishing community while sustaining the values of democratic society. And that has its history.

NOTES

1. I claim no originality for this comment. Max Weber developed the distinction between *gemeinschaft* and *gesellschaft* early in the century as he worked out a sociology for the evolution of industrial societies.

2. For a discussion of the way the "third sector" works by one of its leading analysts, see Peter F. Drucker, *Managing The Nonprofit Organization* (New York: Harper Collins, 1990).

3. George Bush, "Presidential Remarks: New York Partnership," June 22, 1989, pp. 2–3.

4. Points of Light Foundation, "A Declaration of Commitment to Community Service," *New York Times*, April 15, 1991.

5. The William T. Grant Commission on Work, Family and Citizenship (1988), Samuel T. Halpern, Study Director, "Pathways to Success: Citizenship Through Service," *Combining Service and Learning*, Jane Kendall and Associates, Ed., Raleigh, N.C.: National Society for Internships and Experiental Education, 1990), pp. 451–452 *passim*. See also, in the same volume, pp. 417–418, "A Resource Guide for States" (1989), issued by the National Governors' Association.

6. "Foundation Launched For Volunteers," *The Garnet Letter*, December 1987, p. 1.

7. For example, see Marc J. Ventresca and Anna L. Waring with Jeanne Wahl Halleck, Saphira M. Baker and Melissa Auchard, "Collegiate Community Service: The Status of Public and Community Service at Selected Colleges and Universities" (1987), *op. cit.*, Jane Kendall and Associates, vol. I, p. 610.

8. Alan L. Stoskoff and Margot Stern Strom, *Choosing to Participate*, (Brookline, Mass.: Facing History And Ourselves National Foundation, 1990), pp. 301–302.

9. Susan J. Ellis and Katherine H. Noyes, *By the People*, (San Francisco: Jossey Bass, 1990, Revised).

10. Brochure, "StarServe," Kraft General Foods Foundation, A Points of Light Initiative, 1990.

11. Citations are from the Constitutional Rights Foundation, "National Scene," *School Youth Service Network*, 3, 1 (Winter 1991), p. 3.

12. Howard B. Radest, *Can We Teach Ethics*, (New York: Praeger, 1989), pp. 37–38.

13. "Course of Study," The Fieldston School, New York City, 1991, p. 35.

14. Dianna Friedman, "Introduction," *Helping Hands: A Family and School Guide to Volunteering* (New York: The ECS Community Service Committee, 1986), pp. 3–4.

15. The Council for Religion in Independent Schools, *A Guide to Representative Community Service Programs*, (Washington, D.C., 1987). Citation is by Barbara Picco of The Bishop's School, no page numbers.

16. Catherine D. Sands and Michael J. Gorman, editors, *Award Winning Com-*

munity Service Programs in Independent Schools, Revised 1990 Edition, (Washington, D.C.: The Council for Religion in Independent Schools, 1990).

17. "Community Service Program," Bethlehem, Pennsylvania, April 2, 1990. The program is outlined in a "curriculum course guide" form with a set of "course objectives," a description of "course content," provision for "course evaluation" and assignment of "course credit." I suspect the program will be carried on by students and teachers in spite of the structure.

18. Robert B. Longley, "School Seeks to Encourage Community Service," *The Lakeville Journal,* Canaan, Conn., February 13, 1992, Section B, p. 1.

19. "Child Care Helper Program," brochure published by the Early Adolescent Helper Program and the Center for Advanced Study in Education, New York City, the Graduate School and University Center of The City University of New York, no date but probably 1989 or 1990.

20. These and many other examples are to be found in a 1987 informal report, "Background Information on Campus Compact: The Project for Public and Community Service."

21. Citations are from literature circulated by "Into the Streets," with its national office at the University of Minnesota, St. Paul, Minnesota, 1991.

22. "NYC Corps Proves Young People Care To Make A Difference," *Spotlight On Service,* Washington, D.C., Youth Service America, no date but probably published in 1987.

23. David Nyhan, "City Year: An Inspiration for the Nation," *Boston Sunday Globe,* December 30, 1990.

24. "Local Urban Peace Corps Is a Workshop for National Service," *City Year* 1, 1 (Winter 1991), p. 1.

25. "Youth Community Service," fact sheet, no date, probably 1988 or 1989.

26. Donald Kennedy and David Warren, "The Faculty Role in the Public Service Initiative," memorandum Campus Compact Presidents, March 9, 1988, Action Steps, p. 1.

27. James G. Driscoll, "Point Students in Right Direction by Requiring Them to Serve the Community," *The Fort Lauderdale Sun-Sentinel,* June 20, 1990.

28. Jean Hohman, "The Requirement of the Moment," *op. cit.,* The Council for Religion in Independent Schools, 1990, pp. 55–56.

29. Finny Akers, St. Patrick's Episcopal Day School, Washington, D.C., in *Why We Serve,* a "sampler" compiled by the Council for Religion in Independent Schools, 1990.

30. "Profile: At Susquehanna U. Service Is a Way of Life," *Streams* (Washington, D.C., Youth Service America, February/March 1989), p. 1.

31. *"240 Hours that Change the Life of High School Students,"* Spotlight On Service, Washington, D.C., Youth Service America, no date.

32. "Report, National Service Act," Committee on Education and Labor, House of Representatives, H.R. 4330, August 15, 1990.

Chapter Four

Looking Backward

TROUBLED LEGACY

Community service did not come suddenly upon the scene. It had its roots in nineteenth-century America. We must pay attention then to the mixture of practicalism and myth, of self-seeking and idealism which sound the counterpoints of that period. This, in an admittedly selective manner, is what I propose now to do.

I have already noted the traditional themes still heard in the language of community service. We try to fit community service into a vanishing American script and thus to legitimize it. Thus, community service is justified as a free market good by "realists" and as a response to human need by reformers, as character-building by conservatives and as moral development by liberals. It is praised as a vehicle for recapturing the past and for reconstructing the future. Advocates tend to align themselves with one or another tradition, conservatives announcing a return to a "kinder gentler" America and liberals proclaiming a new age of reform. Critics take sides as well. Conservatives are fearful that community service is an attack on individualism and liberals are fearful that it is but an excuse for evading society's responsibilities. It will help us in our search for the meanings of community service to pay attention, then, to self-reliance and community. We locate the sources of community service when we realize that these characters in the American story were radically altered with the demographic, social, and technological changes of post-Civil War America.

Of course, any starting point is arbitrary. Self-reliance and community arrived with the colonists. To be sure, theirs was not the democratic community of the American dream. They accepted religious discrimination, limited the vote to property owners, and had no qualms about the presence of the poor, the slave, the indentured servant. Women had their place in the household. Presence in the community, then, did not necessarily carry membership in it. Nor was Jefferson's "honest farmer" guaranteed success. Farming was—and still is—a harsh and risky way of living. Self-reliance, for all the exaltations of Emersonian rhetoric, did not insure economic or cultural achievement. Yet, the images, celebrated in the American story, come easily to mind: the pioneer in the wilderness and the Pilgrims building the "City on a Hill." Exemplars of self-sufficiency and community, Benjamin Franklin competes with Cotton Mather in the mind's eye.

As long as self-sufficiency and community were embedded in the relationships of the family farm and the small town, little tension existed between them. The good neighbor often provided a home for the poor relative, the unmarried woman, the homeless child. Indeed, this was a common expectation and a token of the responsibilities of the free man. Failing that, poor-houses and work-houses—following the English model—offered grudging shelter, clothing and food although most towns protected themselves against permanent "guests" by requiring proof of blood relationship or by demanding that the "guest" plan to move on after a limited stay. Later, Calvinist "election," a combination of individual salvation and Christian community, evolved into a justification for economic success. Theology served as witness to the secular marriage of community and self-reliance just as events were calling both into question.

> Two doctrines drawn from the Christian tradition were especially emphasized: the concept of the individual as a free moral agent, and the doctrine that God has determined the success or failure of each of His children. . . . Men like James McCosh, president of Princeton University and a power in Presbyterian circles, opposed social legislation on the grounds that God-given abilities were to be used freely and any attempt to interfere with their use was "theft." Equally common was the emphasis of the famous New York preacher, Henry Ward Beecher. "God has intended the great to be great and the little to be little," Beecher cried. If this meant that Henry Ward Beecher received forty thousand dollars a year and a laborer one dollar a day, there was no cause for whimpering at God's decisions.[1]

Of course, *laissez faire* served for those less given to theology. By the beginnings of the second century of the American experiment, however, the family farm and the small town were being threatened by the new industrial city and the millions of immigrants from Europe. Defending the "status quo" in other words was, as it usually is, evidence of a politics under attack although it might pose as a theological—or as in the case of social Darwinism, a scientific-truth. As Richard Hofstadter summed it up,

> From 1860 to 1910, towns and cities sprouted up with miraculous rapidity all over the United States. Large cities grew into great metropolises, small towns grew into large cities, and new towns sprang into existence on vacant land. While the rural population almost doubled during this half century, the urban population multiplied almost seven times. Places with more than 50,000 inhabitants increased in number from 16 to 109. The large cities of the Middle West grew wildly. Chicago more than doubled its population in the single decade from 1880 to 1890, while the Twin Cities trebled theirs, and others like Detroit, Milwaukee, Columbus and Cleveland increased from sixty to eighty percent.[2]

The habits of a rural past were simply inadequate. Personal charity could not comprehend the size of things. And the economy was confounded by the development of a boom and bust business cycle with its massive unemployment and its threat of wide-spread starvation and homelessness. Relationships of family and place were dissolving. In fact, America's farm and town were themselves reflecting the changes visible in the urban center.

> Rural and small-town America ... were no idylls, though they often seemed so to men peering out of the smoky pall of the cities. Local community had often been fragile; now men were unambiguously bound to a commercial chain which united them to the centers of industry and trade and divided them from each other. Vulnerable to changes in the market, often overmortgaged or over-expanded both the farmer and the tradesman were caught up in all too Darwinian competition ... the stablest of communities, all felt it; throughout the East and especially in New England, farmers were forced off the land by competition from the West, and the towns began to die. And the West itself, partly the creation of railway promotion schemes, was in little better straits.[3]

Even as the American scene was being transformed, new Americans with different habits were arriving in ever greater numbers from Europe. Always a nation of immigrants—although the "first families" tended to forget that—a vastly enlarged mix of languages, cultures, and styles made its appearance. City neighborhoods became ethnic enclaves; Italian and Russian and Polish and Czech and Hungarian and Yiddish competed with English. The new Americans brought with them unfamiliar sects, entertainments, diets, costumes and life styles. Crowded into the industrial city, they were soon trapped in the urban slum. Of course, the newcomers were blamed for causing the noise, dirt and disease which was their lot. Uprooted and exploited, they tried to re-create in the new land the resources of the old. At the same time, having arrived in the "golden" land, they were driven by their hopes to become "Americans." A "melting pot" ideology sneered at the values and practices they had brought with them. Victimized, they were also victims of the tension within themselves and not least of all of the tensions between the generations.

Again, the numbers can only hint at the stories they had to tell.

> Between the close of the Civil War and the outbreak of the First World War, the rise of American industry and of the absence of restrictions drew a steady stream of immigrants which reached its peak in 1907 when 1,285,000 immigrant entries were recorded. By 1910, 13,345,000 foreign-born persons were living in the United States, or almost one seventh of the total population. The country had long been accustomed to heavy immigration, but the native Yankee was not prepared for the great shift in the sources of immigration, especially noticeable after 1900, from the familiar English, Irish, Scandinavians and Germans to the peasantry of southern and eastern Europe.[4]

Neither self-reliance nor community had much of a chance under these conditions. To be sure, neighborliness managed to survive among the victims, at least for a time. Ethnic self-help groups grew rapidly. Often centered around church or synagogue and located in the neighborhood, immigrant burial societies and charity organizations flourished. It seemed almost a desperate effort to hold on to what was vanishing or had vanished with the old country. The earlier immigrant, long settled in the countryside or town, was not immune. Indeed, modern events were for him and her doubly puzzling. Involuntarily uprooted, he or she suffered a loss of what had seemed both natural and secure.

> It was the great age of the fraternal orders which sprang up across America in the townsman's search for some safe retreat from his daily life of competition, insecurity, and hostility. The lodges did not try to conquer that environment; rather they allowed men to escape from it into a world of pure affection, a momentary place of romance....
>
> ... Allowing the individual a faint romantic echo of fraternity, they [the lodges] also suggested that in the gigantic and expanding nation he was not alone and insignificant, but one of a band of brothers with lodges about the land.... The communities were passing, men were becoming small units of a great system, and more than passwords and regalia were required to remove anxiety.[5]

The themes of the American story no longer met the realities. Successful and victim alike now lived in a world of lost connections where individualism was praised while corporatism was rewarded. Great personal fortunes could still be and were made. Technical invention was still the province of an Edison or Bell or Howe. And success stories could be told about immigrant fortunes too. All of these were added to the lore of the American story. Yet, a function-filled society was already visible and with it, collectivity in place of community.

Human needs were evident and unmet, and this evoked the passions and energies of the reformer. At the same time, the "boss" and the club house made their appearance. In return for voting—"early and often" as the phrase goes—the boss provided a job, an apartment, food. In a sense, both boss and reformer forecast the coming of the "third sector." They anticipated, too, the struggle between "case" and "cause," the conservative-liberal debate over responding to the personal need or reforming the social structure. Everywhere, needs seemed to grow larger and to multiply in number.

> Along with extremes of wealth came walls of impersonality. By the Eighties, a large percentage of factory hands worked in big plants where the owner was as remote as any feudal lord had ever been from his serfs. The dry-goods shop was becoming the department store, and in department stores the clerk did not first-name the boss or presume to take his daughter to church. Without the familiar relations, callousness was easy, almost inevitable. An inventor remarked that he could sell a time-saving device in twenty places and a life-saving invention scarcely at all. Doctors thought nothing of charging two dollars a visit to workingmen whose wages were a dollar-and-a-half a day. The first move to protect children from the vice and disease of the slums came from the president of New York's Society for the Prevention of Cruelty to Animals who, as a kind of afterthought, founded the Society for the Prevention of Cruelty to Children. "Land of opportunity, you say," a Chicago worker snarled at a spread-eagle speaker. "You know damn well my children will be where I am—that is, if I can keep them out of the gutter.[6]

America's classical age was over and, with that, new needs and new responses were in the making.

THE SOCIAL SETTLEMENT

The reformers are a fascinating lot and their actions a crazy-quilt: the city clubs, and good-government clubs, the utopians and socialists and single-taxers, the establishment of a civil service, the building of model apartments, the beginnings of a labor union movement, the struggle against child labor, the development of visiting nurses and legal aid, the establishment of a public school and on and on. In this whirl, the "social settlement" is most suggestive for a discussion of community service. Here indeed was a movement of the young and the able seeking purpose and participation for themselves. Here too was an effort to re-establish the lost connection. As Jane Addams put it,

> what a Settlement attempts to do. It aims, in a measure, to develop what-ever of social life its neighborhood may afford, to focus and give form to that life, to bring to bear upon it the results of cultivation and training; but it receives in exchange for the music of isolated voices the volume and strength of the chorus. It is quite impossible for me to say in what pro-portions or degree the subjective necessity which led to the opening of Hull House combined the three trends: first, the desire to interpret de-mocracy in social terms; secondly, the impulse beating at every source of our lives, urging us to aid in the race progress; and third, the Christian movement toward humanitarianism.[7]

The social settlement is still with us but in different form. Today, when I visit a neighborhood house or a community house—which is what the "social settlement" is usually called—I am as likely as not to meet with a staff member. He or she will probably have a degree in social work or community organization and will probably be bi-lingual. The bulletin board will provide information about athletic contests, hobby groups, dramatic and musical performances, excursions. There will be offerings of "English as a second language," and adult literacy classes and programs for "senior citizens." Often, the settlement will be part of a housing development, perhaps in a basement area or other nonrentable space. Some of the settlements will be well endowed, most will be struggling to survive.

The pioneer settlement house worker would be quite at home—at least for a while. To be sure, the languages will have changed—Black English or Spanish or Haitian or Vietnamese. An Irish brogue or Italian or Yiddish, the languages of the founding period, are not likely to be heard. Yet, it will still be the languages of the streets and that will be familiar. The activities will be different. But the energies will be the same and the frustrations too. Above all, many young and old will remain on the streets and not come inside.

The professionalization of the settlement house worker—typically, professional and volunteer develop together—would be both a pleasant and an unpleasant surprise. On the one hand, the cause of a profession of social service was very much alive for the pioneers, Jane Addams, Stanton Coit, John Elliot, Henry Moskowitz, Lillian Wald and their col-leagues. At the same time, the apartness of the professional would be deeply troubling to them. They knew the benefits of amateurism al-though they were certainly not amateurish. Their talks, letters and notes report the isolation of "up-town" and "down-town." To counter it, they chose not only to work in the neighborhood but to live there—indeed, failure to become part of the neighborhood, they felt, would insure failure to achieve the goals of the settlement.

> In those early days we were often asked why we had come to live on Halstead Street when we could afford to live somewhere else. I remember one man who used to shake his head and say it was "the strangest thing he had met in his experience," but who was finally convinced that it was "not strange but natural." In time it came to seem natural to all of us that the Settlement should be there. If it is natural to feed the hungry and care for the sick, it is certainly natural to give pleasure to the young, comfort to the aged, and to minister to the deep-seated craving for social intercourse that all men feel. Whoever does it is rewarded by something which, if not gratitude, is at least spontaneous and vital and lacks that irksome sense of obligation with which a substantial benefit is too often acknowledged.[8]

These founders would appreciate the struggle of the settlement "worker" for a personal life. They had tried, not always successfully, to make spaces for themselves in an ever-demanding environment. And they would understand quite well the inescapable need for funds and volunteers, and with it the dependency on "up-town."

The founding generation of settlement house workers would, of course, find much that is unfamiliar. In particular, the loss of a sense of political mission would be very disappointing. In its original, modeled after Toynbee House founded by a group of Oxford graduates in London, the settlement house was part family, part social service and part political movement. As Stanton Coit, founder of the Neighborhood Guild (today the University Settlement) in New York City in 1886, put it,

> Undirected and unorganized, the instinctive generosity of the working people is inevitably sentimental, fanciful, easily fatigued, and excited only by the most palpable forms of want. The poor as well as the rich need enlightenment in their charity; when awakened to responsibility and instructed, their impulsive kindness becomes a persistent principle of all-round care for one another; and if neighborhood be linked to neighborhood, each organized in its own guild but all united in those efforts which are too comprehensive for any one to undertake alone, the whole life of the metropolis will be raised. And, can it be raised in any other way?[9]

For the founding group of college-educated men and women in their twenties, the dream was populist and participatory. Despairing of politics and business as usual, these few—and they were very few—soon came to know each other whether they worked in New York or Chicago or Philadelphia or St. Louis. They were moved to build an alternative life for themselves as much as to help others. Some of our current catchwords like "empowerment" and "participation" would be natural among them. Essentially, they tried to combine meeting the needs of the individual or family in trouble with an effort to "reconstruct" society as John Dewey, who volunteered for a time at Hull House, might have put it. Another reformer caught the mood, when he wrote,

> We had been a band of guerrillas, the incentive proceeding usually from Dr. Felix Adler, Mrs. Josephine Shaw Lowell, or some one of their stamp; and the rest of us joining in to push that cart up the hill, then taking time to breathe until another came along that needed a lift. The social settlements, starting as neighborhood guilds to reassert the lost brotherhood, became almost from the first the fulcrum, as it were. . . . If parks were wanted, if schools needed bettering, there were at the College Settlement, the University Settlement, the Nurses' Settlement, and at a score of other such places, young enthusiasts to collect the facts and to urge them, with the prestige of their non-political organization to back them.[10]

The settlement was a city movement motivated by a sense of the community's historic ability to provide for people. But despite the efforts of those middle-class idealists to transcend class and caste, the community of the poor was remedial more than generative. When the new immigrants became American "success" stories, they left the neighborhood—often regretfully and sadly—for a place that was more "American" and more bourgeois. To be sure, many kept up a money tie but that only emphasized the substitution of function for connection, of symbol for relationship.

Meanwhile, there was always too much to do. I recall, by way of example, my study of the work of John Lovejoy Elliott.[11] I wonder at the number and variety of demands that were reported in his notes, letters, and "day book." Thus, a recent essay described the founding in 1894 of the Hudson Guild,

> The neighborhood [New York's Hell's Kitchen] was a slum: noisy, crowded, violent, and filled with the unemployed, the ill-fed and the ill-housed. Gangs of crap-shooting teen-aged boys roved the streets, a threat to others and a danger to themselves. These were the Hurly Burlies, which under Elliott's guidance became a boy's club. . . . Other clubs evolved as did libraries, gymnasiums, job-training programs, a kindergarten, a mothers' club, many educational classes, and two employment bureaus, all largely staffed by young members of the New York Society [for Ethical Culture].
>
> Elliott succeeded, too, in founding a print shop, sponsored in part by the Printing Trades Union and in part by the New York Society and which became the School for Printers' Apprentices. The employment bureau for unskilled women was sufficiently successful to have been taken over by

the New York State Employment Service. . . . These activities, collectively, became Hudson Guild.[12]

In the end, society could not accommodate community. But, the story is not simply a tragedy. The "subjective necessity," as Jane Addams called it, that is, the urge of the young reformers to model authentic lives, became one of the great achievements of the social settlement as did the establishment of a legitimate place for the "helping" professions. There were needs to be met—always more and more of them—and the social settlement was there when little else was.

AGENCIES OF CRISIS: UMT, THE CCC AND THE NYA

Our search for the meanings of community service cannot be advanced without noticing the development of the military, the New Deal, the post-World War II shift in our sense of place and, later, the evocations of John Kennedy's Peace Corps. They are punctuation marks for a still to be written social history of the young. Of course, I do not mean to suggest that nothing relevant to our story was happening between the founding of the social settlement and the depression-born Civilian Conservation Corps. The public school was coming into its own. The helping professions were taking root. Social experiments were to be found in the states and cities, highlighted by progressive politics in Wisconsin and progressive administrations in New York. Labor unions were making their bloody way onto the national stage. A generation had gone to war in 1917; another was to suffer the terrors of the depression. Youth-serving programs developed like the Boy Scouts and Girl Scouts, and the "muscular" Christianity of the YMCA. Nevertheless, our story takes its twentieth-century shape in the crisis of depression and war.

Young men have always gone to war. With the military draft and technological warfare, however, the notion of the citizen soldier *en masse* made its appearance. To be sure, the colonial militia were citizen soldiers too, but they fought on home territory, under officers who had been their neighbors, and for a limited enlistment period. The Civil War draft conveyed a mixed message of military service. Every young white male was eligible for the draft. However, draftees were permitted to purchase substitutes and the war could, in any case, be interpreted as self-defense. With World War I, however, mandatory military service marked a radical move away from voluntary militias and self-defense. For the first time in the American story, it was legitimate to require a generation to surrender its personal goals to the larger goals of society. A new language of service was initiated and with it the now familiar notion of calling on the young to serve the general good.

If 1917 was the first time this happened, it was not to be the last.

Hitlerism, the depression, and the invasion of Poland set the scene for
the first of many efforts to adopt permanent universal military training
(UMT). A National Service Act was proposed by Representative Jerry
Voorhis of California in August 1940. Every young man between eighteen and twenty-four would be required to give up to twelve months
of service in a designated National Service Agency: the CCC, the NYA,
the Public Health Service, the U.S. Forest Service and the various military
branches. No action was taken in the 76th Congress and the bill was
not re-introduced. The Selective Service Act of 1940 was, however,
adopted and there were suggestions that after the war it could be converted into a permanent universal military training and service program.
As New York attorney Grenville Clark, one of the authors of the Act,
wrote to Professor Eugen Rosenstock-Huessy of Dartmouth, "it is not
too early to begin thinking about a revision . . . on a longer term basis."
He envisioned a program whereby every young man, eighteen to
twenty-four, would give a year of service, some in the military and others
in work-service.[13] When the war was over and demobilization well under
way, President Harry Truman appointed a commission to look into
UMT. In 1947, with Karl Compton, president of MIT as its chair, it
recommended that all eighteen-year-olds have six months of military
training and a long-term reserve obligation. However, the public did
not support the idea and the bill did not get out of committee.

During the "Cold War," military service did become a "normal" occupation for several million young men and women; Korea saw the re-
introduction of conscription; and Vietnam continued it. Once, it was
unusual to see someone in a military uniform in our cities and towns
before World War II. Today, the uniform is a regular feature of the
American landscape and the benefits of a military career advertised in
the media. Of course, the young were not consulted. Blacks and other
minorities, until the early 1950s, were expected to serve in segregated
units with limited opportunities for promotion. Young women were
restricted even more severely. The draft was hardly universal.

The end of World War I had brought with it the end of conscription
and things went back to "normal," for a while. It took a domestic crisis
to bring the idea of service back into view. Depression programs, however, waffled between work relief and community service. For many,
service was only a way of providing sustenance and jobs. For others,
the crisis was a chance to build a "youth movement" that crossed lines
of class and caste, to find ways of bridging the gap, as the settlement
worker might have said, between "uptown" and "downtown." The new
reformers saw a chance for a revived democracy that in the 1920s had
lost its way and that in the 1930s might well lose its existence in the face
of international and domestic fascism. Unlike their settlement worker
ancestors, however, they were not prepared to depend on the charity

of "uptown" and the virtues of the people in the neighborhood. The activism of the New Deal was an opportunity for community reconstruction. Government was a fit instrument. The tensions of the new alliance were hardly noted.

It is not surprising that the language of war was appropriated to these purposes in an ironic variation on William James' call for a "moral equivalent to war." The needs of young men—and in some instances of young women—could not be ignored. If nothing else, there were simply too many young people to permit invisibility. Symptomatically, the administration in Washington created two new agencies—the New Deal was perhaps the most prolific generator of agencies in the history of the modern industrial state. The National Youth Administration (NYA) offered part-time work. Both men and women participated. About one in eight were college students, and participants typically received about $15 per month. The Civilian Conservation Corps (CCC) was aimed at a rural population. Unemployed young men, ages eighteen to twenty-five and with no criminal record could enroll for six months and continue for up to two years. About 10 percent had completed a high school education and 8 percent were black. Placed in camps run by the army and segregated racially, participants were fed, housed, and clothed, and received a monthly payment of $30, two-thirds of which went directly back to the family. In the mid–1930s, about half a million were enrolled and by the time the program was closed in 1942, nearly 3 million men had participated.

Like the NYA, the CCC was also suspect. The militarism of the Nazi Youth Corps and the German Labor Service came readily to mind.

> By 1935, enrollment in the (German Labor Service) was compulsory for all young men between the ages of 18 and 26, regardless of their economic situation. Its function had also broadened. No longer simply involved with relief and conservation, it was now concerned with the molding of character along Nazi lines through massive indoctrination and with preliminary military instruction. The martial caste of Hitler's camps was frankly admitted. . . . The CCC did not develop similar characteristics. . . . The Corps always remained a voluntary organization concerned primarily with relief and conservation, with its wider functions never clarified. Despite military participation in its organization, it was essentially nonmilitary in concept.[14]

A vignette of the period serves to set off the typical CCC program with its immediacy from one of its more curious expressions. This was the aptly named "Camp William James," a CCC project initiated by six newly graduated students from Dartmouth in 1940 and endorsed by Franklin and Eleanor Roosevelt. The camp was to serve as a testing ground for what the CCC might become after the crisis. I learned about it in 1990 when I conducted a memorial service for Louis "Bud" Schlivek, an old friend and one of the camp's student founders. As I explored its brief career in the letters and documents he had left behind, I saw the search for community in the midst of totalitarian attack on one side and bureaucratic functions on the other. The project was inspired by Eugen Rosenstock-Huessy, professor of Social Philosophy at Dartmouth who had tried to develop democratic work-service in Germany after World War I. With the rise of Hitler, he left Germany and came to the United States. In a letter to W. W. Alexander, chair of the National Defense Commission, Huessy wrote,

> American youth is educationally overfed, and vocationally undernourished.
> In any army, even in wartime, the soldiers spend three quarters of their time waiting. . . . Whereas the army stands and waits, the work-service *performs*. . . . However, although the army cannot be a model for work service, a still greater disaster would befall the CCC if it were handed over to social workers, educational advisors, or a civil bureaucracy. At present the CCC camps are an appendix of the army; boredom, playing cards, loafing are the result.[15]

To be located at an abandoned CCC site in Tunbridge, Vermont, the Camp was to be civilian run, to include college graduates along with the working-class and rural population typical of CCC projects, and to involve the local community. Naturally, it ran into trouble—politically and bureaucratically—despite the support of the White House and other influentials like Dorothy Canfield Fisher, Dorothy Thompson and Vermont's Senator Aiken. Responding to an attack by Congressman Albert Engel, Claude Wickard, Secretary of Agriculture wrote,

> One of the severest criticisms of the CCC is that . . . it has tended to develop an un-American sort of class system. . . . Since all the boys were from relief, or near-relief families, there has been a strong tendency among the enrollees and the general public to regard the CCC as a sort of dumping-ground for youth of a special social class. . . .
> One of the most important aspects of present CCC operations has been the lack of cooperation, and the occasional bad relations, between the camps and the local communities . . . we feel that the camps can and should be making a real and permanent contribution to the community life. To work toward this ideal, it has been suggested that the local people should sponsor the camps and assist in the planning of the work they do.[16]

Camp William James lasted less than a year, a victim not only of its nonconforming habits but of the coming of World War II. Politically unique, its work-service features were by no means original. Indeed, some few privately sponsored work camps were making similar efforts to prepare young people for democratic citizenship.

For some years, the Friends Service Camps have provided summer opportunities for young people from colleges to work and to work hard. Thus,
this summer there is a work camp in northern Georgia. . . . It will devote
itself to the construction of a dam for a small cooperative community. . . .
Last summer at the Hudson Guild Farm there was a work camp . . . of
young people . . . who worked . . . on the reconditioning of a house to be
occupied by tenement families of the Hudson Guild district. . . .

    . . . At the present time there are similar educational experiments under
way in ten CCC camps. Thus with under-privileged youth and with privileged youth, there is under way a utilization of work as a significant
aspect of democratic experience.[17]

In 1938, the Farmers Union had experimented with a camp program
at Estes Park, Colorado. Several labor unions had offered similar programs for children of their members. The 4H clubs, the National Association of Manufacturers, the American Legion, and countless
religious groups were responding. All stressed the urgency of democratic
citizenship. By July of 1940, Algernon Black had led the Ethical Culture
Society to establish four work camps organized as Work Camps for
Democracy,

whereas many of the non-work camp programs for youth . . . promoted
programs having to do with their own viewpoints . . . this project would
have no special narrow concern. . . . Its common ground . . . would be the
meaning of democracy and the meaning of democratic citizenship.
Whereas some of the other youth projects had a pacifist spirit and emphasis, this one would be uncommitted to any one program for peace.
And whereas some projects were maintained by a particular political party,
this one would be completely non-partisan.
    The (first) Work Camp for Democracy was held at West Park, New York,
in the summer of 1939. The 60 campers were from 17 to 24 years of age.
They came from 12 states and 5 foreign countries. This coeducational
camper body was diverse in religion, color, vocation, and income level.[18]

Suspended during the war, the project was revived in a more dramatic
and long-lived way as The Encampment for Citizenship which, despite
the vicissitudes of budgets and time, exists to this day.[19]
    For some, reliance on education and community service for an alter-
native politics did not seem to address the forces which were shaping
the modern world. So, Columbia sociologist Robert Lynd commented
privately to Black,

I am for any non-fascist youth movement and therefore for Work Camps
for America. I like the "work-camp" idea. But I had a feeling the movement
is more social worky than trenchant. There seemed to be a kind of mystical

reverence for "working together." It *is* good, but working together for what? . . . we're in a time when youth must be mobilized to take the offensive against this bumbling world we older people have tolerated. . . . I certainly won't sabotage any useful liberal movement. . . . But, it all sounds so doggone "respectable," and if youth organization tries to be too respectable now, it'll simply be taken into camp. . . . I think we're entering a time of real danger to people who urge "more radical" action upon respectable organizations . . . It's a bitter period we're entering and those of us who believe large changes are inevitable are in for trouble.[20]

The partnership of citizen and state was typical of the period and quite different from the attitudes that shaped the social settlement. It was, at one and the same time, a source of strength and of weakness.

ASK NOT . . . THE PEACE CORPS AND ITS CHILDREN

Speaking at the Cow Palace in San Francisco on November 2, 1960, candidate John F. Kennedy called for the creation of a "peace corps" saying,

I therefore propose that our inadequate efforts in this area [the underdeveloped world] be supplemented by a "peace corps" of talented young men willing and able to service their country in this fashion for three years as an alternative to peacetime Selective Service . . . We cannot discontinue training our young men as soldiers of war—but we also need them as ambassadors of peace.[21]

After the election, the Institute of International Education convened a committee to discuss transforming the campaign idea into a workable proposal. Chaired by Harlan Cleveland, dean of the Maxwell Graduate School of Citizenship and Public Affairs at Syracuse University, the proposal called for an "International Youth Service" that would "enable talented young American men and women in their twenties to provide specific services overseas in the development programs of other nations, under conditions that broaden the international understanding of the participants and give them meaningful and useful experiences."[22]

In January, a task force appointed by the president-elect and headed by Max Millikan of MIT presented a blue-print for a peace corps and "urged a cautious beginning with a 'pilot' program to test and develop preferred methods. 'The fact is that we simply do not know a great deal about how to make a program of this kind a success,' Dr. Millikan conceded."[23] In March of 1961, President Kennedy issued an Executive Order establishing the Peace Corps on a "pilot" basis as an agency of the Department of State. It would be responsible for the training and service abroad of men and women of the United States in new programs of assistance to nations and areas of the world, and in conjunction with or in support of economic assistance programs of the United States and of the United Nations and other international organizations.[24]

With the Executive Order, Kennedy sent a message to the Congress asking for legislation making the Peace Corps permanent. Obviously well orchestrated, the order was accompanied by the announcement that Rafer Johnson, the Olympic decathlon champion, had volunteered as had Sally Bowles, daughter of Under Secretary of State Chester Bowles, and Nancy Gore, daughter of Senator Albert Gore of Tennessee. The *New York Times* reported,

> Today, within an hour or two after President Kennedy had announced the establishment of the Peace Corps on a pilot basis, the switchboard at headquarters could not handle the calls from volunteers and inquirers.
>
> The response to the idea of a voluntary organization in which American men and women could help the developing countries of the world has exceeded all expectations.
>
> President Kennedy is reported to have received more letters about the peace corps than about any other issue—some 6,000 letters of suggestion, inquiry and open application. None mentions salary.[25]

It is difficult today, some thirty years later, to convey the excitement many of us felt at the time. Vietnam and Watergate had not yet shaped a certain cynicism toward government. American idealism still seemed genuine and our good intentions indubitable. The Cold War was a moral crusade; Korea and McCarthyism had been mere aberrations; and we were ready at last to re-affirm American virtues in place of the defensiveness of the previous decade.

> "We were Kennedy children," said Pat O'Connor who majored in philosophy at St. Mary's College near South Bend, Indiana. "I can't say I went to Africa because President Kennedy was shot, but there was a sense of carrying on something he started. Now we'd be considered naive, but back then I really thought I could set the world on fire."
>
> Time has changed her thinking. "I loved Africa, but I can't imagine going there again," said Mrs. O'Connor. "Now I'd want air-conditioning."[26]

Hindsight may see in the Peace Corps the dying echoes of the "City on the Hill." To us, the American dream was still alive . . . or so it seemed in that brief moment. And we would demonstrate finally the powers of the young and the ideals of democracy on a global scale. To be sure, there were skeptics,

To the restless and large hearted young, of course, distant misery is always more attractive than misery close to home . . . I know true believers in Washington (D.C.) who travel 10,000 miles to be moved by the sufferings of black men Dr. Albert Schweitzer is trying to help, but who never set foot in the Negro ghettos of southeast Washington . . .

The "peace corps" recruiters must rule out two types at the start—the romantics and the eager beavers. Both will simply get their hearts broken and return as cynics, a posture the young carry off but awkwardly.[27]

Less kindly commentators on the right were not merely skeptical but vicious.

Sarge Shriver has announced that the Peace Corps will "take the world by surprise." He's dead right. No amount of screening will close the Kiddie Korps to wild-eyed juveniles who like to picket to sell pimply ideals in the name of peace; cool opportunists who will want to give it a whirl just for the ride; foot-free rovers who just crave to see the world; and a vast number of young men who don't want to bother with college and will do anything to get a free ride out of Horner's Corners—especially if this emancipation from rubery does not include a stint in the armed forces.[28]

The Peace Corps never involved large numbers. But, limited and selective as it was—at its height the Peace Corps enrolled less than 20,000 volunteers in a given year—it set a tone for an entire generation. Despite the doubters, Shriver and his staff recruited carefully and established a demanding discipline. Training at universities and colleges before going overseas included language and applied anthropology, orientation to the kinds of communities the volunteer would encounter, survival skills. A strenuous physical education program helped prepare the volunteers. Most of the 16,000 who applied in the first year were liberal arts graduates with few technical skills. And most of those who were accepted were assigned to teaching projects. By the end of the first year, 1,000 volunteers had been sent overseas, 1,000 more were in training and a goal of 5,000 was set for 1962 and double that number in 1963.

Already, in its first year in the field, the corps has had teams of American men and women teaching school in the Philippines, surveying roads in Tanganyika, working in clinics in Malaya, and showing farmers how to raise geese on the West Indies island of St. Lucia. . . .

There will be midwives in Bolivia, tractor operators (replacing Czech technicians) in Tunisia, agricultural extension workers in Chile, fisheries experts in West Africa, and thousands of college graduates of all ages teaching school in a dozen lands. . . .

In short, the Peace Corps, despite dark fears expressed by Congressional critics a year ago, has become a success.[29]

The American encounter with peoples who had been, at best, an esoteric footnote in a geography text, often led to confusion and misunderstanding. The fact that the Peace Corps was a government sponsored project raised suspicions, at home and abroad, that it was a mask for spying. The pool of applicants did not include enough people with skills as mechanics, plumbers, sanitary inspectors, farmers, and health professionals so the recruiting program had to be re-shaped. And even with technical skill, the volunteer could not always adapt industrial habits to a different and rural context. So, a report from Pakistan read,

> "I think it would be safe to say," wrote Robert E. Burns, "that I have made every mistake possible pertaining to tube (driven) wells." This is an extract from a report by an irrigation engineer at the Academy for Village Development in Commila, East Pakistan. Mr. Burns, 24 years old, is from St. Louis . . .
> Seven other Peace Corps volunteers are also employed at the academy. . . . Through research, training, and the direction of pilot projects over an area of 100 square miles, it aims to develop the most effective possible ways to speed Pakistani rural development.[30]

By the end of the first year, President Kennedy was calling for increased appropriations and larger numbers. This is not the place, however, to continue the story of the Peace Corps. It will continue to be a subject of research and report.[31] Its beginnings, however, expose the enthusiasms and vulnerabilities of the young and the contrast with the picture we find only a few short years later.

By 1968, the press was reporting that "Peace Corps Recruiters Find Most College Students Apathetic," and that the number of applicants had declined for the second year.[32] Vietnam was eroding support for any government-connected program. By 1970, the less than enthusiastic backing of Mr. Nixon had still further cut budgets and undercut morale. As a Louis Harris poll reported, "a large number of volunteers who have now returned said that the Peace Corps had become less idealistic, less able to attract qualified volunteers, more conservative, and more part of the Establishment."[33] Yet, the Peace Corps, having survived the ministrations of the Reagan years, continues today although with much less fanfare and visibility. The program is about one-third the size of what it once was. The volunteers are older—in 1985 the average age was 28.5; in the early years, it was 23.5—and about 80 percent are skilled specialists.[34] In the first twenty-five years of its life, about 120,000 men and women served in more than 90 countries.

With each new administration, another service agency was born. So, we witnessed Lyndon Johnson's VISTA, the "domestic peace corps"; and Jimmy Carter's the Young Adult Conservation Corps; and along the way the Teacher Corps, the National Health Service Corps, the Job

Corps. Mr. Nixon signalled the shift from community service to "volunteerism." Claiming "expanding opportunities," he established ACTION, merging the Peace Corps, VISTA, the Housing Department's Office of Volunteer Action, the Small Business Administration's Action Corps of Executives. As Harlan Cleveland wrote in 1977,

> During the six years as holding company for the Peace Corps, ACTION has drastically reduced the Peace Corps visibility, sharpened its recruitment dilemma, decreased the number of volunteers, increased their attrition rate, allowed their costs to rise to politically precarious levels . . . and in general made the Peace Corps a more routine, less exciting adjunct to the foreign aid business rather than a uniquely valid and vibrant expression of "the best that is in us."[35]

For a brief moment, the Peace Corps announced a successful partnership of democratic government and youthful activism. All too soon, however, this partnership was seen as tainted by a generation that learned that governments including their own lie and kill and defend their interests even against their citizens. It is possible to see the Peace Corps as an encapsuled moment of idealism never again to be repeated, of echoes growing fainter and fainter of a Kennedy "Camelot." But that would be to miss a story, important in itself and for understanding the possibilities and difficulties of community service. Clearly, the Peace Corps has become part our mythic past. It can be found by reference in the explosion of community serving agencies—governmental and voluntary—that seek to capture the elan of the Peace Corps by using a cognate name—a citizen's corps, a youth corps or what have you. More significantly, the Peace Corps demonstrated the vitality and ability of the young in a way unique to the American story. Prior demonstrations had come in crisis and most often with the military needs of a nation at war.

Young people are now invited to participate in civil society. Even where the invitation is withdrawn or grudgingly given, the young expect participation of themselves—and this even for that majority of them who in fact do not participate. So, Nader's Raiders counts on the young for action and energy in ways that early reform movements scarcely thought to do.[36] PIRGs (Public Interest Research Groups) are everywhere. And as we see on city streets and on campus alike, young people are not waiting for the invitation of the old. They energized and often afflicted their older colleagues in the "peace movement" and the "civil rights movement." If the CCC and the NYA were fearful of being accused of leading a "youth movement," the present age has experienced it. Not merely content to serve, to meet adult specifications, young people now play an autonomous role in civil society. Quite simply, they are visibly present. It is difficult to designate any single event that brought this into being. But it is not difficult to locate the military draft, the New Deal agencies, and the Peace Corps as seminal moments in the process. The efforts at reconstructing the lost connection are tangible in the activism of the sixties and in its legacies. A certain romanticism, a failure of political construction, and a lack of reflection are also visible. Yet, old themes found different tonalities with the sudden and active presence of the young in the American story.

NOTES

1. Eric F. Goldman, *Rendezvous with Destiny*, (New York: Vintage Books, 1955), p. 69.

2. Richard Hofstadter, *The Age of Reform* (New York: Vintage Books, 1955), p. 174.

3. Wilson Carey McWilliams, *The Idea of Fraternity in America*, (Berkeley: University of California Press, 1973), p. 379.

4. Hofstadter, *op. cit.*, p. 176.

5. McWilliams, *op. cit.*, p. 380.

6. Goldman, *op. cit.*, p. 29.

7. Jane Addams, *Twenty Years at Hull House*, (New York: MacMillan, 1910), p. 125.

8. *Ibid.*, pp. 85, 109.

9. Stanton Coit, *Neighborhood Guilds*, (London: Swan Sonnenschein, 1892), pp. 7–8, 19.

10. Jacob A. Riis, *The Making of an American*, (New York: MacMillan, 1901), p. 204.

11. Howard B. Radest, *Toward Common Ground*, (New York: Ungar, 1969).

12. The Social Service Board, *115 Years of Social Service at the New York Society for Ethical Culture*, (New York: The New York Society for Ethical Culture, 1991), pp. 12–13.

13. Letter, Grenville Clark, December 3, 1940, cited in Jack J. Preiss, *Camp William James*, (Norwich, Vt.: Argo Press, 1978), p. 88.

14. John A. Salmond, *The Civilian Conservation Corps, 1933–1942: A New Deal Case Study*, (Durham, N.C.: Duke University Press, 1967), pp. 86–87.

15. Letter, Eugen Rosenstock-Huessy to W. W. Alexander, November 6, 1940, cited in Jack J. Preiss, *op. cit.*, pp. 68–69.

16. Letter from Claude R. Wickard to Michigan Congressman Albert J. Engel, January 24, 1941, cited in Jack J. Preiss, *op. cit.*, p. 126.

17. "Idle Youth and American Education," an address by V. T. Thayer (New York: The Society for Ethical Culture, May 14, 1939), pp. 6–7 *passim*.

18. Algernon D. Black, *The Young Citizens*, (New York: Ungar, 1962), pp. 28–29.

19. During the 1960s I served on the Board of the Encampment for Citizenship. Earlier, I had visited the program in New York City, later in Puerto Rico and San Francisco. Practicalities forced a shift from serving the young college-age student to the high school student. The economic needs of the 17–22 year-old

changed, and a program dedicated to liberal democratic education did not seem radical enough during the civil rights struggle and the Vietnamese war. For a while in the 1970s, the project simply disappeared to be revived in the late 1980s by several of its alumni with its headquarters now in the San Francisco Bay area.

20. Letter from Robert Lynd to Algernon D. Black, November 6, 1940, Ethical Culture Archives.

21. Campaign speech, John F. Kennedy, November 2, 1960, Cow Palace, San Francisco. The idea was originally suggested by Representative Henry S. Reuss, Democrat, Wisconsin.

22. Committee on Educational Interchange Policy, New York, December 15, 1960.

23. W. H. Lawrence, "Peace Corps Sets 'Tough' Criteria," New York Times, January 9, 1961.

24. "Establishment and Administration of the Peace Corps in the Department of State," Executive Order, John F. Kennedy, March 1, 1961. (Source: Higher Education and National Affairs, American Council on Education, 10, 7, March 6, 1961.)

25. David Halberstam, "Recruits Flocking to Join Corps," New York Times, March 2, 1961.

26. Joyce Maynard, "Peace Corps Veterans Step Ten Years into the Past," New York Times, August 18, 1976.

27. Eric Severeid, "Peace Corps Analyzed," The Chicago Sun Times, January 22, 1961.

28. Robert S. Ruark, "What Price Peace Corps?," New York World Telegram, March 17, 1961.

29. Peter Braestrup, "Peace Corps Thrives in First Year Abroad," New York Times, June 25, 1962.

30. Paul Grimes, "Peace Corps' Job Felt in Pakistan," New York Times, February 25, 1962.

31. Among the texts I have run across are: Moritz Thomsen, A Peace Corps Chronicle, (Seattle: University of Washington Press, 1970); Robert B. Textor, ed., Cultural Frontiers of the Peace Corps, (Cambridge, Mass.: MIT Press, 1976); Harlan Cleveland, The Future of the Peace Corps, (Palo Alto, Calif.: Aspen Institute Publications, 1977); and more recently, Karen Schwartz, What You Can Do for Your Country, (New York: William Morrow, 1991). Newspaper and magazine articles, particularly in the decade following the Kennedy inaugural in 1961, are simply too numerous too cite.

32. Deirdre Carmody, "Peace Corps Recruiters Find Most College Students Apathetic," New York Times, March 22, 1968 and Joseph Loftus, "Peace Corps Shows Drop in Volunteers," New York Times, June 24, 1968.

33. Robert M. Smith, "Less Zeal Found for Peace Corps," New York Times, April 4, 1970.

34. William R. Greer, "Face of Peace Corps Today," New York Times, January 23, 1985.

35. Harlan Cleveland, "A Fresh Start for the Peace Corps," The Washington Post, April 24, 1977.

36.

In 1965, a Connecticut lawyer wrote *Unsafe at Any Speed*, a critique of the American auto industry based on his work in litigating car accident cases. This publication catapulted its author, Ralph Nader, and its cause, consumerism, into the limelight. Nader recruited student volunteers, soon dubbed "Nader's Raiders," to do independent research on the effectiveness of government regulation of a wide variety of health and safety issues. . . .

In time, Nader and his "public interest research groups" brought consumerism into the political vocabulary. They examined everything from the ingredients in hot dogs to issues of industrial safety. The consumer movement eventually affected the purchasing decisions of most Americans and the production decisions of a large number of industries.

Susan J. Ellis and Katherine H. Noyes, *By the People* (San Francisco: Jossey Bass, Revised Edition, 1990), p. 261.

Chapter Five

Needy People

TO HIM (HER) THAT HATH...

Need is a leading character in community service. Where I am in the story, however, shapes its meaning for me. It was the personally "felt" need that moved the settlement house worker into the neighborhood and the Peace Corps volunteer into the "third world." Of course, the settlement workers were not indifferent to questions of policy. Indeed, the discipline of urban sociology had its roots in their research. Yet, meeting poverty "with a human face" was their starting point. They claimed an objective basis as well and that was the tangibility of need itself—in a tenement neighborhood, a third-world country, a ghetto. Something was missing in the life of a human being while in another place the ability to meet that reality was present. The task of community service was to bring these two together through a person and a passion. With the encounter, however, the idea of need becomes problematic.

At first glance, need and response seem self-defining. It is only common sense to feed the hungry, clothe the naked, house the homeless. However, I have to decide on the way "I" will do something about someone else's need. I may turn to collectives and surrogates. Useful as that is, for community service something else is required. Meeting another's needs expects me to enter an alien world at some risk to myself. This is a puzzle and comes to the surface in debates about mandatory and voluntary service, in the choice between community service and political action, participatory and expert strategies, and so on. The risks of the personal encounter stir anxieties although these are not often acknowledged.

Even the simple act of providing food can be complicated. We soon grow numb to famine, grow comfortable with surrogates. We learn, usually too late, that demanding a choice between "case" and "cause" can also be an alibi. In the choosing, however, we face ourselves, encounter ourselves and that feels dangerous. So we retreat to the familiar. We are easily charitable which means helping the needy while leaving society alone. Ignorance, too, is an available retreat. As Peace Corps volunteers discovered when they came to alien places, we need to know what is acceptable as food and what is unacceptable. It is possible to starve in the midst of plenty as an Australian aborigine said to me in commenting on the strange dietary preferences of white people. Feeding the hungry, then, requires sensitivity to the broad range of agricultural, culinary, aesthetic, and religious habits of our life worlds. But that knowledge is painful.

Needs are not absolute. Today, indoor plumbing is a need. But, not so long ago, it was a luxury. Similarly, a telephone or a radio or a TV set become needs. Schools and hospitals and transportation become needs depending on when and where we live and work. When we move to less tangible needs like association and literacy, the difficulties multiply. I might conclude that "need" really stands for that which lags behind the way most well-satisfied people are living. Or, more cynically: for me yesterday's choices are today's needs while for others the day before yesterday's choices are today's needs. At work is the elusive notion of expectation, and expectation is a moral idea. Need, in other words, reveals us to ourselves as much as it names what is missing for another.

The way we think about needs depends on where we are in the worlds of having and not having, of giving and getting. We have a higher standard for ourselves and a lower standard for our beneficiaries. Implicitly, we attribute greater value to our lives than to the lives of others. So, it is often our leavings which we dump on others. But we are offended by a "welfare" family that dares enjoy the luxury of an automobile or a large-screen TV set at "our expense." We often seem entirely indifferent to the welfare of those who are done-to, all the while proclaiming our charity.

In fact, we set one norm for ourselves—call it a norm of privilege— and another for our recipients—call it a norm of neediness. Trying to avoid this was one reason for the settlement-house workers' decision to live "in the neighborhood" and their worry about being identified with "up-town." This concern was built into Peace Corps training and lifestyle. Despite genuine efforts to be one with those done-to, however, the doers could always leave. Frustrated, we might say, "beggars can't be choosers." Save for martyrs and saints, we attach a certain priority to our own needs or the needs of those close to us. For community service, this fact of human experience is reinforced by the non-equality between doer and done-to. Have and have-not is part of its structure. At the center of community service then is the problem of the lesser stranger.

Who shall say what a need is and for whom? The colonialist has no trouble deciding since the "primitive" and "benighted" natives simply do not know what is good for them. We take up "the white man's burden" when it suits us. By contrast, the democrat announces that the person being done-to is the only one legitimately allowed to determine his or her needs. Thus, the doer ought to respond only to those needs which the done-to identifies. More generally, then, the democrat adopts a stance of non-interfering availability. This attracts us because it seems to cohere with liberal notions of a respect for autonomy, free-market notions of self-interest and libertarian notions of hands-off.

Community service tempts us with the illusion that other people have needs while we don't. Needs, then, are signs of weakness—as in the connotation of "neediness." The ability to respond is a sign of our powerfulness. Although this is denied in the language of community service, it is a likely outcome of its practice. We thereby reinforce the alienation that marks the lost connection while claiming that we are trying to reconstruct that connection through community service. In a world where needs become an economic and political agenda, community service too easily becomes another specialized function.

> Increasingly these volunteers do not look upon their work as charity; they see it as a parallel career to their paid jobs. . . . Above all, they see in volunteer work access to achievement, to effectiveness, to self fulfillment, indeed to meaningful citizenship. And for this reason there is more demand for well-structured volunteer jobs than there are positions to fill. . . .
>
> . . . nonprofits have to learn how to raise money. The American public has not become less generous—there is little evidence of the "compassion fatigue" nonprofit people talk about. . . . Unfortunately, a great many nonprofits still believe that the way to get money is to hawk *needs*. But the American public gives for *results*. It no longer gives to "charity;" it "buys in."[1]

We are convinced that we are the able ones who do for and to needy strangers who remain strangers. Surely that is a troubling thought. Yet, there are legitimate distinctions of competence and admitting it is not simply self-serving. Nor should a commitment to multi-cultural respectfulness lead us to deny that we are more likely to find, in a democratic and technically sophisticated society, the resources and motives necessary for meeting the needs of others however defined. At the same time, it is chastening to remember that figuring out what counts as a resource depends on what counts as a need. We seem to be trapped in a democratic vicious circle.

The obvious result is to choose up sides and that is just what the advocates of community service do. The liberal speaks of self-determination that is a mixture of prudence and principle. After all, we'll only be able to do a few things in any event. Why then not maintain our democratic integrity by respecting the autonomy of the recipient. Others justify community service on grounds of economic realism. There are indeed social needs to be met and it is simply cheaper to meet them through un-paid and low-paid service. To be sure, the advocates on all sides are moved as much by their interests as by their reasons and so we are not surprised to find differences over control and power everywhere at work in community service.

Finally, a look at community service programs tells us that advocates on all sides share the view—often unspoken—that really to meet the needs generated by an incompetent society is beyond the capacity of community service. Granting that there are good things being done, they turn their attention to the doer of service. Implicitly, they admit that the done-to's needs are not really central to community service at all but only the occasion of it. A concern with reforming the doer accounts for much of the interest in community service. Of course, we encourage talk about "making a difference." However, service is promoted as a way of changing the nature and values of the doer. We hear about citizenship, character-building, personal development, educational practice or what have you. Rejecting the grand enthusiasms of the Peace Corps and the political dreams of the settlement-house, our attention is drawn to the fact that giving of oneself to others is itself a need. In a strange and troubling way, the need that justifies community service becomes the psychological and moral need of the privileged. Nowhere is this attention to personal change more clearly at work than in justifications of universal service. Thus, in an exaggerated but by no means untypical statement, William F. Buckley, Jr. wrote,

> The objective of national service should not be considered in the tender of Good Deeds. Tending to the sick, teaching illiterates to read, preserving our libraries are desirable ends. But the guiding purpose here is the spiritual animation of the giver, not the alms he dispenses. The person who has given a year in behalf of someone or something else is himself better for the experience. National service is not about reducing poverty; it is about inducing gratitude.[2]

We seem to have concluded that we will not significantly change the world of the other. Our goal, then, is not really to change the world but to change individuals and in particular the individuals most accessible, the young. Community service, then, lacks a politics. So-called non-partisan strategies abound as we can observe in the coalition which supported the 1990 National and Community Service Act. We are doing good because in the doing, we do good to ourselves. The stranger is met apart from the world he or she inhabits. We do not expect to dispense with our own cultural and social baggage, or ask whether it is worthwhile to do so. In a deliberate choice of interpersonal isolation, we are scarcely interested in trying to do so.

The move from the needs of the done-to to the needs of the doer is not surprising. So, service becomes an instrument of personal development. Young people are told that they are missing something and this rings true because it confirms their experience of a competitive education and work-life. Confusing the matter, however, we also deliver the message of interdependence. Or, as a popular song once had it, "People Need People." Yet, we hold back from the risk of the genuinely interpersonal and the politics of a plurality of life-worlds by encapsulating the former and ignoring the latter. Community service is caught in an environment of mixed messages again.

We know that we turn to others—a parent, a brother or sister, a friend, a teacher—for help. And, if we are fortunate, they are there, they are able and they respond. That, in its most primitive sense, tells us that we are communal animals. At the same time, these familiar others may not be there for us. Yet, we still need help and if we are fortunate, strangers respond. And that tells us that we are social animals. In turn, each of us can be a familiar-other for those we know or a stranger-other for those we do not know. Or, to put this somewhat paradoxically, among our needs is the need to be needed. Since our world is a scene of distorted individualism and distorted collectivism, however, this need is seldom adequately met. Community service becomes a therapy for the doer. The need of the other that stirred the moral passion of the reformer is transformed into self-service.

FROM NEEDS TO NEEDINESS

Community service is not a single thing which becomes clear when we shift our perspective to the worlds of persons in need. Those who do the service and those who are done-to live in different and shifting worlds. For example, when a "crime" like insanity or a "sin" like drunkenness becomes a disease, we move from the worlds of the prison and the pulpit to the world of the patient. But, often, need is also structural and social. We identify those being done-to by some generic label—as the young, the old, the school drop-out, the illiterate. The names we give to such worlds seem to be neutral descriptions. But, "old," or "young" or "poor" or "black" are not just demographic categories. They are shaped by social and moral decisions. "Benign" names like "nuclear family" carry moral and political values. The feminist argument over gender-based language touches upon a nontrivial issue. Generally, then, community service is determined by the world the doer lives in, the world the doer enters and the world the done-to inhabits.

Many of those being done-to are caught in inaccessible worlds. To be Black or Chicano or Native American is to increase the chances of being found in them. We know, too, that a "culture of poverty," the world of a growing underclass, is perpetuated by the habits of dependency passed on from generation to generation and by policies which reinforce those habits. The energies of the doers are at work in such places but their goals and their achievements are frustrated by impermeable world boundaries.

In short, community service meets different peoples under different life conditions often without following through on the implications of these differences. Political and economic analysis and action is not only absent but even threatening. So I am forced to ask: Is community service with its bias for "one-to-one" tangibility and its deliberate blindness to structural inequalities an appropriate response to needs? And why is community service so congenial to the doer and the policy-maker?

Such questions open up the hidden place of social class in community service. Both practice and literature hardly notice it. Yet class clearly plays a role in defining those "in need." At the same time, given our American denial of class, we find it difficult to disabuse ourselves of the notion that good will and personal effort can change social realities. This helps explain the fact that we continue to act as if the needs of others can really be met. This adds a tone of frustration and a note of anger to community service for both doer and done-to. Good will, genuine though it may be, is accompanied by self-doubt and aggression. Nor is it surprising that the individual success story is celebrated without confessing that another person in need is already in place. In this, community service seems but an incarnation of the myth of Sisyphus.

In fact, during the Reagan "prosperity," the economic worlds of doer and done-to grew even more radically apart. Income is one index. In the 1980s, families in the lower 10 percent of the population experienced an income decline from $4,791 to $4,295. "The richest 1% got 12.4% of all after-tax income in 1989, compared with 8.4% received by those in the top 1% in 1980 and 7.3% in 1977."[3] More recently,

The number of Americans below the poverty line increased in 1990 by two million, or nearly 6% according to the Census Bureau. In addition, inflation-adjusted median household income declined for the first time since 1982.

The official poverty line, which varies according to such factors as family size and age, averages $13,359 for a family of four and $6,652 for an individual. . . .

. . . A separate report issued yesterday by the Census Bureau found that several "experimental estimates" of non-cash incomes and benefits showed a significant increase in poverty rates from 1989 to 1990.[4]

The efforts—energetic, serious, and continuous—of community service really did little to reduce the number of homeless or hungry or jobless. As it were, community service created its own momentary world even as doer and done-to continued to live in different worlds.

Economic differences do not of themselves define social class. But they do mark social spaces and social chances. Significantly, the very choice of community service as a normative type of social conduct is a sign of the role of class in the lives of the doers. Assumptions about the individual clearly shape what is being done. The language of civic consciousness and of character development supports this conclusion. In a way, community service is a secular rendering of the Protestant notion of salvation by good works. Traditional middle-class virtues attach to community service. For example, if we wish to find those to whom community service makes its greatest appeal, we will increase our chances by looking to college populations, to college preparatory high schools, to the well endowed economically, educationally, and socially. In community service we see played out a complicated drama of middle-class privileges and middle-class deprivations.

We would still need to explore the meanings of such a middle-class effort. Often, it is a replication for the young of the typical volunteer activities of adults, busy activism doing what would otherwise be paid for by a minimum wage. Were that all, community service could hardly warrant the claims for restoring civic virtue, building character and nurturing moral development which are made in its name. The attempt to reduce community service to social function, however, does not usually succeed. Like the volunteer, the doer tutors, visits the sick, reads to the old, teaches a skill, and so forth. But, in community service these activities force an intersection of worlds in ways that volunteerism does not. That is what is most transparent in the passions of the young wherever we find them. Ironically, the assignment to the young brings with it a surprise.

The doer feels the pain of the other. This becomes a challenge, even a threat—and, no doubt, guilt at undeserved good fortune plays its role too. Deep down, a strong dose of misery shapes the world of the done-to and radically separates him or her from the doer. But the doer learns even this. Poverty becomes real; life worlds become real.

Sometimes, it seems as if community service is designed to evade the responsibilities of wealth by forcing the needy to help the needy. Illustrative is the unintended demography of today's "all-volunteer" military service. For example, blacks and other minorities were 38 percent of the army's enlisted men and women (1988). The Brookings Institution reported that in 1982, 42 percent of qualified black young people enlisted while only 14 percent of qualified white young people did. The concentration of community service on the young can itself be interpreted after the model of neediness and class. As it were, the powerless are expected by the powerful to aid the powerless. To be sure, we mask the conditions of the young by exaggerated—and self-serving—stories of indulged middle-class teen-agers. But, the world of the young and the world of the poor are likely to intersect. Even "privileged" young people recognize this in their language, music and costume. A visit to an urban high school or a drive through city streets on a hot summer evening is tangible experience of the fact. It becomes evident, too, once we look at the disproportionately large number of children and young people living below the poverty line.

> The "juvenilization of poverty" is just as real as the "feminization of poverty." We have dramatically altered the way in which we allocate social resources to different portions of the life cycle in this country. The result is that proportionately, the elderly are doing better, and the young much worse. In 1970, for example, about equal shares of the gross national product were spent on health and on education. A dozen years later, expenditures for health had grown half again as large as those for education. That, in itself, indicates a major proportional shift of resources from young to old. But even within the health sector, the new commitments have been heavily concentrated on such diseases of age as cancer, heart disease, and stroke. The result is that from 1968 to 1980 mortality rates for Americans between the ages of 70 and 80 were reduced about four times as much as mortality rates for the age group between 10 and 20.[5]

There are many service programs undertaken by those who themselves live in a world of neediness. For instance, urban service corps projects like the CCC before them attract those from the ghetto. Typically, they include some form of payment—cash allowances, college scholarships—and some form of job training. For example,

> When 15-year-old Staci Mango first learned she was one of 50 students chosen for the Academy of Public Service at Anacostia High School [Washington, D.C.], she thought it must have something to do with the military.
>   Instead, the 10th grader has discovered she is part of an innovative three-year program that links one of the city's most troubled high schools with the Federal Government. It is an attempt to train a new generation of public servants with an enriched curriculum, a specially trained core of

teachers, field trips to Government agencies, paid summer internships and future job placement.[6]

In this way, we mobilize those in need to help others who often have the same needs. To its credit, this avoids some of the risks of alienation that endanger other forms of community service.

Getting the poor to help the poor casts doubt on the notion that we can interpret community service only through the lens of middle-class privilege. However, the mobilization of the deprived still feeds the processes of separation by leading the doer toward the normalization of middle-class values. Community service can serve as the continuation in a different form of a "melting pot" ideal with all its ambiguity of acceptance and arrogance. In a way, then, community service reflects the norm of a homogeneous society, a genuine functional ideal. The limited mobility of the needy doer is so little noted in the language of community service, that it further reveals our blindness to its class implications. This alerts us to the fact that community service is not simply a plurality of activities but a plurality of types. It means one thing under conditions of middle-class life and yet another under conditions of ghetto life. Transcending the plurality of types, however, are the roots of community service in middle-class goals of personal salvation and social conformity. It is the individual who is the goal. The lost connection is still untouched.

Where the poor serve the poor another separation appears. The projects that mobilize the young of the ghetto are not the ones that mobilize the young of the middle-class neighborhood. The appeal of a city youth corps falls on deaf ears in the college preparatory high school. I can recall that the announcement of the New York City Service Corps was simply uninteresting to our students and, parenthetically, to our faculty as well. I recall, too, the "Helping Hands" program developed on the initiative of our elementary school parents, children and teachers. I knew of their sensitivity to the dangers of paternalism and their commitment to caring and to equality. Yet, a review of the outcomes reveals an unwitting message of separation. Its list of agencies inescapably conveys the apartness of neediness.[7] More generally, community service projects themselves tend to be separated by social class both as to type and as to practice despite near-heroic efforts to overcome those separations.

The National and Community Service Act of 1990 tried to address this issue. In the report of the Senate Labor and Human Resources Committee we find

> A national service program should be inclusive in nature. It must become neither an elite preserve for the affluent and well educated, nor a subminimum wage holding pattern for the poor and disadvantaged. For this

reason, S.1430 does not eliminate incentives altogether, but avoids the type of incentives that make service attractive only to the non-affluent. On the other hand, its stipend, voucher, and reimbursement provisions show awareness of the fact that economic barriers to participating in long-term service programs do exist for many segments of the population and tries to reduce or eliminate these barriers to the degree possible.

And it adds, hopefully,

The [Senate] Committee is aware of the benefits of student community service programs for at-risk students. We have refrained from limiting these programs to those involving only at-risk students as volunteers because it is the Committee's strong belief that all Americans, not just those with limited incomes, should develop an ethic of service.[8]

Thus far, we have puzzled over needs to which the doer responds, and the multiple worlds where the action is played out. These tell a story of separations. The lost connection remains elusive and community service may even contribute to its perpetuation.

GOOD INTENTIONS

Community service is a story of interpersonal relationships and we need to take a closer look at them. The following is by no means unusual.

Daniel Maimin, a student at the Dalton School in the Upper East Side [New York City], always knew that one day he would be a developer. When he was 14 years old, though, he started working as a volunteer in a soup kitchen to meet a school requirement for social service . . .

"Building a building is like a monument to yourself," the 16-year-old said. "I had a big ego then. I never really thought about the people." The people, he found, sometimes are left homeless because developers destroyed their houses. "Now I'm interested in working with the city in developing low-income housing," he said.

Daniel is one of 30 or so Dalton students who have worked with the homeless and the hungry as part of a three-year-old program intended to make one principle clear: that people owe a debt to their communities. Increasingly private and public schools nationwide are requiring students to do some kind of volunteer work. "You're seeing a lot of this happening across the country," said Angela G. Vassos, who directs the community service program at the Fieldston School and shows other schools how to set up similar programs.[9]

Again, the story of community service is told from the side of the doer. The silence of the done-to shapes the narrative, building in us the belief that he or she is essentially passive. As it were, we are not looking at interpersonal relationships at all but at the relationships of a person and an object of interest. We are caught in community service's "Catch 22." If we fail to act, then we are unresponsive to need and fail to meet our own need to be needed. At the same time, life in a world of neediness is marked by the inability to take initiatives.

> The noted University of Pennsylvania psychologist, Martin E. P. Seligman coined the term "learned helplessness" to describe passive and defeatist attitudes and behaviors that result from repeated failure. It is a truism to state that overcoming feelings of learned helplessness among the poor and disadvantaged is crucial if their lives are to be made better.[10]

The struggle for inclusiveness—for hearing all the voices—is frustrating. For example, a meeting sponsored by the Johnson Foundation at its Wingspread Center developed "Principles of Good Practice in Combining Service and Learning" supported by just about all of the major national community service agencies. Among other things, these principles included calls to engage "people in responsible and challenging actions for the common good" (Point 1), to ask "for those with needs to define those needs" (Point 4), and a commitment "to program participation by and with diverse populations" (Point 10).[11] However, one of the partners to the dialogue was absent, as usual. But that is not surprising. Conferences are characteristic of professional, that is, middle, classes. Street languages and street voices are alien to the conference milieu.

The struggle for inclusiveness is also reflected in community service planning but the situation of the absent partner recurs. For example, in a collection of suggestions under the heading, "Making community service curriculum work," we find,

> Community service curriculum requires a dedicated partnership among youth, teachers and community members. . . . The classroom expands into the outside community, the "real world." Community members become valued educators alongside the classroom instructor . . .
>
> Curriculum must encourage students to challenge belief systems and attitudes—ageism, racism, etc.—and view themselves as collaborators *not* missionaries, and resist the "you need my help" attitude.[12]

An urge to inclusiveness motivates public and private school partnerships.

> University High School [San Francisco] is one of a growing number of independent schools nationwide that are forging stronger ties with the public-school system, through such means as public-private school part-

nerships and special summer or weekend programs for disadvantaged students in the surrounding community . . .

John C. Esty Jr., president of the National Association of Independent Schools, estimates that there are some 200 to 300 collaborative programs of varying types between public and independent schools.[13]

I remember the meeting convened by then New York Mayor Edward Koch. Except for several upper echelon public school administrators, the twenty or so people around the breakfast table represented New York City's more successful private schools. A repeated theme of our conversation—and of many that followed—was the necessity for participation at the "grass roots" as the jargon had it. The outcome was the development of twenty-five partnerships of teachers and students in paired public and private schools. But the initiative remained, by and large, with the private school leadership despite efforts to transfer it elsewhere. No doubt, part of the reason for this was the complexity of the public system. But it was also true that interest in the project was highest among those who felt a need to serve and who were accustomed to perceiving themselves as a "leadership" if not as an elite.

Finally, military service has played a number of variations on the theme of inclusion. In war, the need to be met is common across the society. So, military service, for all its authoritarian structure, meets the participatory requirements of community service. This became quite visible with the development of an "all-volunteer" force. The military ceased to be inclusive and, except in time of war, remains as it has been historically, a function of class. For example, during the Vietnam War, high school dropouts were likely to enlist or to be called to serve. An elaborate deferment policy helped many college and university students avoid service. In other words, an "affluent" world does not enlist and hardly serves.

Not all efforts at community service are caught in the trap of the silent partner. For example, the American Friends Service Committee, a long-lived and vital agency of the Quakers, has developed around an ideal of mutuality although it cannot entirely escape the problem of "learned helplessness."

See the pride in the faces of 75 black farmers in western Kentucky who have kept their land and survived. . . . AFSC is organizing Kentucky farmers, helping start black chapters of the Community Farm Alliance to increase their power and representation in regional policy making . . .

See the pride in the faces of the Sioux people in South Dakota after defeating the Department of Energy and its plan to give them a nuclear waste dump . . .

You know we're a Quaker agency but you don't have to be Quaker to like AFSC and its work. . . . the Quaker founder George Fox spoke to the whole human family when urging us "to walk cheerfully over the earth, answering to that of God in every person."[14]

Nor are we entirely without deliberate efforts to give voice to voiceless people although such efforts are still unusual.

> This fall, 10 teenagers from the tiny Appalachian town of Ivanhoe, Va., have a bit of after-school paper-work to attend to—an application to the Federal Communications Commission to operate their own radio station.
>
> In rural Lawrence County, Ala., meanwhile, eight Cherokee Indian youths are forming a corporation and continuing negotiations in an effort to buy a local movie theater they hope to renovate.
>
> The two projects—part of a first-of-its-kind effort by the Appalachian Regional Commission—were among 16 youth-leadership programs to receive funding from the A.R.C. last summer . . .
>
> Ms. Ennis (Ella Ennis, the A.R.C. coordinator) said the commission decided to create the youth project because many young people end up leaving Appalachia when they realize that they are powerless to bring about change in the region or even to make a decent living.[15]

In short, when we look at the persons present in community service, we are again confirmed in our beliefs about our own potency and others' impotency. We try to move away from the arrogance of piety, but do not succeed. Community service is caught in the demands of giving and getting, the demands of neediness. The benevolent intention is, no doubt, genuine. As genuine is the unwitting elevation of some and derogation of others.

IN ANOTHER'S PLACE

It is not possible to speak with the voice of another any more than it is desirable to speak for another. Yet, community service tries to do both. To be sure, recent criticism, most notably from feminist sources, has led to greater acknowledgment of the democracy of participation. Professionals no longer can easily arrogate to themselves the authoritarianism of expertise. Reformers, who once perceived their object as a community-to-be-reformed, can no longer see themselves apart from a reforming community. No doubt, there are those who would prefer things as they were. But that is to be expected. More troubling is the structure of participation itself. Democratically inclined experts in medicine, law, business, engineering and social service are caught in the paradoxes of "full disclosure" which almost seem to require the non-expert to become expert in order to benefit from it. And reformers are caught by the condition of "learned helplessness."

Implicit in the response to need is a notion of what ought to count as good for everyone. Despite much talk of diversity, we do not avoid the temptation of spelling out the good life for others. It is unsurprising then that this results in the tensions which characterize community service. When I reflect on my own experience, I am aware, too, that these tensions are often denied and hidden—some might even say, conveniently hidden. I wonder at the sheer activity of the programs. We are so busy doing good things that we do not stop to ask about their goodness and we are so oppressed by the number of good things yet undone that we do not take the time to ask. Busy-ness becomes our defense of choice. Even where we are sensitive to the integrity of the other, we are driven to override these sensitivities in the name of our urgencies. And we believe that our urgencies are really everyone's. So, perhaps the voices of the others may not be silent at all; we just cannot hear them.

Some decades ago, I served as chair of a health and welfare council in a well-to-do suburban county. There came a time when it was popular among agency professionals to talk about the weaknesses of minority families. The children were truants. Of course, we failed to ask whether or not the school deserved its truants. Rent was unpaid and apartments dirty. Diets were inadequate. Health needs were ignored. At times, the list of things undone read like an indictment. We blamed the problems of the family on the absence of the father. Of course, we did not pay attention to the demeaning jobs that were available to Black and Chicano men when available at all. The few Black and Chicano members of the council were, if anything, more condemnatory than we were. But they, occasionally, reminded us that we knew little of the strength of the family and particularly of the mother who held things together while working, usually at a harsh and unrewarding minimum-wage job. Of course, all of this was another way, no doubt unwitting, of blaming the victim.

We were working within the norms of the middle class family and the virtues of middle class life. That these norms and virtues might deserve to be universalized could be argued but they could not simply be assumed. We did not see that our conclusions about the ineffectiveness of minority families excused our failure to provide support for all families. It was a time, as the common wisdom from Washington had it, of "benign neglect" although I'm not sure how benign it was. In short, before concluding that the done-to are silent, I need to be aware of my own part in creating the condition of hiddenness, interpreting it as silence and then using it to justify myself as a professional. As an article on community service, rare for its critical candor, noted

In his book *Power in the Helping Professions*, Adolph Guggenbuhl-Craig describes a kind of drama that often takes place in a helping relationship.

As one person gives and another receives help, certain qualities constellate in the helper: power, goodness, health, strength, etc. In the person with needs, the negative is constellated: weakness, sickness, incompetence. As each person becomes accustomed to his or her role, it becomes increasingly difficult to leave it . . .

Guggenbuhl-Craig's analysis contains an element that is often missing from our conversations about service-learning. The element is power. . . . Many of us have operated with the naive belief that service reflected upon is good in itself. In the process, we have failed to look deeply enough at . . . the ways in which service-learning may reinforce injustice and produce what John McKnight has called "disabling help."[16]

Meanwhile, the "street" speaks its own language. Like the language of the oppressed everywhere, it serves as a way of including and excluding. Community service, however, is embedded in organizations that can only hear certain kinds of sounds—less tangible in their reference and more abstract in their generality. So, it is set apart from the "street." When the "street" breaks through into our consciousness, we scarcely understand it and even are annoyed by it. We imitate without quite "getting it" as when we adopt and ultimately exploit working-class costumes or styles of popular music like "rap" today and "blues" in an earlier day. The young, of course, are much better at this than we are and can be said to be more assimilative than imitative.

We notice that the street—the poor, the unemployed, the deprived— is also a self-contained cultural world even as its members victimize each other and are victimized by the other worlds around it. Understood by the street as extensions of those other worlds, the reformer and the professional are objects of suspicion, humor, indifference and aggression. Community service, then, because it works through professionals in service agencies and schools appears as an intrusion from outside.

From time to time we hear about what we are doing from those who are done-to and not just from those who claim to speak for them. A study of settlements in 1920 reported,

Nearly all expressed a good-natured friendliness for settlements . . . But as to the settlement's really representing them and their groups in any substantial sense, their comment was all to the contrary.

"They're like all the rest. . . . A bunch of people planning for us and deciding what is good for us without consulting us or taking us into their confidence. No one but a member of our own race can really understand us." . . .

Another woman felt that settlements were " . . . just scratching the surface . . . and not trying to get at the bottom of things."

An editor of racial cast [i.e., a black leader] was more sweeping: "No outside agency can undertake to tell my people what to do. . . . This must come from the people themselves through their societies and education after their own ideas. The influence of the settlements in our life is negligible."[17]

Less gently, Ivan Illich, addressing a group of U.S. college students in Guernivaca, Mexico, said,

> By definition, you cannot help being ultimately vacationing salesmen for the middle-class "American Way of Life," since that is really the only life you know.
>
> A group like this [the Conference on Inter-American Student Projects] could not have developed unless a mood in the United States had supported it—the belief that any true American must share God's blessings with his poorer fellow man. The idea that every American has something to give, and at all times may, can and should give it, explains why it occurred to students that they could help Mexican peasants "develop" by spending a few months in their villages.[18]

What then shall we make of all this? Shall we simply give up community service as a bad job? Shall we continue, despite all our doubts? Shall we re-direct our attentions to nature, leaving the worlds of needy to some other kind of ministration? Shall we identify community service only with relationships of equals?

We know that community service loses its élan absent the worlds of the needy. But that dependency, in itself, is a commentary on its lack of meaning. Need, in other words, may initiate programs but confounds their meaning. William James saw our problem. To be sure, he brought to its solution a romanticism about military life which those of us who have lived in it find hard to swallow. He sensed, nevertheless, the need to restore the lost connection and the salience of the personal experience. As he wrote in "The Moral Equivalent of War,"

> There is nothing to make one indignant in the mere fact that life is hard, that men should toil and suffer pain. The planetary conditions once [and] for all are such, and we can stand it. But that so many men, by mere accidents of birth and opportunity, should have a life of *nothing else* but toil and pain and hardness and inferiority imposed upon them . . . —*this* is capable of arousing indignation in reflective minds. . . . If now—and this is my idea—there were, instead of military conscription a conscription of the whole youthful population to form for a certain number of years a part of the army enlisted against *Nature*, the injustice would tend to be evened out and numerous other goods to the commonwealth would follow. The military ideals of hardihood and discipline would be wrought into the growing fibre of the people; no one would remain blind as the luxurious classes now are blind, to man's real relations to the globe he lives on, and to the permanently sour and hard foundations of his higher life. . . . To coal and iron mines, to freight trains, to fishing fleets in De-

cember, to dish-washing, clothes-washing, and window-washing, to road-building and tunnel-making, to foundries and stoke-holes, and to the frames of skyscrapers, would our gilded youths be drafted off, according to their choice, to get the childishness out of them and to come back into society with healthier sympathies and soberer ideas.[19]

Our experience with an all-volunteer army tells us that the needy not be consigned to a permanent category of neediness even if transition to the worlds of privilege is denied. It also tells us of the unmanageability of modern collectives. Despite James, there is no "moral equivalent of war." The communalism of community service is surrendered to functionalism under conditions of large numbers. We seem to be left with self-defeating possibilities amid grand intentions. Community service becomes a merely personal instrument even if its ideal is the reconstruction of lost connections. Need and neediness lead us then to ask the complementary question: What does it mean to serve; who are the servers and who are the served? And, is the idea of service as problematic as the idea of need?

NOTES

1. Peter Drucker, "It Profits Us to Strengthen Nonprofits," *The Wall Street Journal*, December 19, 1991.

2. William F. Buckley, Jr., "National Debt, National Service," *New York Times*, October 18, 1990.

3. David Wessel, "The Wealthy Watch Gains of 1980s Become Political Liabilities," *The Wall Street Journal*, April 8, 1992.

4. Timithy Noah, "Number of Poor Americans Is Up 6%, Real Income Is Off 1.7%, Agency Says," *The Wall Street Journal*, September 27, 1991.

5. Donald Kennedy, former President of Stanford University, "Can We Help? Public Service and the Young," keynote address, National Conference on Higher Education, 1986.

6. Barbara Gamarekian, "Public Service Stressed at a Troubled School," *New York Times*, October 10, 1990.

7. See The Ethical Culture Schools Community Service Committee, *Helping Hands: A Family and School Guide to Volunteering*, (New York: The Midtown Ethical Culture School, 1986).

8. Citations are from the Report of the Senate Committee on Labor and Human Resources included in a background booklet prepared by the office of Senator Edward M. Kennedy, Chair of the Committee, *About the National and Community Service Act of 1990*, Washington, D.C., pp. 75, 76, 82.

9. Trish Hall, "Young, Privileged Volunteers Learn that Hunger Has a Face," *New York Times*, May 13, 1987.

10. Ira Harkavy and John L. Puckett, "Toward Effective University-Public School Partnerships: An Analysis of a Contemporary Model," *Teachers College Record* 92, 4 (Summer 1991), pp. 556–557.

11. The conference was co-sponsored by the American Association for Higher Education, Campus Compact, Constitutional Rights Foundation, Council of Chief State School Officers, National Association of Independent Schools, National Association of Secondary School Principals, National Society for Internships and Experiential Education, and Youth Service America. See *Combining Service and Learning*, Jane C. Kendall and Associates, Ed., (Raleigh, North Carolina: National Society for Internships and Experiential Education, 1990), Volume I, p. 40.

12. Cathryn Berger Kaye et al., "Behind the Scenes, Curriculum Concepts," *School Youth Service Network*, 1, 3 (Autumn 1989) (Los Angeles: Constitutional Rights Foundation), p. 4.

13. Mark Walsh, "Independent-Public School Links Breaking Down Wall of 'Elitism,' " *Education Week* 9, 40 (August 1, 1990), p. 1.

14. Untitled booklet, American Friends Service Committee, Philadelphia, Pennsylvania, Spring 1990.

15. Millicent Lawton, "Youth-Service Effort 'Opens Eyes' to Appalachian Region's Prospects," *Education Week* 10, 9 (October 31, 1990).

16. Steven Schultz, "The Shadow Side of Service," *Experiential Education* 17, 1 (January-February 1992), p. 9.

17. John Daniels, *American Via the Neighborhood*, (New York: Harper and Brothers, 1920), pp. 222–223.

18. Ivan Illich (1968), "To Hell with Good Intentions," Kendall, *op. cit.*, p. 316.

19. William James, "The Moral Equivalent of War," (New York: American Association for International Conciliation, Number 27, February 1910).

Chapter Six

They Also Serve

AT YOUR SERVICE

There is something paradoxical about the relationship of community service and democracy. When I bring images of service to mind I see pictures of servants, of menials, of lesser breeds. I meet relationships of inequality. Like neediness, service emphasizes distinctions of potency and impotency, activity and passivity. However, it is now the possessors of goods and position who are done to, the impotent who are doers. Abilities and powers are still distributed unequally but it is the well endowed who are served and the needy who do the service.

Ordinary language describes service as a relationship between superiors and inferiors. So, I enter a restaurant or a department store and am greeted by the message, "at your service." I take my car to a "service station" or my toaster to a "service center" where I call the tune. When I stay at a hotel, a maid cleans my room and makes my bed; a desk clerk assures me that the staff will make my stay comfortable and pleasant. A brochure on the desk describes the various other "services" that can be provided at my request. The illustrations multiply. At bottom, then, I find myself dependent on the services of others and yet it is a privileged dependency. I am, after all, free to use or not to use the service. Those on whom I depend, in turn, know something I do not. Or, they have a position that enables them to be of service to me. In that sense, they enjoy a certain power over me. This becomes evident when services are withheld as in a strike or when service personnel are in short supply.

These services are impersonal. So the waiter at my table, the maid in

my room, the mechanic in the service center are nameless despite the
ubiquity of name-tags and introductions—"Hello, my name is Wendy,
and I'll be serving you today." No doubt, if my students who "wait
tables" to earn their college tuition can be believed, I am as faceless to
them. The exchange is functional, role-based, utilitarian. We pass each
other by, stopping a moment to do or be done-to.

These relationships do not seem to have very much to do with community service. The exchanges of the market place are private, economic
and functional. At the same time, the market exchange is tinged with
moralism. So, it is not unusual to find us praising the effects of holding
a regular job, any regular job, with its disciplines and responsibilities.
Blurring the lines in the other direction, we adopt the values of the
market place in describing community service or in defending proposals
for doing it. As Charles Moskos, whose work provided much of the
basis for Senator Kennedy's interest in national service legislation, notes,

> The major political obstacle to national service becoming a reality is the
> laissez-faire bent of many conservatives . . . the real nub of the matter is
> ideology. Congressman Jack Kemp, Republican of New York and a 1988
> presidential hopeful, belittled the whole idea by asserting: "At the age of
> eighteen, you should be focusing on your dreams and ambitions, not
> picking up beer cans in Yellowstone." A similar sentiment was reflected
> in the comment of Donald T. Regan when he was Secretary of the Treasury,
> who said the question of national service had to be answered in terms of
> whether the nation needs youth "Picking up trash rather than earning
> their first million."[1]

Yielding to our temptation to measure things by their cash value, it
is not unusual to justify community service as a way of meeting social
needs at low or no cost. Yet, the economics of community service are
said to be secondary. So we praise self-sacrifice and commitment. Moreover, many of the programs—like the CCC in an earlier day and the
Youth Corps program today—deliver a mixed message of idealism and
practicalism. Often, too, they mix community service and job programs.

When we look at the things we do, we find another reminder of the
market place. Most services for hire demand limited and minimal skills.
They are, as it were, permanent "entry-level" positions. There are of
course elite services like plumbing, carpentry, auto mechanics. But these
are the exceptions. Most service work is routine; indeed its virtue is to
be routine. Advancement means promotion out of one service and into
another or into the management of services. Service jobs, therefore, are
reserved for those who have little choice and little future. Of course,
people in service jobs may enjoy their work. The social environment of
the work place may take on communal characteristics. For some of us,
and for some of the time, service work may even be a relief from re-

sponsibilities. Dependent though we may be on their performance, however, we tend to hold service and service people in low esteem.

With little change, this description can readily be transferred to many of the activities of community service—routine, minimal skill, temporariness, low esteem—although use of a moralistic rhetoric blurs the connection. The debate surrounding the 1990 national service legislation was typical. In Senator Kennedy's proposals, in President Bush's "call to action," and in the legislation finally adopted, a familiar and revealing list of targets appeared: the homeless, the illiterate, the school drop-out, the drug user, the pregnant teenager, the AIDS victim, the nursing home resident. Tasks were to be restricted to those for which few economic resources were available; participants were to be restricted to unskilled helping activities.

The cash rewards of the market place were absent or at best reduced. Instead of a wage, we found small stipends, scholarship grants, forgiveness of college tuition loans. Not least of all, non-economic rewards were emphasized. Thus, "The President said he planned to establish an awards program for outstanding volunteers, and to appoint 'youth ambassadors' to promote volunteerism among the young."[2] Above all, national service must not cost us very much. So, we speak in two ways about community service: that it is worth so little that society does not choose to provide for it; that it is worth so much that the status of young people as persons and as citizens depends on their willingness to participate. These messages are reflected in Ernest Boyer's wry recollection of a youngster's description of his summer job, "Last summer I got a job working at McDonald's. It didn't pay too well, but at least I felt needed for a while." Boyer added, "There's something unhealthy about a youth culture where feeling needed is pushing Big Macs at McDonald's."[3] That this double message introduces a note of skepticism, if not cynicism, into the most well-intentioned efforts of community service should not be surprising.

We compound the double message by how we think about the young who are the targets of community service programs. The connection we make between youth and service is all too easily understood as a cheap way of adding to the ranks of those we can use to meet our needs. So, the double message is reinforced by telling the young that they are both precious and exploitable. To be sure, adult concern for what is going on in a so-called youth culture is legitimate; it is often understood, however, as manipulative and patronizing by the young. As Joe Nathan and Jim Kielsmeier sum it up,

Unlike earlier generations, which viewed young people as active, productive, and needed members of the household and community, adults today tend to treat them as objects, as problems or as the recipients (not the deliverers) of services. Young people are treated as objects when they are routinely classified as a separate group, isolated in age-based institutions, and beset on all sides by advertising—though not otherwise recognized or treated with respect. They are treated as problems when they are feared, criticized, and made the focus of preventive and remedial programs. They are treated as recipients of services when they are viewed as creatures to be pitied, "fixed," and "controlled."[4]

The usages of "service" tell us that it is difficult in a developing service economy, to insulate community service from the values of a market culture. Even the public good, the differential mark of community service, is shaped by those values. So the tasks of the public good look very much like those of the market place except that we're unwilling to pay for having them done; the rewards of community service come to look like the superficial gimmickry of all other public relations campaigns.

THE DUTIFUL SERVANT

In our anxiety about being practical, realistic, hard-headed—all the shibboleths of a culture that measures its values by the "bottom line"— we easily corrupt community service. We acknowledge this by using two kinds of discourse. In our public rhetoric, we attach service to larger and more imaginative ends like character, citizenship, moral development; we appeal to our latent idealism. When policy decisions are made and resources allocated, however, we quickly revert to the habits of the market place.

It is striking to find how little reference is made to a rich religious and political tradition of service. The languages of faith are found, of course, where service projects are attached to religious institutions but even here a so-called realism calls the tune. Indeed, it sometimes seems as if the worst we can say of another is that he or she is a "do-gooder." No doubt, one of the reasons for our silence about religiously motivated service is the importance in a pluralistic society of providing a secular basis for community service. Even religiously sponsored projects—with the exception of missionary efforts—try to escape parochialism for the sake of inclusiveness. In so far as they seek a share of public funds or engage in general fund-raising they must avoid crossing the line between church and state or the appearance of sectarianism. No doubt, too, the historic identification of community service with social reform in politics and progressivism in education tends to underplay conservative sources of value like religion and republicanism. Like President Bush, conservatives tend, instead, to offer us a mix of *laissez faire* political economy, hucksterism, and moral sentimentality.

There are, of course, a few exceptions. Among the latter, William F. Buckley, Jr., who takes his republicanism seriously, is characteristically articulate.

On obligations: It is realistic to conclude that a national service program entirely voluntary in nature . . . is likely to founder. There is no reason to be surprised by this, given that most of what human beings do is in response to sanctions or inducements of one kind or another: God, self, family, health, patriotism. Organized inducements are appropriate and are not in conflict with a conservative understanding of the relationship between state and citizen whose education is to a certain stage properly required; whose service in the military is, in extremis, conscriptable; whose taxes are reasonably exacted.[5]

Buckley reminds us that neither the menial tradition nor the habits of the market place exhaust the usages of service. At the same time, our situation makes it difficult to get hold of these transcending meanings. Although I am a Humanist and a secularist, I cannot reflect on service without calling to mind the Hebrew tradition of the *mitzvah* or "good deed" and the Christian tradition of "caritas" in the West or the Buddhist tradition of "compassion" and the Confucian tradition of "respect" in the East. Each establishes the notion of service as calling and elevates service from servility to moral ideal. Each is both a practice and a symbol. As a practice, service under a religious inspiration is a way of connecting persons to each other and to the universe, de-alienating them as it were. Thereby, it provides a mode of mutual recognition. As symbol, service carries the message of a common root and a common destiny that transcends the accidents of living in the world. Service, in other words, is the way in which god-like powers—the powers for doing good, for escaping the bonds of ego—become accessible to mortals.

Like social reform, Christianity centers attention on the poor and the needy. In its ideal of sainthood, from St. Francis to Mother Teresa, it offers a model of service to the point of a near disappearance of self. Paradoxically, the need of the doer reappears in the tension between self-sacrifice and self-development. For us lesser folk, however, Christianity encourages a more modest behavioral—but not spiritual—connection between self and other. It celebrates the commonality of all persons as children of God but it makes a puzzling demand on the contemporary psyche. The modern connection is functional and contractual and self-interested. The religious idea of service is communal and we are not accustomed to communities. We are face to face, once again—but now from a different angle—with the lost connection.

Unfortunately, Christian service appears in ways that reinforce our ambivalence. For example, service appears in *Luke* as a household obligation. The language of duty and role is revealing.

> Which of you, with a servant plowing or minding sheep, would say to
> him when he returned from the fields, "Come and have your meal im-
> mediately?" Would he not be more likely to say, "Get my supper laid;
> make yourself tidy and wait on me while I eat and drink. You can eat and
> drink yourself afterward?" Must he be grateful to the servant for doing
> what he was told? So with you; when you have done all you have been
> told to do, say, "We are merely servants; we have done no more than our
> duty."[6]

Doing service is as unremarkable as doing chores. Community service
as a boundaried and identifiable activity, as a project, really doesn't
exist. Volunteerism with the implication that I may choose or not choose
to respond, wouldn't make sense either. By an interesting inversion,
service is portrayed—in *Matthew*—as a sign of leadership,

> When the other ten [disciples] heard this they were indignant with the
> two brothers. But Jesus called them to him and said, "You know that
> among the pagans the rulers lord it over them, and their great men make
> their authority felt. This is not to happen among you. No; anyone who
> want to be great among you must be your servant, and anyone who want
> to be first among you must be your slave, just as the Son of Man came
> not to be served but to serve, and to give his life as a ransom for many."[7]

We are expected to live up to a sacred ideal. Yet, the competition
among the disciples invites a struggle for power with service as its
method and position as its reward. We can hear echoes of a political
leadership that poses as a "servant of the people." A more benign interpretation of the same text, however, takes shape as a movement for
"servant leadership." Its founder, Robert Greenleaf, describes it,

> The servant-leader is servant first. . . . It begins with the natural feeling
> that one wants to serve, to serve first. Then conscious choice brings one
> to aspire to lead. . . . The difference manifests itself in the care taken by
> the servant—first to make sure that other people's highest priority needs
> are being served. The best test, and difficult to administer, is: do those
> served grow as persons; do they, while being served, become healthier,
> wiser, freer, more autonomous, more likely themselves to become ser-
> vants? And, what is the effect on the least privileged in society; will they
> benefit, or at least, not be further deprived?[8]

John McKnight, however, rejects the term entirely and suggests a third
Christian model,

> When I'm around church people, I always check whether they are misled
> by the modern secular vision. Have they substituted the vision of service
> for the only thing that will make people whole—community? Are they

service peddlers or community builders? Peddling services is unchristian—even if you're hell-bent on helping people . . .

We all know that at the Last Supper, Jesus said, "This is my commandment: love one another as I have loved you. There is no greater love than this: to lay down one's life for one's friends." But for mysterious reasons, I never hear the next two sentences. "You are my friends if you do what I command you. I no longer call you servants because servants do not know the business of the one they serve. But I have called you friends because I have made known to you everything I learned from God."[9]

Christian models, then, offer differing ideals of service. At the same time, Christianity is caught in paternalism; we are all "children" of God, the Father. And this is less than convincing in our secular democratic culture.

THE PUBLIC GOOD

There is an affinity between the religious images of service and the secular images of *res publica*. In contrast with market and menial images, both religion and republican politics embed service in transpersonal values—cosmic or worldly. By way of example, Thucydides recreates the funeral oration of Pericles,

> So died these men as became Athenians. . . . And not contended with ideas derived only from words of the advantages which are bound up with the defence of your country . . . you must yourselves realise the power of Athens, and feed your eyes upon her from day to day, till love of her fills your hearts; and then when all her greatness shall break upon you, you must reflect that it was by courage, sense of duty, and a keen feeling of honour in action that men were enabled to win all this, and that no personal failure in an enterprise could make them consent to deprive their country of their valor, but they laid it at her feet as the most glorious contribution they could offer.[10]

Patriotism and loyalty are the context for a politics of community and not of social contract. Using that theme, Socrates describes the demands of a transcendent Athens. Replying to the urging of his friends to escape the sentence of death, he imagines that the Laws of Athens speak to him,

> For having brought you into the world, and nurtured and educated you, and given you and every other citizen a share in every good which we had to give, we further proclaim to any Athenian by the liberty which we allow him, that if he does not like us . . . he may go where he pleases and take his good with him. . . . But he who has experience of the manner in

which we order justice and administer the state, and still remains, has entered into an implied contract that he will do as we command him. And he who disobeys us is . . . thrice wrong; first, because in disobeying us he is disobeying his parents; secondly, because we are the authors of his education; thirdly, because he has made an agreement with us that he will duly obey our commands.[11]

Citizenship and its duties take a somewhat less exalted pathway in the move from Greece to Rome. Service still attaches, however, to the proper role of the citizen in the community. In his *Meditations*, the Roman Emperor, Marcus Aurelius, writes,

Every moment think steadily as a Roman and a man to do what thou hast in hand with perfect and simple dignity, and feeling of affection, and freedom, and justice; and to give thyself relief from all other thoughts. And thou wilt give thyself relief, if thou doest every act of thy life as if it were the last, laying aside all carelessness and passionate aversion from the commands of reason, and all hypocrisy and self-love, and discontent with the portion which has been given to thee.[12]

Set in the context of an Aristotelian image of the person as *zoon politicon*, as a political animal, reason and observation establish the intentions of human nature. The duty of the human being to serve the common good is the theme of a classical view of citizenship. And citizenship is a necessary outcome of human nature under conditions of freedom.

This Graeco-Roman tradition was renewed with the emergence of a political science in the work of Macchiavelli and his Enlightenment successors.[13] Consequently, it was much alive for the founders of the American republic. They knew their Greeks and their Romans. As Saul Padover reminds us,

Even those who had no formal education would refer to classic writers or historic personalities. . . . Franklin, who was self-taught and "fond of reasoning," seems to have read, as judged by the references in his writings, Cicero, Epictetus, Herodotus, Plato, Pliny, Pythagoras, Sallust, Seneca, Tacitus, and Xenophon. Similarly, George Washington, a man of little schooling and not ordinarily given to literary references in his correspondence, showed an awareness of antiquity . . .

The writings of the more learned and formally educated Founding Fathers are replete with citations from and references to personalities of antiquity. In James Madison, one finds mentions of the outstanding classical writers, such as Plato, Plutarch, Polybius. . . . Indeed, Alexander Hamilton was in the habit of using classical pseudonyms in his polemical writings—"Camillus," "Pacificus," "Publius."[14]

I encountered these Greek and Latin roots in a striking way during a visit to Charlottesville, Virginia. The connection of politics and person became tangible in the architecture of Jefferson's University of Virginia with its neo-classical collonades, its courtyards, its statuary, its rotunda modeled on the Parthenon. I was reminded that we children of the Enlightenment are thereby grandchildren of Greece and Rome.

The common good of classical republicanism is not simply a collection of private goods. It is to be found by the exercise of rational inquiry into the history and meanings of political morality much as Aristotle examined various states and Macchiavelli studied the Roman republic. In the name of the common good—variously, the public good, the general welfare—the Founders made a revolution. No small part of their motivation was their sense of a deteriorating British commonwealth. In making the transition which we call the "industrial revolution," England had lost its genius in the sacrifice of common goods for private interests. The Founders understood the demands of the common good then as both a criticism of the deteriorated present against which they rebelled in the name of the "rights of Englishmen," and as an ideal drawn from the classical past. So it was that,

> it was not as a scholarly embellishment or as a source of values that antiquity was most important to Americans in these revolutionary years. The American's compulsive interest in the ancient republics was in fact crucial to their attempt to understand the moral and social basis of politics . . .
>
> To make the people's welfare—the public good—the exclusive end of government became for the Americans, as one general put it, their "Polar Star," the central tenet of the Whig faith, shared not only by Hamilton and Paine at opposite ends of the Whig spectrum, but by any American bitterly opposed to a system which held "that a Part is greater than its Whole; or in other Words, that some Individuals ought to be considered, even to the Destruction of the Community which they compose." No phrase except "liberty" was invoked more often by the Revolutionaries than "the public good."[15]

The common or public good was the objective ground for service. Fading echoes of this transcending sense of citizenship remain with us in the near-sacred regard we give to the Constitution while often ignorant of its detail and dismissive of its commitments. While giving patriotism a psychological and pedagogical "spin," this republican tradition clearly informed William James' call for a "moral equivalent to war" and allows us still to understand the connection between citizenship and service.

The interpretation of community service as civics service is an attempt to breathe new life into the republican ideal. Morris Janowitz of the University of Chicago is a long-time and articulate spokesperson for this view. Within the Jamesian tradition, he comments,

> I contend that there has been decline in the vitality and clarity of civic education in the United States. . . . The United States was born in armed political revolution, but the American Revolution was more than a military battle; it served as a powerful agency of civic education. . . .
>
> Civic education limited to inculcation of traditional patriotism or conventional nationalist ideology is obviously inadequate. . . . I find the words *national* and *patriotic* limiting, and offer the term *civic consciousness*. . . . It involves elements of reason and self-criticism as well as personal commitment. . . .
>
> Since classroom teaching is insufficient for civic education, the interesting question is whether the particular educational experience of national service with real-life content will strengthen popular understanding of civic obligations. . . . National service should operate to balance the pursuit of economic self interest against collective civic obligation.[16]

In a society which has fragmented itself into a collection of separated worlds, however, the duties of the citizen like the obligations of *caritas* or *mitzvah* do not come comfortably to us. Indeed, these often seem but museum exhibits. So community service leaves behind this tradition with its tie to a transcendent and transpersonal good. But even when we escape the effects of the market, we only replace a transpersonal good with the subjectivity of interpersonal relationships. For example, in its influential report, the William T. Grant Foundation begins with the following familiar sentences, "At the core of citizenship is the willingness to contribute to the common good. When young people are asked to channel their idealism and energy into helping others and solving community problems, they build respect for themselves and attachments to others."[17]

The burden of the recommendations that follow, however, is a call for familiar list of governmental and school-based programs. All of us are caught in the modern trap. Over and over again we replace service for the common good with interpersonal acts between doer and done-to who continue to live in worlds apart. To the ambiguity of neediness, we add a pseudo-republicanism by invoking citizenship without insisting on the transcending commitments it entails. Citizenship becomes but another function.

A SERVICE ETHIC

Efforts to draw upon a religious or a republican tradition for the meanings of community service seem to be an exercise in nostalgia. As two consultants to the Educational Service Cener (Region 13) in Austin, Texas, remark,

Citizenship education is the aged great-uncle at a family gathering. Everyone treats him with respect and some are genuinely fond of him, but few want to sit next to him at the dinner table. . . .

The respect accorded citizenship can be traced to the early days of public education in America. Thomas Jefferson, in supporting the establishment of schools at public expense, argued that students should learn to read, write, and figure so that they would be ready for the responsibilities of citizenship. . . .

Gradually, the subjects taught in schools came to be ends in themselves, however, and the attention given to citizenship education declined accordingly.[18]

The marketplace view of services undercuts our ability to fulfill the grander promises we attach to community service. Even when the less lovely features of the market—greed, self-seeking, competitiveness—are minimized, it works against a community-creating ideal of service. For example, in 1970, the Gates Commission reported on a proposed all-volunteer military service. Its recommendations, inspired by free-enterprise economists like University of Chicago's Milton Friedman, called for converting military service from a civic duty into an ordinary occupation. Pay scales were to be raised to market-place levels in order to compete with civilian job offers. Skill was to be rewarded according to its sophistication and scarcity. Cost-benefit analysis was to be used in assessing productivity. The paraphernalia of the military continued to be used—rank, time-in-grade, the symbols of patriotism, and so forth—but these became another language for economic reward.[19] Military public relations campaigns, for example, "Be the best you can be in the Army," are continuing signs of this conversion of civic duty into private purpose.

The busyness and repetitiveness of community service may not,then, be a testimony only to our penchant for imitation or our wisdom in reproducing workable programs. Nor are they only the result of compromise between differing but sustainable visions of community. Above all, they are not, as Rachel's dilemma points out, evidence of our security about the meanings and ends of the community service idea. Instead, our busyness and repetitions, in large measure, are a method of blindness. The confusing kaleidoscope of activity is the result of our inability to grasp the religious and civic possibilities of community service.

Another model of service arises from that very inability. Those of us engaged in community service try to move toward what may be called a "service ethic," to take a step beyond activism. For example, Anthony Richards notes the implications of re-conceiving community service on transpersonal grounds. In a case study of "We Care and Share," a demonstration project in Nova Scotia, he comments,

> The ideal outcome of any service/learning program is that the participant
> has developed a service ethic. This service ethic has also been a long time
> goal of most traditional programs, most of the learning has been vicarious
> and as a result of strong role models or specific environments. It is only
> recently that such courses as "community service" and programs like "We
> Care and Share" have deliberately set out to have a service ethic as a major
> goal of the program. Even well known national service programs such as
> the California Conservation Corps have the work ethic as paramount rather
> than the service ethic.[20]

Unfortunately, the language of citizenship is used to manipulate the
young. But, there is more to the story. I recall that Angela Vassos,
Fieldston's Director of Community Service, insisted on calling our program "service ethics." Puzzled by what looked like a clumsy name, I
came to understand it as the search for a connection between transpersonal purpose and personal experience. There are many students and
teachers who take their citizenship seriously. They really want to embed
service in what is genuinely valuable and agree that we have not yet
succeeded in doing so.

Latent in much of the discussion of community service, then, is a
"feel" for this transcending ground. A look at the various models of
service thus tempers the skepticism that emerges from an analysis of
the self-serving features of need. Participants in community service like
policy makers attach concrete programs to transcending ends. But for
the participant, unlike the policy maker, this is not just an incidental
exercise or a public relations ploy. Let me cite some sentences by Richard
Lodish, assistant headmaster of the Sidwell Friends School in Washington, D.C.

> Perhaps after all is said and done, we are left with our original question:
> "What do you want for the world? What do you want for yourself?"
> "For the world, I want enough food and shelter for everyone. For me,
> I want to help others to have food and shelter." If we receive this answer
> from our young children and if they mean it, understand it, and act on
> it, then the lesson of service learned in youth will last a lifetime.[21]

Calls for an "ethos of service" or a "service ethic" take various forms.
Among educators, service is connected to learning so that the very nature
of schooling itself is to be transformed. For others, community service
is embodied in national service so that the very nature of the society is
to be transformed. And for still others, service is embedded in a normative psychology, a notion of altruism, so that the very nature of
human nature is to be transformed. These share the attempt to work
out a model of community service that speaks to us in the present and
that yet benefits from the traditions of *caritas* and the common good as
well as the tradition of reform.

The idea of a service ethic reflects the attempt to connect community service with a religious or a republican inspiration in weakened form. Nor is this weakness regrettable. A service ethic is limited in a way that the commandments of God or *res publica* are not. It takes account of a culture with many centers of value, that is, it converts the separated worlds of the lost connection into affirmative life-world opportunities. So, such an ethic cannot expect the sacrifice of self in service of another. It is not a directive to sainthood. Nor can it expect the common good—except in times of emergency—to demand the surrender of self for collective purposes. It is not a directive for heroism. For all of its faults, the market place is a useful corrosive, subverting traditional models that can, unchallenged, become the disasters of fanaticism or totalitarianism. As we surely know, church and state can demand all loyalty and all service in their name. William James' call for a "moral equivalent to war" can all too easily turn emergency into a steady diet.

Unchecked by a messy worldliness, transcendence becomes tyranny. Even under ideal conditions of faith and patriotism, for example, the equality of all persons as children of the universe or as citizens of the Republic, service can lead to the surrender of liberty in the name of a greater good. Paradoxically, then community service can be destructive of democracy and this is likely when it is sanctioned by conservative tradition and motivated by liberal good will. A Philippine student reminds us,

> I resist the notion of service learning for U.S. students in the Philippines, my country of origin, because I think it perpetuates a "colonial mentality" among Filipinos and a kind of "manifest destiny" among U.S. students. To my way of thinking, the results of the history of U.S. dominance in the Philippines is so overwhelming that it is almost impossible for a U.S. student doing what is regarded on both sides as "service" not to deliver a message of superiority.
>
> There is an incipient racism in the practice of service that cannot be avoided even if the conceptualization of it includes values and ideals we can respect and the virtues of people who practice it are above question.[22]

I am struck by the interplay between interpersonal and transpersonal motivations. And, I notice that the reality of direct connection is accompanied by the desire that it also connect to something more than the present moment of doing and done-to. "Making a difference," which is the message of the notion of "need"—I am needed, the need to be needed—is joined by the notion of making a difference "to the world." It is not enough to serve only this or that particular person in this or that particular place and moment. At the same time, community service becomes a mere abstraction without this directness of the moment.

Exposure is what most students experience during their involvement in community service. The vast majority of programs aim to expose students to people who are less fortunate than they are—people with whom they would not ordinarily come into contact. Yet, some programs aspire to go beyond such exposure, to *engage* students. *Engagement* implies intensity. In such programs, students take service seriously, they are intellectually engaged. Programs that engage students demand not only that students use their hearts (e.g., sympathize or empathize with clients); they also insist that students understand intellectually the "broad social dynamics" underlying the situations of the people they serve (the plight of the elderly, causes of poverty, racism, etc.). Engagement programs require more commitment from their students that just fulfilling the required number of hours.[23]

Need and service are two sides of the same coin, the language of psychological and social reality. Need dramatizes the unreality of mere "exposure" and service dramatizes the unreality of mere "doing." For community service unlike social analysis, however, persons and not merely forces and powers are gathered. It is this encounter which the various models have in common. The background of any of them is existential, passionate, tangible. Locating service in self, school, and society is the next step in exploring the lost connection and in resolving Rachel's dilemma.

NOTES

1. Charles C. Moskos, *A Call to Civic Service*, (New York: The Free Press, 1988), pp. 169–170.

2. Lisa Jennings, "Kennedy Unveils $330 Million Plan for Volunteerism," *Education Week* 8, 40 (August 2, 1989).

3. Charles H. Harrison, "Foreword," *Student Service: The New Carnegie Unit* (Princeton, N.J.: Carnegie Foundation for the Advancement of Teaching, 1987), p. vii.

4. Joe Nathan and Jim Kielsmeier, "The Sleeping Giant of School Reform," *Phi Delta Kappan* 72, 10 (June 1991), p. 740.

5. William F. Buckley, Jr., *Gratitude* (New York: Random House, 1990), pp. 58–59.

6. Luke, 17:7–10, *The Jerusalem Bible* (Garden City, N.Y.: Doubleday, 1968), p. 98.

7. Matthew, 20: 24–28, *The Jerusalem Bible* (Garden City, N.Y.: Doubleday, 1968), p. 31.

8. Robert K. Greenleaf, cited from *The Servant as Leader*, in "Building Better Institutions Through Servant-Leadership," pamphlet (Indianapolis, Ind.: The Robert K. Greenleaf Center, no date).

9. John McKnight, "Why 'Servanthood' Is Bad," *The Other Side* 25, 1 (January–February 1989).

10. Thucydides, *The Peloponnesian War*, trans. R. Crawley, intro. Joseph Gavorse (New York: The Modern Library, 1934), p. 107.

11. "Crito," *The Dialogues of Plato*, 2 vols., trans. Benjamin Jowett (New York: Random House, 1937) vol. 1, pp. 435–436.

12. Marcus Aurelius, *Meditations*, 2, 5, *The Stoic and Epicurean Philosophers*, ed. Whitney J. Oates (New York: Random House, 1940), p. 498.

13. For example, Macchiavelli, *Discourses on the First Ten Books of Titus Livius*, trans. Christian E. Detmold, (New York: The Modern Library, 1940).

14. *The World of the Founding Fathers*, ed. Saul K. Padover, (New York: A.S. Barnes and Company, 1977), pp. 29–30.

15. Gordon S. Wood, *The Creation of the American Republic, 1776–1787*, (Chapel Hill, N.C.: The University of North Carolina Press, 1969), pp. 50 and 55.

16. Morris Janowitz, "The Good Citizen—A Threatened Species?" *University of Chicago Magazine* (Summer 1985), pp. 7–13, cited in Morris Janowitz, *The Reconstruction of Patriotism: Education for Civic Consciousness* (Chicago: The University of Chicago Press, 1985).

17. *Citizenship Through Service*, a pamphlet issued by The William T. Grant Foundation Commission on Work, Family and Citizenship, November, 1988, (excerpted from Chapter 4 of *The Forgotten Half: Pathways to Success for America's Youth and Young Families*, Washington, D.C.), p. 90.

18. Greg Farman and Etta Hollins, "Citizenship and the Infusion Game," *Phi Delta Kappan* 62, 7 (March 1981), p. 510.

19. Thomas S. Gates was a former Secretary of Defense. The Commission was charged with exploring alternatives to a military draft given the military "peace-time" obligations of the United States. A discussion of the evolution of an all-voluntary force can be found in Charles C. Moskos, *A Call to Civic Service*, (New York: The Free Press, 1988).

20. Anthony Richards, "Developing a Service Ethic," Dalhousie University, Halifax, Nova Scotia, Canada, unpublished and undated, probably 1988. See also, Anthony Richards and Edward Scrutton, "Progress Report to Halifax School Board," 1980.

21. Richard Lodish, "A Lesson for a Lifetime," unpublished paper, undated but probably Fall 1989; the title is drawn from Senator Edward Kennedy's comments in introducing the proposed National Service Act on July 27, 1989.

22. Nadinne Cruz, "A Challenge to the Notion of Service," *Combining Service and Learning*, Jane C. Kendall and Associates, Ed., (Raleigh, N.C.: National Society for Internships and Experiential Education, 1990), vol. 1, pp. 321–323 *passim*.

23. Lee M. Levison, "Choose Engagement Over Exposure," Jane C. Kendall and Associates, *op. cit.*, vol. 1, p. 69.

Chapter Seven

Familiars and Strangers

THE TROUBLE WITH PEOPLE...

Need and service raise questions about altruism and selfishness and invite confusions between ego development and egoism, selflessness and self-seeking. We also run into the habit of excusing human beings for their failures with the phrase, "that's human nature." Typically, we are surprised when we find someone doing for a stranger, and ask cynically, "what's in it for him or her?"

To be sure, we suspend our cynicism when we respond to the victims of an earthquake or flood although a persistent crisis soon finds us losing interest. Usually, however, bad news about people is *the* news. We are fed a steady diet of information that encourages us to mistrust human beings. And, we accept its accuracy. In doing community service, then, we seem to go counter to our normal habits and our normal expectations.

Community service assumes that we are capable of being moral agents. We can enter into relationships, make choices, take initiatives, exhibit abilities and assess what we and others are up to, and we can do all these things on principled grounds and not just for our own benefit. Community service presumes that there are doers and done-to; that there are distinctions between them which allow us to speak of their relationships in moral language. We are, in other words, histori-cally, imaginatively, psychologically and practically a capable species. Among our capabilities are moral objectivity like fairness and a sense of justice and moral empathy like caring and concern. Given these assumptions, community service also presumes that people can change and, above all, that they can change themselves.

Obviously, assumptions can be wrong. Nevertheless, the story of community service tells me that freedom, good will, and moral ability can develop and change over time. Thus, I do not think it possible to make sense of community service and at the same time to believe that human nature is "a something" once and for all. Of course, there are determinate things we can say about ourselves but not the least of the things we can say is that we are plastic, malleable, corrigible. Absent that, and it would simply make no sense to praise altruists or to blame egoists or to worry about whether we were teaching people to be passive or authoritarian or what have you. Community service would simply be the name of an event which, like other events, would have to follow whatever causal laws existed.

We enjoy a rich vocabulary that points to a human nature that is, in some measure at least, under our control and finally nonpredictable. So we speak of development and character and value as if these did not have to come out in any one determinate way. We refer to goals, norms, desires, hopes, dreams, fears, angers, disappointments, achievements, failures. And these do not convey notions like hard or round or heavy or granular or green. We expect, ultimately, to be responsible for changing ourselves. The *inability* to do so—whether by reason of political or economic arrangements or for the lack of the tools or because of some handicap—is taken as a diminution of human nature and so becomes a moral-political statement. The *refusal* to do so is taken as a betrayal of our moral capacities. Taken together, this provides a rough distinction between objects and persons. Of course, we may be mistaken in this— our vocabulary may only point to a self-serving illusion—in which case a person is simply another kind of object.[1] But, if that is the case then terms of choice are emptied of their meaning and we are left, at best, with a descriptive social psychology.

Community service is also built on assumptions of relationship. So, we assume that it is both possible and appropriate for culturally diverse persons to move, although not without difficulty, into each others' worlds and to have a shared world as well. On that ground, neither biology nor class nor culture is destiny. However, the argument against determinism—whether theological, behaviorist, or Marxist—is unresolvable and confusions between determinateness and determinism will continue. William James had it right, I think, when he wrote,

> I thus disclaim openly on the threshold all pretension to prove to you that the freedom of the will is true. The most I hope is to induce some of you to follow my own example in assuming it true and acting as if it were true. . . . Our first act of freedom, if we are free, ought in all inward pro-

priety to be to affirm that we are free. This should exclude, it seems to me, from the free-will side of the question all hope of a coercive dem-onstration—a demonstration which I, for one, am perfectly contented to go without.[2]

Community service requires making concrete choices against deter-minism. At the same time, because of our experience—particularly the resistance to change we find in both doer and done-to—determinism is always a temptation. If we fail to make the choice against determinism, however, the done-to can never be anything but an object and the doer can never be anything but an unwitting actor and so, in a sense, equally passive. More serious than the old and tired argument about free will is the supposition in action that time and place and history do not necessarily predict a person's pathway through life. If they did, then community service could only be a palliative, a way of making a person's lot tolerable without any hope of changing his or her condition. This ontological conclusion about the nature of community service is quite a different matter from sociopolitical criticisms of it in practice, that is, that it reflects an imposition on others of middle-class values or is a conservative ploy used to avoid collective responsibility. The assumption of freedom affects the doer's initiative as well, leaving him or her with the choice of conservatism or reform although, again, this does not preclude deciding that community service as such cannot be an effective agent of reform. At any rate, the assumptions of freedom are essential to community service. Summing up John Dewey on the theme, Robert Westbrook remarks,

> It is worth repeating that this dialectical relationship between individuality and community, self-realization and social service, did not necessarily require conformity to the practices of one's particular community. Reform could be as much a service to a community as other functions. Dewey did insist, following Hegel's notion of *Sittlichkeit* or concrete ethics, that reform be ground in the "ought" that was already apparent in the "is" of pre-vailing practices of existing communities rather than the abstract and purely formal injunctions of Kantian ethics, but this limitation left plenty for the reformer to do.[3]

Until recently the ability to be an agent had to be defended against those who were inclined to one or another kind of positivism. The moral validity of plasticity had to be established against assumptions about the fixity and universality of human nature and human society. Of course, determinism and cultural arrogance masking as objectivity are still very much alive in the languages of "welfare dependency" and of race and gender. Today, however, we also face a different problem which, ironically, emerges from the very success of the defense of di-versity. It shows up in ordinary discourse when we hear that "it's all a matter of taste," or "that's only your opinion." And the same view is evident in our intellectual romance with "deconstruction" and "post-modernism." On the liberal side of things, we seem to be left with no dependable reference points outside of the accidents of our culture and moment. From a moral point of view, we are told that all cultures are equal to all other cultures and with them their values, hopes, organizations, and life-styles.[4]

If a "post-modern" conclusion is valid, then it makes no sense to assume that the transcultural exchanges characteristic of the relationship between doer and done-to are morally desirable although they may be aesthetically and psychologically interesting. If all cultures are equivalent to all other cultures, then notions of need, service and community cannot be defined except from within a culture and only for its own members. We might be able to exchange a minimum amount of information about our respective cultures and in that sense we might gain some limited understanding of each other. But we surely could not justify using that information to respond to a need identified in one culture on behalf of another. As a caution against arrogance, a respect for the integrity of diverse peoples and cultures makes good sense as we have seen in our discussions of the settlement house and the Peace Corps. But, converting this respect into an absolute leaves us with few human connections and indeed enshrines the lost connection in the very being of social relationships. In short, if relativism run wild is truthful, then the notion that some cultural habits are preferable to others loses intelligibility.

On one side, community services presumes a certain benevolence in human beings that goes counter to our popular expectations. On the other, it presumes a certain freedom that goes counter to those philosophic habits which have denied it in a burst of scientism or which have taken it to the extreme of pure arbitrariness.

THE POSSIBILITY OF DEVELOPMENT

The assumptions of community service show up in the actual relationships between strangers. These relationships are nourished in a dialectic of self and other. Further, these relationships are not just happenings but can be aimed in a direction or else they would not be chosen at all. That is also why we are able to speak of success or failure, of effectiveness or ineffectiveness, of learning or failing to learn from our experience. Community service assumes that certain forms of conduct are morally right or less right or wrong. So, we criticize projects as arrogant and praise others as participatory. In short, persons in community service whether as doers or done-to are expected to develop in some way—as citizens, as individuals, as students. Concretely, the decision to address community service to the young—however much I may criticize its arrogation of power—is a restatement in practice of the notion of development. The young stand for tomorrow in the present and attention to them stands for the aim of shaping that tomorrow by what is done in the present. Development is built into the very way in which community service is understood.

Development presumes that we are going somewhere, not just "hanging around." Now within a life-world, that "somewhere" takes form as conventional goals, expectations and values. Generally, we have dependable ground on which to stand as long as we remain at home. Indeed, issues of direction are hardly raised although issues of meeting standards of practice will be. In a sense, when we are at home we know exactly where we are going and why. Even conflicted goals are intelligible.

Leaving home, however, we experience the anxiety of relativism. We step aside as observers or enter as visitors from another place. Like the tourist, we are fascinated by the esoteric but cling to the familiar. A neat separation between being at home and being a stranger doesn't hold up in our experience, however, certainly not in modern experience. We are simultaneously at home and alien, and in many places at once. Diversity is a fact of our personal lives and not just of collective life. Despite its anxieties—who am I when I am so many things at once, who are we and which "we"—this experienced diversity can have its benefits. Thus, in a study of "experiential education," Diane Hedin and Dan Conrad report,

> Students in 24 of 28 programs increased both *general self-esteem* and *self-esteem in social situations*. The results suggest that the increased interaction with a variety of people, new places, and novel responsibilities tended to give these young people more confidence in themselves in social situations—speaking in front of a class, meeting new people. General perception of self-worth, such as feeling more useful and more able to do things well, also increased.[5]

Consideration of familiarity and strangeness suggests that the idea of culture itself has really left its comfortable anthropological niche. It may now be interpreted in an extended sense to include differing and decreasingly connected life-worlds drawn together around generational, gender, geographical, communal, and political economic values and customs as well as around traditional ethnicity and race and class.[6] Concretely, this shift can be heard in the report of a student,

> A long time ago, when I was a small child of about six or seven years old, I learned what it meant to be Black in America.... As I grew up in the ghetto, I remember feeling the frustration around me—frustration that many people don't understand. I knew then that if I wanted to feel like

my life had any meaning, I would work to change the perceptions on both sides of the fence. . . .

My [community service] projects were an extension of that commitment to uplifting the race, and all minorities. I can look back on them with satisfaction, and say that I did my best for a short while to do something to help the people in my community while gaining something for myself.[7]

An extended idea of culture shows up too in the claim that the rest of us cannot know what minority experience is like. A similar message is conveyed by feminists in debates about rape or abortion. More radical nationalists and feminists have even called for a deliberate politics of separateness based in a notion of alienated race and gender communities.[8] Less extreme, but no less striking, is Carol Gilligan's view,

Since masculinity is defined through separation while femininity is defined through attachment, male gender identity is threatened by intimacy while female gender identity is threatened by separation. Thus, males tend to have difficulty with relationships, while females tend to have problems with individuation. The quality of embeddedness in social interaction and personal relationships that characterizes women's lives in contrast to men's, however, becomes not only a descriptive difference but also a developmental liability when the milestones of childhood and adolescent development in the psychological literature are markers of increasing separation. Women's failure to separate then becomes by definition a failure to develop.[9]

Today's discourse of diversity is characterized by the absence of common values even where common language signs are used.[10] This separateness includes but is not limited to the more obvious differences of class and income. The differing life-worlds establish us in our separateness and suggest the arrival of a radical pluralism of cultures. Among other things, using the idea of culture as life-world offers a way of interpreting the evolution of "stranger-ness" among persons said to be living in the"same" time and place. For example, it is simply unhelpful to approach the following description of "people like us" (PLUs) in moralistic terms.

T. M., a 44-year-old tax attorney, is sitting in his English Tudor home . . . talking to himself.

Actually, the conversation is with his earlier self—a fondly remembered 20-year-old who worked for Eugene McCarthy in 1968, worried about the poor and thought he could change the world . . .

Mr. F. falls silent . . . "Did we all grow up," he murmurs, "or just grow away from the things we really believe?" I guess he'd (the 20 year old self) say I've become part of the problem and he'd be right."

Pelham Manor . . . is an island of prosperity in a volatile urban sea. . . .

Like a number of residents in well-to-do enclaves across America, many people here in Pelham Manor have retreated not only into a geographical but a psychological suburbia. They pulled up the drawbridge and, perhaps reluctantly and unconsciously, recoiled from growing societal problems.[11]

To yield to liberal self-righteousness or to traditionalist nostalgia is to ignore a process which cannot be changed by simply asking individuals to will things differently. I have already noticed the more obvious differences between middle-class and under-class cultures in discussing need and neediness. A look at intergenerational projects illustrates the point of difference, too, although more benignly. For example, participants in a "partners" program commented,

When you work with a senior citizen about a part of history, you learn something about difference, that person's feelings and how it was to grow up during that time. [David Grossman, Columbus Academy, N.Y., N.Y.]

I expected to find mean, old people who were boring and people who didn't like teenagers; people who thought we should come in and take over the place. I found, instead, people who were alive and who enjoyed our company and were very nice. [Nia Payne, Marie Curie Middle School, Queens, N.Y.]

The person who impressed me was the old man who climbed on chairs to get his pipe. He hopped onto that chair as if he were young; I didn't expect him to do that. I had a talk with a man who likes to go fishing. I told him that I fish too. We discovered we fish at the same place. [Paul Giangreco, Marie Curie Middle School, Queens, N.Y.]

I think it is amazing how history to one person is a life experience to another. . . . For example, to me the depression was a huge stock market crash. To somebody who lived through it, it was a tragedy that made them lose all hope and confidence. [Suzanna Saul, Columbus Academy, N.Y., N.Y.][12]

The emergence of life-worlds is also illustrated by this comment about a program involving high school students and pre-school children.

"When we first started, we talked down to them, like 'Oh, you're so cute,' " Erin said of the children as she wiped some muffin mix from the face of Sam Feinberg, one of the 3-year-olds. But she said she changed her thinking after a while.

"They are only 3-years-old and they already can carry on a conversation and they understand you," she explained. "They are just like regular people."[13]

We talk easily these days about "life-styles." We do not often recognize the remarkably rapid move we have made—particularly in a gathered society like our own—in pluralizing and separating not just our actualities but what count as acceptable values in living and what are described in our images of them. Costumes, languages, sexual relationships, family configurations present us with a kaleidescopic reality. To be sure, there are passionate moments of resistance to this pattern of change. But few, I think, really expect us to return to a single homogeneous image—the "typical" American, say, or "the" American way. Our revisionist evaluation of the "melting pot"—once an ideal, now a problem—is further testimony to that fact.

Being embedded in a plurality of life-worlds is now "normal." So, the community service project always involves crossing some cultural line and entails a meeting of strangers. Not the least of its puzzling features, however, is the encounter within myself, so to speak. Diversity appears not only between myself and others but in a confusing way within the "self" by itself. In the meeting of strangers I also meet myself as a stranger. I have seen it when the youngster enters a nursing home, or the healthy enter a hospital, or the sighted meet the blind, or the adolescent re-visits kindergarten. There is a personal shock in the encounter and there is a collective alienness too. An effective encounter begins when this strangeness is acknowledged and when the temptation to hide our otherness behind abstraction is avoided.[14] Indeed, one of the virtues of community service is the erosion of defensive abstractions which are all too tempting and all too misleading. We are caught in a problem now made even more obvious and dramatic. Community service relies on development that is somehow to be shared between strangers. What then can count as an effective encounter when sharability is denied and diversity moves to the extreme of relativism run wild?

THE SEARCH FOR DEVELOPMENT

In an impacted world, the relative absolutes found in the goals, values, and life-plans within any single life-world no longer serve. If direction is to make any sense, then I need some common human ground that can have a transcultural or intercultural meaning. Obviously, I could turn to religious claims of universality and cosmic validity—except that religion itself is one of the more obvious instances of diversity. Unless, therefore, I am prepared to engage in holy war for the one true faith, I cannot find common ground in religion. And unless I am prepared to interpret community service as a missionary effort—a mission to the heathen in modern costume—I am required to respect the integrity of diverse life-worlds. I could, perhaps, look toward traditional philosophic notions of universality but I confess I cannot find any coherent set of them on which we can all agree. Indeed, the story of our philosophies, like the story of our religions, is inherently pluralistic and argumentative.

There are several ways to go forward. For example, when community service is looked at from the standpoint of the doer, development can be identified by the values and goals of his or her life-world. Of course, this is an imperfect choice since each of us these days is party to more than one life-world and at the same time has been to a greater or lesser degree deracinated by our society's separatism and competitiveness. So, many of us try passionately to restore our "ethnicity" and at the same time cannot really live within the restoration. As a rough and ready limited strategy, however, it is possible to arrive at a usable meaning for development on this narrowed ground.

The persons done-to would, from this point of view, neither develop nor regress and the only necessary transcultural guidelines might be, "do no harm,"[15] or else the done-to would vanish and the development of the doer become impossible. Even "do no harm" is problematic since harm is itself a matter of judgment and, once again, some minimal common standard would have to be invoked. Nevertheless, a pragmatic interpretation of such a rule might lead to training the doer to understand when the done-to said "ouch." The elementary transcultural literacy this requires should not be that elusive although mistakes will happen. While imperfect, learning what "ouch" means in a multi-cultural setting may well be the best we can do. Community service would then be a rather unpretentious activity but it would still have a useful purpose, the development of the doer's character. This, despite its conservative ring, can make sense to progressive too. As Robert Westbrook notes,

> [John] Dewey was not reluctant to assert that "the formation of a certain character" was "the only genuine basis of right living." Individuals, he continued to argue, achieved self-realization by utilizing their peculiar talents to contribute to the well-being of their community and hence the critical task of education in a democratic society was to help children develop the character—the habits and virtues—that would enable them to achieve self-realization in this fashion. . . . An "interest in the community welfare, an interest which is intellectual and practical, as well as emotional—an interest, that is to say, in perceiving whatever makes for social order and progress, and for carrying these principles into execution—is the ultimate ethical habit to which all the special school habits must be related if they are to be animated by the breath of moral life."[16]

Character development, however, has its own problems even under a minimalist suggestion. It is not clear to me whether it would be possible to develop the "habits and virtues" of the doer if he or she could not expect some kinds of "good" effects on the "welfare of the community" as a result of his or her actions. As we have heard a number of times in reviewing the record, "I want to make a difference," plays an important role in the motivations of community service. But the attempt to arrive at an assessment of the difference we make would plunge us right back into the morass of the transcultural encounter of strangers. Of course, we might try some variation on the "noble lie" and persuade the young of an effectiveness which is neither actual nor knowable.[17] Perhaps, like the exercises and scales required of novice musicians, the habit of "doing" itself would be implanted, in which case character development becomes a practice without performances, without outcomes, and is then only preparatory. This would indeed be an ironic conclusion to the Deweyan suggestion given his passionate commitment to schooling as life-experience and not merely as preparation for life-experience. Conservatives, of course, would have no difficulty, because schooling for them is essentially preparatory.

A more direct response to the need for a transcultural basis for development can be found in efforts to ground it in cognitive psychologies like those of Piaget and Kohlberg.[18]

These require, however, the introduction of some non-empirical standard or end-in-view in order legitimately to move from mere change to change in a direction, that is, as maturity, identity, moral development, reasoning capacity, or what have you. Kohlberg, for example, borrows—albeit uncritically—from the imperatives of Kantian ethics as reworked by his Harvard colleague, John Rawls.[19] He uses a universalist notion of "justice as fairness" as a normative standard for moral development.[20] Progress from "stage" to "stage" is measured by the increasing adequacy of a sense of justice and this adequacy is specified on the grounds of greater inclusiveness and the ability to use universal principles in moral reasoning. Behind this standard, of course, is the assumption that we can speak intelligibly of the "rationality" of human beings as exhibited in their capacity to formulate, understand, and live according to principle. More dynamic than classical, Kohlberg and his colleagues do not claim that human beings are necessarily rational but that they can become so. Unlike Plato's bronze, silver, and gold souls which are fixed at birth, the modern psyche can "progress."

> This attitude of respect for persons is then shown to take a principled form at Stage 6, one which entails the seeking of consensus through dialogue, and one which is constituted by a set of cognitive operations. We identify these operations as "sympathy," "ideal reciprocal role-taking," and "universalizability," and we explicate these operations in the order listed to show how they are coordinated in the form of Stage 6 principled thinking. . . .
>
> At Stage 6 there is an additional aspect of respect for persons which consists of a concern for the way in which people with differing views and principles discuss with each other their disagreements. This is the attitude of recognizing the necessity of entering into dialogue in the face of disagreement about what is right.[21]

Universalization and rationality could in fact provide us with a bridge across the gaps of life-worlds. Studies in various cultures have shown that ideas like "fairness" are understandable and usable within those cultures. The discursive use of moral "dilemmas," which was Kohlberg's instrument for measuring development, is also understandable and usable.[22]

> One of Kohlberg's most stimulating and controversial claims concerns his contention that moral reasoning develops according to a universal sequence of stages that transcends or cuts across culturally specific ethical value systems, religions, political ideologies, and conceptions of the cosmic order. The cross-cultural empirical validation of his approach and related approaches has made considerable progress in recent years. . . . More than fifty studies employing the MJI (moral judgment interview) in a wide variety of cultures are available, while more than thirty studies using the Defining Issues Test (DIT) outside the USA have been reported.[23]

Developmental psychologies, therefore, seem quite promising as solutions to the problem of finding transcultural ground. However, a number of conceptual and practical issues plague such psychologies. Piaget, for example, has been criticized for the narrowness of his sample (his son and his son's friends) and for cultural parochialism. Both Kohlberg and Erikson have been criticized for gender bias. As Carol Gilligan remarks, "But about whom is Erikson talking? Once again, it turns out to be the male child."[24]

If critics like Gilligan are correct in urging "caring" as a feminist alternative, then putting "justice" or "identity" or "autonomy" at the moral center limits the universality of developmental psychologies. In other words, at least half of the human story is ignored. Similarly, measuring development by rationality becomes questionable too. As a review of a recent series of essays on caring summed it up,

> [Mary] Braebeck's introduction grounds the contributions to this volume in two parallel shifts in contemporary thinking: (a) recent critiques of human nature as being autonomous, independent, individualistic, and rational, with the concurrent move toward defining the self in terms of relationships and the moral ideal in terms of connection and compassion, and (b) feminist theorists' shifts from viewing males and females as similar toward a "celebration of gender differences."[25]

Feminist critics advance the notion that a "web of relationships" is a much more usable description of human existence than the principled individuality described by Kohlberg and others. Without realizing it, however, the notion of a "web" because it is based on intimacy undercuts its use as a universalizable criterion. So, we are in a sense no better off than we were with a cognitive rationality criterion. Except at a level of abstraction which feminists tend to reject in reaction to masculine "objectivity" and "indifference," "caring," like "justice," does not help us find direction across cultures. Webs of relationship—intimacy and the encounter of familiars, not strangers—are specific and concrete. I do not establish relationships with families in general but with my family, with friends in general but with my friends.[26]

In the feminist critique of cognitive rationality, there are, however, hints that might help us ground development in transcultural experience. What began with Gilligan as a criticism of a way of doing psychology's business has escaped its more parochial disciplinary boundaries and raised the question of an "ethic of care," the move from an intimacy of familiars toward an intimacy of strangers. Clearly, if this could be worked out it would be particularly appropriate to community service. It is even more appropriate historically when we recall the significant role of women in developing the settlement house and social work.[27] And since caring is an event that is inherently transactional, an "ethic of care," if it could escape the traps of an intimacy of familiars, might not need to limit the idea of development to a minimalist attention to the avoidance of harm.

At its most rudimentary level, caring means that I acknowledge that I live in a universe with at least two members, myself and another. Caring happens between us. In reporting that I care, I report that I put another person's (or persons') welfare in play along with my own. Only at the extremes, however, do I put another's welfare in place of my own as a martyr or saint does, or do I insist that the universe I live in has only one significant member as an egoist does. I can, by extension, care for non-persons like animals, things like paintings or ideas like truth-telling. When I care, I reveal my values in the sense that I show myself in a relationship. It is possible, of course, to challenge me when I report that I care by asking me what I am doing about it. In other words, caring ordinarily entails the activity of caring and not just the language or the attitude of caring.

It is likely that in caring I will sooner or later experience conflict, that is, I will find that I am unable to care for another human being or animal or thing or idea because I must choose between competing persons, animals, things, or ideas that I care for. At that point I learn about my limitations, experience frustration, and am forced to arrange my carings in some ordered form. I will also learn that I cannot care for myself, on occasion, without coming into conflict with caring for another. When that happens—as it will—then the arena of caring and the degree to which another is at play in that arena for me will begin to be boundaried and shaped.

Because when I care I am in a universe with at least two members, I am invited by the presence of the other, as it were, to imagine what it is like to be another for someone else.[28] And I imagine his or her response as if it were my own. Kohlberg called this "moral musical chairs." When I put myself in another's place, I am also unsure. I realize that I can be more secure about myself than another, more secure about my feelings, thoughts, acts. Of course, if I care for another, then I can inquire, as it were, in order to decrease my unsureness. But that inquiry need not—does not—use ordinary language since that is already problematic in an encounter of strangers. I can, however, observe, seek reciprocation, locate common consequences. So caring for person, animal, thing, or idea in an experience of caring can dissolve the "dumbness" of the other for me. Sooner or later, too, my acts of caring will need interpretation in order to have meaning for me. Caring thus forces me to use my intelligence and is not only a matter of feelings, emotions, and actions.

In an "ethic of care," a family model is at work. For all its apparent innocence, such a model is also a form of social criticism, for example, it contradicts the individualist models of our society. Thus, reporting on a study of young adolescent boys and girls, Carol Gilligan and Edith Phelps write,

> The messages to students in these institutions is often an ambivalent one that speaks increasingly of diversity, caring, and cooperation but that rewards individual competition, hierarchical ranking, and the survival of the fittest. Our culture and its institutions affirm the belief that care is a preferable way of looking at life but in practice, care solutions are often regarded as naive, idealistic, and unworkable. In one high school, students of both sexes said that they preferred care-based solutions but had learned to consider them utopian or outdated.[29]

The universe of caring reflects the primary relationships of mother and child which provide its stimulus and interpret its content. In an ethic of care, I try to generalize these. Almost, they provide a "concrete universal"; that is, something that is both immediate and tangible, and at the same time pervasive, species-wide and independent of time and place. With that, I do seem to have available a transcultural and comprehensible standard for development.

In so far as caring derives its meaning from family and, in particular, from mothering, it shares both species-wide accessibility and the ambiguities of cultural experience. I cannot interpret the family relationship in a psychologically or culturally neutral way. A caring perspective proposes that the direction of change is toward warmth, acceptance, helping, self-sacrifice, nurture, nourishment, growth; that is, the sociobiological features of mother and child connection are re-interpreted as standards of development. These features are not without their own

special problems. Mothers need not be unambiguously committed to
their children. The manipulative mother whose care is more self-serving
than child-serving is not unknown to us. The interference of others and
of events beyond the control of the relationship leads to failures of
intention which, in turn, can reshape the relationship. So caring may
wind up in dismay, anger, rejection. In summing up Nel Noddings
discussion of this problem of interference, Berenice Fisher writes,

> The heart of Noddings' endeavor lies in what she calls a "phenomenology
> of evil," the terms of which she draws from women's experience of caring
> for others. In what she calls the "mother model" of caring, evil is pain,
> helplessness and separation—the "elemental terrors" we experience as
> infants and to which mothers respond. Noddings notes that a certain
> amount of pain, helplessness and separation is required for survival and
> growth, but she emphasizes the maternal struggle against these evils:
> mothers' attempts to diminish children's suffering through reflective, com-
> passionate, and perhaps instinctual caring. "Natural evil," she writes can-
> not be totally eliminated, so the "mother model" of caring entails a "tragic
> sense of life."[30]

Caring has diverse possibilities in any given relationship and in any
given setting. And, the more elaborated family relationships become—
for example, with the introduction of the father, the presence or absence
of elders and other children, the imperatives of a family's social obligations, and so forth—the more complicated the understanding of direction is. Like character and justice, an "ethic of care" leaves us still in
search of development. At the same time, each moves us toward possible
transcultural ends-in-view. No doubt this move is still unsatisfactory.
For example, I do not pretend to resolve the "is/ought" dilemma of
philosophers nor avoid the so-called "naturalistic fallacy."[31] Yet, character, justice, and care do present themselves in experience as both *prima
facie* goods and as guiding principles of action. On the positive side,
they suggest directions to be explored in the doing; on the negative side,
they establish the grounds of caution needed for doing well while doing
good.

ALTRUISM AND EGO

In the search for development, character, justice, and care emerge
from their social and psychological roots and acquire moral and political
status. But, before I can go forward, I need to look briefly at the ground
in which these notions are embedded. For all the difference of emphasis,
history, language, and even of the temperament of their proponents,
these developmental ends-in-view have a common requirement. They
expect us to transcend the "natural" obligations that arise in relation-

ships of the familiar and to establish obligations among those who do not know each other. For example, the characterful person "behaves well" with and toward other persons as such.[32] There is no virtue, as it were, in simply doing well only with and for those to whom we already are connected. Nor does the characterful person expect a return. The give and get of a market ethic demonstrate no special moral virtue. Similarly, justice as fairness gets its meaning from its impartiality, the very "indifference" for which it is faulted by feminist critics. And care requires an indefinite extension of the web of relationship if it is to serve in a pluralist world. There is no moral credit in simply "doing what comes naturally" as son or daughter, mother or father, brother or sister, although the commandment to "honor thy father and mother" reminds us that even intimate relationships are not simply instinctive. All three, then, are relevant to an encounter of strangers although the strategies of that encounter differ as one or another is emphasized.

In short, character, justice, and caring point in common to the problems of altruism. I realize that in considering altruism I run the risk of sentimentality or wishful thinking. I realize, too, that my very doubts tell me that I am culturally unaccustomed to taking it seriously. I am well trained in the contractual notion of bargained obligations and benefits.

So, given the conditions which are normal to our society, altruism is a threat to our claimed values. We may be many things—conformists or do-gooders, kindly or cooperative—but we celebrate ego and competition as the heart of virtue. Yet, I cannot make sense of community service as an encounter of strangers unless I can find some convincing way of replying when asked: "Why is it that many people from diverse life-worlds do care for others whom they never knew and whom they will never know?" In some sense or other, there is a capacity in us of doing for another just as there is a capacity in us of recognizing that this is being done. Altruism seems to be exhibited in fact.

Clearly, altruism denies that "man is a wolf to man" and suggests that the possibilities of human relationship are not exhausted by a Hobbesian war of each against all. It even challenges the more benevolent notion of a social contract agreed to by rationally self-interested individuals. Altruism represents, therefore, a polar alternative for human conduct which we otherwise interpret as essentially self-concerned. In this connection, I do not think it productive to extend the argument about the identification of altruism with enlightened self-interest. If the calculation involved in an extended sense of self-interest takes only my interests—long or short term—into account, then it is not identical with altruism at all even though it may appear so behaviorally in many instances. For altruism, the calculation must include others for their sakes and not just for my own. The "web of relationships" or some sense of solidarity defines my interests as essentially connected with, but different from, the interests of others. Nor do I think it helpful to confuse the satisfaction that accompanies a job well done with the reasons for doing that job. This is illustrated by the notion of a "calling."

> The alternative idea of work as a calling is conspicuously absent from Brian's [one of the authors' interviewees] pattern of success. Brian sees the value of work in terms of what it yields to a self that is separate from the actual activity work demands of him in return. In this imagery of exchange, the self stands apart from what it does and its commitments remain calculated and contingent on the benefits they deliver. In a calling, by contrast, one gives oneself to learning and practicing activities that in turn define the self and enter into the shape of its character. Committing one's self to becoming a "good" carpenter, craftsman, doctor, scientist, or artist anchors the self within a community practicing carpentry, medicine, or art. It connects the self to those who teach, exemplify, and judge these skills. It ties us to still others whom they serve.[33]

The altruist claims that species-solidarity is both transcultural and personal. This underlies the possibility of interpersonal responsiveness as doer and done-to. We recognize each other. Because of it, we are able to play "moral musical chairs," to feel what others are feeling, to experience what others are experiencing. We never encounter total strangers even if we do not acknowledge the familiarity of the stranger. In that sense, too, the lost connection—exhibited in relativism run wild and diversity become absolute—represents a deterioration of the human being. A moral capacity is atrophied. Given the temptation, by contrast, to interpret the "survival of the fittest" as a biological ground for individualistic competition, it is helpful to recall Darwin on altruism. James Rachels sums it up,

> Following Darwin's suggestions, we might envision a process that takes place in three stages. In the first stage, there is only kin-altruism. . . . The "social instincts" are in place, but they do not govern behaviour beyond one's kin. In the second stage, individuals attain enough "reason and foresight" to understand that aiding nonrelatives might be a good strategy for gaining some benefit for themselves, provided that the nonrelatives can be induced to reciprocate. . . . Thus the social instincts are extended beyond one's kin. In the third stage, this pattern of behaviour becomes more widespread, until it has become habitual.[34]

Recent developments in evolutionary theory continue this Darwinian tradition by interpreting the preservation of genotypes as a ground for cooperation.[35] The evidence for the existence of altruism is both anecdotal and experimental. For example, I do not doubt that each of us has, in one or another instance, exhibited altruistic behavior, although I also do not doubt that we are hesitant to admit it.

In a sense, the need to take altruism seriously arises precisely when, as is true today, we are troubled because its alternative dominates our moral and political values. It is no accident, either, that in our society to be taken seriously means to be taken scientifically. Reflecting both of these themes,

> It was a time when President Kennedy's ringing call—"Ask not what your country can do for you; ask what you can do for your country"—touched off an explosion of idealism; a time when civil rights, aid to the poor, and other humanitarian issues were high on the national agenda; a time when much of American youth was revolted by the war in Vietnam and passionately devoted to peace, cooperative endeavors, and good causes.
>
> First a handful, then dozens, then hundreds of behavioral and social scientists began conducting laboratory experiments and field studies on cooperation, sharing, reciprocity, donating, helping in emergencies, and the like. On altruism alone, by 1970 some 150 studies had appeared in psychology-related journals; by 1982 the total had swelled to 1,050; and today the figure is estimated at 1,200. Scores or possibly hundreds of other studies of altruism have been made within other disciplines and published in other journals.[36]

Altruism like selfishness is finally, however, not a matter of biology but choice. In this instance the choice is not simply a private act of will, a passing moment, but a life-habit.

The facts are not unimportant to the choice, however. As the philosopher puts it, "ought implies can." The evidence tells us that altruism is a choice we have already made and so can make again. There is no ultimate ground, however, on which altruism can be demonstrated. It is finally a decision. Given the facts of our moral experience, this decision, however, is not merely arbitrary. For example, we can imagine the kinds of worlds that follow from our choices. So, we can describe the experience of living in a world of "each against all" as over against a world of solidarity. Here, our moral sources are literature, drama, poetry as well as our reveries and daydreams. The argument turns into an aesthetic activity. In the experience which gives the moral art its content, our feelings of connectedness and empathy appear. Our strengths as persons follow upon our development as caring, just, and virtuous, that is, follow upon giving reality to those ends-in-view which rely on altruism. In turn, altruism is believable just because these ends-in-view are *prima facie* goods. Community service, in this context, is the application of just such a circle of connected choices to the encounter of strangers. It, then, is both a form of applied ethics and applied aesthetics.

If altruism is neither unrealistic nor fated, then it follows that it can be helped to happen. It is not some mysterious transnatural quality that awaits a miracle. Finally, then, we meet ourselves caught in the trap of the life-world and trying to find ways of dealing with a reality that is transcultural. But we are equipped to grasp the problem which means that we are to that extent at least able to stand outside of ourselves and are not fully caught within a single life-world. We meet ourselves, too, as transforming animals. And, we meet ourselves as transitional animals able to grow in a direction. In these various meetings we detect patterns, ends-in-view, grounding points. Our search for development now leads us to the question of how these meetings are and shall be shaped. We turn then to the connection between schooling and community service.

NOTES

1. For example, see B. F. Skinner, *Beyond Freedom and Dignity* (New York: Bantam/Vintage, 1972).

2. William James, "The Dilemma of Determinism," *Essay on Faith and Morals* (New York: Meridian Books, 1962), p. 146.

3. Robert B. Westbrook, *John Dewey and American Democracy* (Ithaca, N.Y.: Cornell University Press, 1991), p. 44.

4. For example, see Richard Rorty, *Contingency, Irony, and Solidarity* (New York: Cambridge University Press, 1989), particularly, Chapter 3, "The Contingency of Liberal Community," and Chapter 9, "Solidarity."

5. Diane Hedin and Dan Conrad (1980), "The Impact of Experiential Education on Youth Development," *Combining Service and Learning*, Jane C. Kendall and Associates, Ed. (Raleigh, N.C.: National Society for Internships and Experiential Education, 1990), vol. 1, pp. 124–125.

6. It seems to me that suggesting the move from the idea of culture to life-worlds is supported by the relative autonomy of groups, the evolution of group-specific languages, symbols, and customs, the development of group myths, the increasing separateness of groups, etc. Our almost compulsive attention to "diversity" and "multi-culturalism" suggests that this move is taking (or has taken) place. The superficiality of "common" elements—most significantly as found in the mass media—points up the fact that depth in living is not found in a common space at all.

7. Judith A. Boss, "The Effect of Community Service on the Moral Development of College Ethics' Students," paper presented at the Conference of the Association for Moral Education, University of Georgia, November 1991, p. 65.

8. See, for example, Alison M. Jaggar, *Feminist Politics and Human Nature* (Totowa, N.J.: Rowman and Allanheld, 1983), particularly Chapter 9.

9. Carol Gilligan, *In a Different Voice* (Cambridge, Mass.: Harvard University Press, 1982), pp. 8–9.

10. For a critical discussion of this theme, see Diane Ravitch, "Multiculturalism: E Pluribus Plures," *American Scholar* 59, 3 (Summer 1990).

11. Ron Suskind, "As Urban Woes Grow, 'PLUs' are Seeking Psychological Suburbia," *The Wall Street Journal*, May 15, 1992.

12. "Reflections on the Partners Program . . . from Participants," *Community Roles for Youth* 5, 2 (May 1991).

13. Ina Aronow, "High School Students Learn from 3-Year-Olds," *New York Times*, December 9, 1990.

14. For an instructive developmental model, see William G. Perry, *Forms of Intellectual and Ethical Development in the College Years* (New York: Holt, Rhinehart and Winston, 1970). Perry's "fourth" and ultimate category (positions seven, eight, and nine) is called "commitment" where a student accepts responsibility for establishing personal identity in a pluralistic world by affirming, choosing, deciding concretely in marriage, career, etc.

15. For example, Richard Rorty, for all that he pluralizes cultures and cultural values, recognizes the need for such a minimal transcultural guideline. See *Contingency, Irony and Solidarity* (New York: Cambridge University Press, 1989).

16. Robert Westbrook, *op. cit.*, pp. 104–105.

17. Sisella Bok in *Lying* (New York: Vintage Books, 1979), p. 176 describes the noble lie as follows,

> A long tradition in political philosophy endorses some lies for the sake of the public. Plato . . . first used the expression "noble lie" for the fanciful story that might be told to people in order to persuade them to accept class distinctions and thereby safeguard social harmony. According to this story, God Himself mingled gold, silver, iron, and brass in fashioning rulers, auxiliaries, farmers, and craftsmen, intending these groups for separate tasks in a harmonious hierarchy.

18. Except for purely descriptive psychologies, if there are any, I know of none that do not make some assumption of direction although it is not always clear that nonempirical value choices are being invoked. Among other developmental schemes, the work of Erik Erikson comes to mind. Clearly, too, the "humanistic psychology" of Abraham Maslow and Carl Rogers presumes direction under the guise of maturity. For example, see Abraham Maslow, *Religions, Values and Peak Experiences* (New York: Viking, 1970). Kohlberg, because of his pioneer work in moral development, is particularly apt.

19. John Rawls, *A Theory of Justice* (Cambridge, Mass.: Harvard University Press, 1971). For a brief discussion of the problematic nature of Kohlberg's strategy, see Howard B. Radest, *Can We Teach Ethics* (New York: Praeger, 1989), pp. 70–71.

20. Kohlberg reveals his intention in his essay, "From Is to Ought: How to Commit the Naturalistic Fallacy and Get Away with It in the Study of Moral Development," *The Philosophy of Moral Development*, Lawrence Kohlberg (San Francisco: Harper and Row, 1981), vol. 1, Chapter 4, pp. 101–189.

21. Lawrence Kohlberg, Dwight Boyd, and Charles Levin, "The Return of Stage 6: Its Principal and Its Moral Point of View," 1985. This paper was presented to the University Seminar on Moral Education at Columbia University which I was privileged to found and chair. Kohlberg, a regular member of the seminar, had for some years given up on "Stage 6" because, as he said, he found so few instances of it. Nevertheless, he was re-introducing it in his thinking if for no other reason than to establish an "ideal" end to the cognitive moral process. I had a sense—almost—that he wanted some kind of aesthetic closure and was not contented with either leaving things at Stage 5 which was simply

to hang matters in mid-air so to speak or to let moral development proceed endlessly. By contrast, John Dewey, whom Kohlberg regarded as one of his essential sources, had no trouble defining direction as the continuing enrichment of experience.

22. Again, drawing on my experience as chair of the University Seminar on Moral Education, I can recall a number of presentations by Uwe Gielen on the validity of Kohlberg's ideas in different cultural settings. See, by way of example, "Moral Reasoning in Radical and Non-Radical German Students," *Behavior Science Research* 20, 4 (1986), pp. 71–109 and "Some Recent Work on Moral Values, Reasoning and Education in Chinese Societies," *Moral Education Forum* 15, 1 (1990), pp. 3–22.

23. Uwe Gielen, "Research on Moral Reasoning," *The Kohlberg Legacy for the Helping Professions*, ed. Lisa Kuhmerker with Uwe Gielen and Richard L. Hayes, (Birmingham, Ala.: R.E.P. Books, 1991), pp. 41–42.

24. Carol Gilligan, *op. cit.*, p. 12.

25. Judith G. Smetana, "Caring About Care," a review of *Who Cares?: Theory, Research, and Educational Implications of the Ethic of Care* (New York, Praeger, 1989), *Contemporary Psychology* 36, 6 (1991), p. 494.

26. In this regard, it is striking that Nel Noddings in *Caring, A Feminine Approach to Ethics and Moral Education* describes the role of care-giver and care-receiver in familial terms and grounds obligation in a relationship of those who know each other. Strangers and others are only indirectly and distantly accounted for through nonpersonal collective agencies but moral relationships are essentially personal relationships. In an insightful critique of Noddings, Barbara J. Walton noted,

> I will also question whether an ethic which depends heavily upon the proximity of the other, which deals exclusively with caring *for* and neglects caring *about* is too narrow in its scope to be broadly useful. One can imagine a kind of caring which precisely because of the "chains and circles" of connectedness which Noddings describes so graphically, applied to others far from our immediate perception or influence. Only by providing for such caring-at-a-distance within a caring ethic can we establish the grounding for an ethic of public as well as personal responsibility.

"The Ethical Dimensions of Service: Nel Noddings and Caring," a paper based on Dr. Walton's doctoral research presented at the University Seminar on Moral Education, December, 1988, p. 8.

27. For a discussion of this theme, see Anne Firor Scott, *Natural Allies, Women's Associations in American History* (Urbana, Ill.: Illinois University Press, 1992).

28. Because of the tendency to polarize the so-called masculine gender-bias of Kohlberg and the feminist critique of Gilligan, it is important to notice that an ethic of caring very early in analysis entails what Kohlberg called "moral musical chairs," i.e., the urgency of being in another's place in order to develop morally. Neither the traditional notions of empathy or sympathy quite catch the active features of being in another's place. A more likely reference might be drama and dramatic play in which I am many selves without pathological consequences.

29. Carol Gilligan and Edith B. Phelps, *Seeking Conversation: New Insights and*

Questions for Teachers (Cambridge, Mass.: Harvard Graduate School of Education, 1988), pp. 17–18.

30. Berenice Fisher, "Banalities of Evil," a review of *Women and Evil* by Nel Noddings (Berkeley, Calif.: University of California Press, 1989) in *The Women's Review of Books* 7, 8 (May 1990), p. 21.

31. Briefly the "is/ought" dilemma appears when we convert a fact into a value. Thus, that mothers care for their children is a fact; that it is good for mothers to care for their children is an evaluation. We cannot, however, deduce the evaluation from the fact by saying that "because mothers love their children then it is good for them to love their children." We distinguish between the "desired" and the "desirable," and cannot conclude that "because something is desired, therefore it is desirable." The "naturalistic fallacy" is the name given to drawing that conclusion. Some of us think, however, that it is possible to develop evaluative criteria from within a naturalistic framework. John Rawls, for example, points to the interplay of "fact" and "value" when he talks about reflexive equilibrium. John Dewey embeds the process of valuing in the socio-biological notion of dis-equilibrium, i.e., a "problem" appears when we experience a disturbance and it is solved when balance is restored. The solution includes an evaluation, i.e., is satisfying, satisfactory just because we are able to proceed.

32. The ambivalence of *caritas* is relevant here. For the Christian, the person as such is also the familiar, i.e., a fellow child of God, the father. Hence, *caritas* really evades the problem of community service, the problem of the stranger.

33. Robert N. Bellah, et al., *Habits of the Heart* (New York: Harper and Row, 1985), p. 69.

34. James Rachels, *Created from Animals: The Moral Implications of Darwinism* (Oxford, England: Oxford University Press, 1991), pp. 156–157.

35. For example, see Edward O. Wilson, *Sociobiology: The New Synthesis* (Cambridge, Mass.: Harvard University Press, 1975).

36. Morton Hunt, *The Compassionate Beast* (New York: Anchor, 1991), pp. 29–30.

Chapter Eight

Knowing Is Doing

RECONSTRUCTING EDUCATION

Since community service is aimed at the young, we expect to find it in the school. But, is it part of schooling or is it just there as a matter of convenience? I find myself back on familiar territory—the classroom, the teacher, the student and the parents—the place where my interest in community service began.

With the move into the field, schooling becomes problematic. The student and teacher find themselves in a puzzling mix of separated life-worlds. Community service, then, only seems easily assimilated with the character education of traditionalists or with the "organized intelligence" of progressives. But there are surprises for both. For the traditionalist, the field begins as another form of preparation. Working in the field also fits well with "learning by doing." At the same time, the disconnected pluralities of our world defy organization and coherence whether by traditionalist or progressive.

Then, too, I am not accustomed to leaving the comfortable walls of the classroom for the dubious securities of an encounter of strangers. So, I try to fit community service into my habits of schooling. My programs take on a certain uncontroversial quality, even have a "goody-goody" air about them. Who, after all, could oppose feeding the hungry, caring for the sick or teaching the ignorant? The problems we worry about are practical—funding, organization, time, interpretation—the typical problems of educational management. Yet, community service is an issue—as we have seen that it can be politically—and the experience of it is a puzzle—as we have seen that it is for our more sensitive students. These puzzles appear, I think, because despite efforts at normalization, when I do community service I find myself on alien ground with an alien epistemology.

As a progressive I am accustomed to the language of "learning by doing." But, I find myself in little better condition than the traditionalist. I do not know how to talk about the move the doer makes from the standard world of discovery—for example, the laboratory, the field trip—to the unexpected world of happenings. Even less accessible are the unknown worlds of the done-to. In discussing the resistance of university faculty members to community service, Howard Seeman offers a hint of the reasons when he remarks,

> We are still a society influenced by an epistemology dating back to Plato's "eternal forms" as the seat of Truth . . .
> The stance has been challenged by Heidegger, among others, who rejected the myth that any knowledge can be purely cognitive: to have meaning, ideas must be involved with a network of affect. Dewey infused into our epistemology the notion that "knowledge" includes action, that "scientific knowing" is only one kind—and not the only kind—of human action that defines truth.
> Though these more recent ideas open the door to experiential learning, we are still in a cultural lag. Purely cognitive learning is often deemed "real scholarship" and precludes subjectivity in education.[1]

And yet, for all its strangeness, the move into the world actualized by community service would seem to be inevitable, particularly as we grow skeptical of academicism. Even the "liberal arts," which can become so abstracted from the world, have their roots and ends in the work of the world—as in the medieval vocations of clerk and cleric. And, as the liberal arts rediscover their sources, their current attenuated definition as aesthetic ends-in-themselves changes too. The move into the world becomes visible,

> In sum, two conceptual developments have been at work in recent years—First, the notion of liberal education has undergone a metamorphosis such that it is increasingly receptive to empiricism, science, and experience and less exclusively scholastic and bookish. And second, the experiential learning movement has become more sophisticated in its conception of experience. It has come to see that the rigidly scientific notions of early experimentalism need to be tempered by a receptivity to surprise and serendipity. These simultaneous trends have now progressed to a point where the compatibility, complementarity, and potential for mutual enrichment of liberal education and experiential learning have become apparent.[2]

On the desirability of a move of schooling into the world both conservative and progressive agree. The former does so when he or she
marks schooling as preparation for work and citizenship; the latter does
so when he or she enriches the idea of preparation with the notion of
"lived experience." But, we no longer face the choice between traditionalist temporality and progressive simultaneity. Today, we must account for other preparations and other simultaneities. I am always
preparing and never prepared, always experiencing and never experienced. So, the progressive rightly called a schooling that was only preparatory incomplete. But the progressive did not, perhaps could not,
go far enough into the puzzle of experience.[3] For all its historicism,
progressive discourse was still universal, and could not account for a
plurality of life-worlds. And, for all its attentiveness to the person, it
missed the first-person singular. An existential reminder to both conservative and progressive is in order,

> Let us imagine a pilot, and assume that he had passed every examination
> with distinction, but that he had not as yet been at sea. Imagine him in a
> storm; he knows everything he ought to do, but has not known before
> how terror grips the seafarer when the stars are lost in the blackness of
> night; he does not know the sense of impotence that comes when the pilot
> sees the wheel in his hand become a plaything for the waves; he has not
> known how the blood rushes into the head when one tries to make cal-
> culations at such a moment; in short, he has no conception of the change
> that takes place in the knower when he has to apply his knowledge.[4]

But this needed reminder is faulted by its radical individualism. Ex-
istentialist themes like alienation, authenticity, choice announce, even
celebrate, the disconnection of person from person. I am to face my
apartness alone, indifferently as hero, villain or fool. A reasoned individualism—in politics, drama, poetry, theology—established the existential problem for both traditionalism and progressivism. But, the
argument between preparation and experience scarcely does justice to
an encounter of strangers living in separated life-worlds. And, we are
more likely to meet strangers than familiars.

Once upon a time, the "old education" and the "new" shared a common social logic.[5] Their protagonists could argue the nature of "community" or of "experience" while referring to a shared reality. To be
sure, inspired by the sciences of development—biology, psychology—
the "new education" had a different sense of educational timing. "Old"
and "new" differed too, in their sense of the potencies of the human
being. And they differed in their generosities. In these differences, however, they hardly hinted at the shift to the world of lost connections that
was to come. That shift has set us on a pathway more radical than the

progressive imagination foretold and against which the traditional imagination defended. Nor is this only a pedagogue's dilemma.

> As we have come to see with increasing clarity over the last twenty or so years, the problems of real-world practice do not present themselves to practitioners as well-formed structures. Indeed, they tend not to present themselves as problems at all but as messy, indeterminate situations. Civil engineers, for example, know how to build roads suited to the conditions of particular sites and specifications. . . . When they must decide what road to build, however, or whether to build it at all, their problem is not solvable by the application of technical knowledge, not even by the sophisticated techniques of decision theory. They face a complex and ill-defined melange of topographical, financial, economic, environmental, and political factors. If they are to get a well-formed problem matched to their familiar theories and techniques, they must construct it from the materials of a situation that is, to use John Dewey's term, "problematic." And the problem of problem-setting is not well formed.[6]

The individual of progressivism like the virtuous "man" of traditionalism has become a much more mysterious person in a much more mysterious world. And our students are unready for that mystery.

> They have always been taught about a world out there somewhere apart from them, divorced from their personal lives; they never have been invited to intersect their autobiographies with the life story of the world. And so, they can report on a world that is not the one in which they live, one they've been taught about from some objectivist's fantasy.
>
> They have also been formed in the habit of experimental manipulation. These students believe they can take pieces of the world and carve out for themselves a niche of private sanity in the midst of public calamity. That is nothing more than the ethical outcome of the objectivism in which they have been formed, or deformed. It is a failure to recognize their own implication with society's fate.[7]

In every culture, schooling aims to continue that culture: to replicate it in traditionalist environments, to reconstruct it in democratic environments. But both assume the accessibility of a knowable shared culture. And that is precisely what is at issue in the lost connection. Community service exposes us to this because of its concreteness. But, it is not alone in the revelation. The lost connection is revealed in arguments about "multi-culturalism." Mysteries of knower and knowing are embedded in complaints about the "information explosion" and in the "subject matter explosion."

We are at sea about what to teach and what is teachable, about who to teach and who is teachable, about why to teach and where to teach it. We try to present these as familiar issues even if on a new and enlarged global scale. It seems quite familiar. We can still hear echoes of a six-teenth-century debate on the merits of Latin or Italian, of modern and classical art, of the new science and the "tried and true" ways of Aris-totle. We can still hear the complaint of secularism and the decay of churchly virtues. We've heard it all before: it is the "modern" argument. The repetition of it today, however, masks the abyss that grows between our pedagogies and our experience. As George Leonard remarks,

> Ironically, the success of a highly publicized school-reform movement has most clearly revealed the failure of school to meet the challenges of these times. The movement began on April 26, 1983, with the publication of a report by the National Commission for Excellence in Education. *A Nation at Risk: The Imperative for Educational Reform* asked for a longer school day and year. It called for the assignment of "far more homework." It de-manded higher standards for college admissions, more rigorous grading, better textbooks, and a nationwide system of standardized achievement tests. Like most of the dozens of reform proposals from other organizations which followed, *A Nation at Risk* was preoccupied with course require-ments at the high school level. . . .
>
> The interesting thing about the National Commission report . . . is that with all of its talk of "fundamental" change, it proposed nothing really new. . . . Let's have the same, but better and more of it.[8]

In an environment of presumed familiarities, community service has a double aspect. It is simply another opportunity for our students, a curricular enrichment which must compete for attention, time, and re-sources with other proposals for enrichment. Joining reflection and ac-tion and integrating classroom and field become the salient educational questions. We debate it under many names: experiential learning, co-operative learning, service learning, field study, and the like.[9] Learning by doing becomes a question of extension but does not raise a novel issue of theory. So, as Ernest Boyer remarks,

> We are moving, in fits and starts, toward a national view of education . . . we need a national commitment to the proposition that every student regardless of economic circumstances will have a quality education. . . . A second goal is proficiency in basic skills. . . . A third priority is a core of common learning to assure that all students are prepared to be civically engaged and economically productive. . . . Another goal should be a healthy climate for learning in every school, with a national commitment to reduce vandalism, violence and drug abuse. And why not agree that all students should participate in community service projects that connect their schooling more fully to the realities of life?[10]

When, however, we encounter "the realities of life" and life-worlds in doing community service, we suddenly find ourselves on radically unfamiliar ground. And we did not invite it. Ordinarily, we protect ourselves by associating with "people like us" in deliberately narrowed settings. Those of us who have worked in schools know the phenomenon. As the headmaster of Moravian Academy (Bethlehem, Pennsylvania) tells it,

> we live now in a time when there are more temptations than ever before to serve ourselves, to be certain we are entertained, comfortable, and having fun. We know this is so. The greater the academic, social, and athletic demands on students' time, the more likely that they will live within a small self-oriented existence unless they can find some way to expand that world of their own. Thus, the perennial curricula dilemma: what do we encourage students to do with their time, and what is important enough for us to require them to do?[11]

But, community service disrupts our comfortable retreat behind the walls of the familiar. And so the typical issues of resources and enrichments and teachabilities are invaded by unfamiliar shadows. To be sure, unable to catch the meaning of these shadows—the problem of problem-formulation again—we withdraw behind the walls of the school. Even in the field, we carry the walls within us, setting them down wherever we are. Schooling opts even more vigorously for narrowed settings and "people like us." The move toward "vouchers" and "school choice" and "basic skills" are scarcely hidden mechanisms for exercising that option.

We force experience into standard formats; report experience with standard protocols; evaluate experience with standard assessments. We continue the hierarchy of teacher and student, the competitiveness of individual achievement. It is not surprising, then, that

> our observations of community-service classes, of students working at their placements, and our student interview data suggested that these goals (citizenship, community awareness, etc.) were often . . . interpreted in terms of *individual* rather than public experience. The explicit focus of many programs on career exploration or experience, for example, is one significant manifestation of this emphasis. . . . Even students assigned to a nursing home, who find themselves less afraid of the elderly and more knowledgeable about the health and psychological needs of the aged, may view this experience entirely in terms of their personal competence . . . the performance of a socially desired service in a technically proficient way will not necessarily result in greater social responsibility, commitment, or political action.[12]

With this conversion of reform into administration, we also grow inattentive to the "lived" experience. The very typicality of the language we use to talk about community service around the country suggests that we are using a familiar rhetoric to hide rather than communicate what is going on. This routinization of pedagogy—progressive or traditional—is a ready temptation. But, in the experience of community service—that is its contribution and its threat—the routine breaks down; the shadows do not vanish. In other words, the ambiguities of need and service come to haunt the school.

Schooling is always a problematic activity. But it is a "normal" problematic. As the progressive might put it, we rebuild schooling so that it will be commensurate with our needs and our life-patterns. The "new education" was, as it were, a reconstruction on its way to becoming a tradition. Its building blocks were drawn from a more varied environment but these were not really alien to us. The language and culture of inquiry permitted us to embed the problem of schooling in stabilities and only rarely do these—as theories and systems and world-views—shift. As Thomas Kuhn put it, we ordinarily do ordinary science.[13]

Community service then can be interpreted as only another building block in an ongoing reconstruction. But, because of its peculiarities—it thrusts us into the world—it is a radically personal experience. Unlike other school "subjects" it escapes our academic habits, even our progressive academic habits. The interplay of doer and done-to, the ambiguities of need and service, break into those habits with encounters of a different sort. As it were, community service alerts us to a next step in the emergence of schooling as "lived experience."

THE TWO-NESS OF SCHOOLING

The double aspect of schooling, as a familiar and as an alien meeting ground, shapes the classroom with its already complicated multiple encounters.[14] Community service makes this double aspect tangible, intense and unavoidable. Ironically, if it becomes part of the curriculum—for example, as with the proposal to make it a "Carnegie Unit"[15]—this double aspect will even carry the stamp of legitimacy. Community service, then, invites the uninvited guest. This is troubling, so our community service models try to minimize surprise. For example,

A Laboratory for an Existing Course. This kind of program has enabled many schools to introduce community service into their academic program with little or no immediate change in curriculum, school structure, or staff deployment.

In this model, students in existing courses do community service as a way to "reality test" course content. . . .

. . . Community Service Class. This model, found in approximately seven percent of U.S. high schools (1987). . . . Here the community experience . . . is the central focus of the course, but it is combined with an ongoing classroom experience where the emphasis is on providing infor-

mation, skills, and generalizing principles to assist students directly in
interpreting their experiences.[16]

Nevertheless, community service helps students to address the classroom from their own actualities and their own discoveries.[17] Thus,

> A service-learning program might encourage participants working in a
> local soup kitchen, for example, to ask why people are hungry, what
> politics in our country do or do not contribute to this problem, and what
> economic, cultural, and logistical factors result in hunger in a world that
> already knows how to grow enough food to feed everyone. Participants
> in a program that focuses primarily on charity, on the other hand, might
> serve food in the same soup kitchen, but they would not be encouraged
> and supported to ask these types of questions. After a direct service ex-
> perience related to local hunger, a young person might then be ready to
> explore the issue of hunger more deeply through work in a government
> agency, a citizens' group, or public policy research project. . . . The "com-
> munity" in the definition of service-learning programs can thus refer to
> the local neighborhood as well as the state, national, or international com-
> munity.[18]

In the classroom, practice struggles to catch up with realities and, at
the same time, to block realities from entering. I can recall my own
conflicts. As a teacher, I was committed to connecting practice and reflection; as an administrator, I complained there was not enough time
and not enough money to do it all. So, all too often, community service
turned into an administrative convenience. And too often, community
service became only another add-on: a co-curricular activity or at best
another "subject." Community service is costly, to be sure, but even
more to the point, it is risky. Disciplines like history, economics, politics
and art would be felt and known. We want and do not want this to
happen. Schools are always caught in this tension between cultural
mission and cultural criticism. Reform moves toward uniformity, authority, skills and the like. We adopt the language of the market place—
talking about competition, productivity, the economies of scale, the use
of technologies. Failing this, we run into resistance.

Of course, our students should learn to work together and to rely on
each other. Thus far we are on familiar reformist ground. But, other
things make their appearance too. I cannot avoid myself and I cannot
avoid the other. Metaphorically, community service holds a mirror up
to the classroom and is a type of criticism. For example,

> In one study, fifth-graders who studied grammar in cooperative learning
> groups were more likely to give away prize tokens to a stranger than were
> those who studied on their own; in another, kindergarteners who partic-

ipated in cooperative activities acted more prosocially than their peers in a traditional classroom. . . . Carefully structured cooperative learning also promotes a subjective sense of group identity, a greater acceptance of people who are different from oneself . . . and a more sophisticated ability to imagine other people's points of view. Cooperation . . . allows [students] to transcend egocentric and objectifying postures and encourages trust, sensitivity, open communication and pro-social activity.[19]

Whatever familiar attitudes have been practiced on the home ground—learning to welcome the stranger, to accept the diverse, to be in another's place—the actual encounter of strangers is both tangible and surprising. Otherness is had, not just pointed to or rehearsed.

Community service reaches us in ways quite different from the distanced and abstracted methods of so much of our schooling. Yet, these too are necessary and legitimate; that is, doing and learning are not coextensive. As the physicist Richard Feynman remarked,

I can appreciate the beauty of a flower. But at the same time, I see much more in the flower than he [the artist] sees. I can imagine the cells inside, which also have a beauty. . . .

There are the complicated actions of cells and other processes. The fact that the colors in the flower have evolved in order to attract insects to pollinate it is interesting; that means insects can see the colors. That adds a question: does this aesthetic sense we have also exist in lower forms of life? There are all kinds of interesting questions that come from a knowledge of science, which only adds to the excitement and mystery and awe of a flower. It only adds. I don't understand how it subtracts.[20]

With community service, the shadows that linger around our standard defenses assume definite form. So, the stranger who was a story-book figure or a statistical entity or an instance of a moral rule takes shape for me. The student and teacher, who are role-takers and observers in the classroom, take shape as participants, intruders, visitors, actors, agents. They appear to each other in all their unfinished complexities as persons. A student described the experience of student-led seminar as follows,

As the class developed, we discovered deeper implications to our new approach than we had envisioned. We involved ourselves in an entirely different epistemology. In previous academic experiences, a detached analytical approach encouraged us to treat what we study as something separate from ourselves. Yet, in this class, we did not pose service as a bloodless abstraction, as a body of material to be identified, isolated, and analyzed. We discovered that we could not study service separate from ourselves. We learned things about the world, but even more, we learned things about our relationship within the world.[21]

The classroom acquires a more numerous cast of characters even if "class-size" remains unchanged. Some of them may always have been there, but we did not know it. Teacher and student diversify into many persons, some only variations on the familiar, others quite strange and even shocking. So, I encounter my self as biased and appreciative, as ignorant and knowing. I am, as we say, a different person there or there or there. And I discover that these are personalities with, hopefully, a certain coherence of connections. I am not merely playing different roles but I am different actors. I am, it almost seems, a community all by myself. Obviously, the opportunities for conflict and for enrichment abound. As it were, community service reveals myselves to myself even as it reveals others to myself and myself to others. The diverse characteristics which are at the same time out-there and in-here themselves become a pedagogy and a curriculum. History becomes literature, becomes autobiography, becomes activity and so on. The walls fall away, are eaten away, even torn away.

The classroom loses its character as the familiar scene of a transference of knowledge and becomes a theater without walls. Knowing becomes "personal knowledge."[22] This is,

> a process Habermas calls "critical discourse": the recursive examination of experience in which students learn to "read" their workplaces as "texts," as "discourse-practices." The skillful post-structuralist instructor engages in what several writers have called "critical pedagogy." Habermas claims that critical discourse requires certain conditions. It must be symmetrical and non-dominated, and all participants must be able to initiate comments, challenge assertions and question theories. The teacher in this model does not provide authoritative meanings, facts or answers, but rather establishes the conditions within which everyone can examine and penetrate the histories, power arrangements and values underlying their work organizations. Participants "criticize" their experiences, trying to discover the full range of interpretations through which their worlds might be understood.[23]

Community service has its dangers and none more serious than the possible loss of objectivity. The encounter of strangers invites an unbounded subjectivism. This may show itself as a retreat from the world as in the notion that everything is just "a matter of taste" or as in the notion that my wants are the only wants that count. Or it may show itself as the transformation of interpersonal relations into a world-view, the conversion of psychology into cosmology. But, the so-called objectivity of text and examination and discipline is also a distortion of the world. When, moreover, these become artifacts of a frozen past—the notorious out-datedness of texts, for example, or the politically motivated intellectual and aesthetic canon—then the distortion is evident and the claim of objectivity unsustainable. The encounter of strangers, of doer and done-to, suggests another objectivity for all the passion which the interpersonal commands and diversity makes problematic. Community service forces us to face the done-to who, by his or her presence, calls attention to what is—the pain of the sick, the neediness of the poor, the ignorance of the illiterate, the anger of the exploited.

The joining of service and classroom is a reminder that schooling is finally a place where choices include the unexpected, even the dangerous. As Maxine Greene comments,

> None of this will have concrete content, however, if we do not think of creating live situations in which there are *actual* uncertainties. . . . A crucial dimension of ethical teaching has to do with the cultivation of the ability to recognize moments of choice. It is not easy. Situations do not come labelled moral situations. And yet, the person who chooses himself or herself as a moral agent . . . must somehow learn how to assess situations, how to constitute situations as situations in which there are indeed alternative courses of action. This requires a mode of wide-awakeness I am afraid many people are lacking today: the kind of wide-awakeness that carries with it a habit of attending to life and its requirements, a habit of *active* attending of the kind we experience when we are trying to carry some project into effect—to execute a plan.[24]

All too often choosing remains only a notion; with community service, the stranger actually appears in the choices I make and in the recognition of myself as the one who is choosing. The stranger's connection to me and the place of his or her residence apart from me is raised. The classroom must focus on the question of community.

SCHOOL AND COMMUNITY

We talk—sometimes *ad nauseam*—the language of community. We refer to the "school community," to the association of parents, teachers, and students in "a community." However, the radical individualism of our view of learning subverts the communities that try to emerge. Where a hint of community appears—as can happen on more than one occasion—the failures of community outside of the schools erode what happens inside. In this contradictory context of language and practice, community service raises a number of questions. Community becomes a matter of pedagogy, that is, the way in which the human relations of familiars and strangers and the encounter with diverse collectivities affect how learning happens. It becomes, too, a matter of school politics, that is, the interactions of schooling with social functions. Community service informs us that the world which appears as accessible through these functions is, at heart, problematic. It opens the issue of membership, an issue of inclusion and exclusion. The question of community, finally, asks whether schooling can be effective in the absence of a more widely shared community.

It was the progressives who generalized the notion of "the school as community" as another criticism of the "old" education. Of course, they did not deny that the school also served society and often blurred the distinction between the two. But, in describing the school as community they were making a pedagogical and an institutional point. They were concerned to embed schooling and democracy in each other. And they intended, thereby, to validate the present experience of students while at the same time integrating experience—making experience seamless—across time and generations. Criticizing the habit of confusing learning with recitation, they called attention the fact that learning is a sociable activity and not simply a lone individual's address to the world as object. Learning is a practice creating and strengthening the habits of sociability. Finally, it creates new sociabilities ranging from the friendly associations of "show and tell" to the shared rewards and pains of critical inquiry. The relationship of learning and sociability were, so to speak, dialectical.[25] This increase of sociability would be measured by a greater and greater inclusiveness of persons as in the notion of human solidarity and at the same time by a greater and greater intensity of relationship as in the notions of mutuality and participation. So, the progressive, as it were, opened the discussion of the "school as community" as a way of reforming our epistemology and our politics.

The sociability of knowing is familiar to us as a traditional virtue as well, although it was reserved for those who were already said to know. We continue that tradition when we symbolize our own arrivals by a hierarchical arrangement of academic degrees which once carried not just distinctions of knowledge but distinctions of power. My diploma, for example, refers to the "rights, privileges and immunities appertaining" to my degree but I've never found out what these were or how to use them. More seriously, we practice the tradition when we break experience in two, as a preparation for and later as a living out of experience. Affirming the privileged status of membership, we isolate students from each other at crucial moments and permit them to come together as scholar-peers only when they are done being students. Homework assignments are not shared inquiries. Examinations are individual obstacle courses. Little wonder then that our students have difficulty taking the language of community seriously. Of course, the progressives did not deny relevant distinctions of authority based in competence. What parted progressive and conservative from each other—and it is no small matter—was a sense of timing and trust and location.

The school as community was for every student at every age; membership was not a grant of privilege. By contrast, for the tradition, the school as community was an achievement that followed advanced study, a reward. Thus, a university faculty—but not its students—describes itself as a "community of scholars." Elementary and high school faculties use community language too but their reference is to teaching and not to scholarship. Here, too, we subvert community by our practices. The teacher closes the doors of the classroom and announces thereby a preferred isolation. The "community of scholars" connects backward in time to the classic academy and lyceum and to the medieval monastery and university. We only symbolize our apartness today in the academic robes we still wear on ceremonial occasions. Finally, in modern form, the "community of scholars" is transformed into the research university with departments, disciplines and subdisciplines that neither understand each other nor want to. Community disappears.

Indeed, the failure to be a "community of scholars" is but one more instance of lost connections. So, the notion of sharing knowledge in pursuit of truth deteriorates into a job requirement, that is, "publish or perish." Students are set on isolated pathways toward qualification for membership in a community that does not exist and for which a lonely preparation would not help them if it did. As doctoral candidates put it, cynically, the degree is only a "union card." The sociability of knowing deteriorates into a functional arrangement or as Clark Kerr, former president of the University of California, once described it, a "multi-versity."

A more sanguine picture of school as community is presented by the elementary school, still uncorrupted by the artificialities of the discipline and the pressures of competition for grades and places. Here, schooling is, more often than not, genuinely sociable with working groups, learning circles, study corners, and the like. As many of us in schools have noticed, however, this picture is present in fewer and fewer places as concern for "success" penetrates to younger and younger students and particularly to their parents. In the upper grades, already infected by lost connections, sociability is likely to appear, if at all, in informal settings—the lunchroom, the club, the athletic team. We can already notice the separations too, the appearance of life-worlds; for example, the cliques and religious and ethnic ghettos so visible in a high school cafeteria. In the classroom, meanwhile, learning and knowing become more and more isolated. So, talk of "school as community" is familiar enough but its practice becomes less and less visible as the student "progresses."

Perhaps the progressives overstated the connections of pedagogy and politics. Yet, the school as community is a political statement, a way of looking at the relationships of the school to what goes on outside of the school. These relationships are particularly rich and interesting in the United States with our history of decentralized schooling and our mix of private and public schools. It is obvious enough that the surroundings shape the school's purposes. A middle-class suburb makes one kind of school, an urban ghetto another. Interest-group politics create relationships that reach to faculty hiring and retention policies, curricula, co-curricular activities as well as to more obvious matters of budget and architecture and location. At the same time, the school is not just a passive recipient of influences. This becomes obvious in exploring the economics, architecture and even the traffic patterns in a "neighborhood"; it is presumed in our anxiety about the economic consequences of an "uneducated" population. Here too, however, the direction of schools like the direction of the society around them is toward "people like us." A shared commitment to schooling hardly exists. Cities and towns populated with citizens whose children have grown up or whose children are in private and parochial schools habitually vote down school budgets. And even the relationships among those said to be alike in values and goals are functional, utilitarian and private. Thus, we join to protect ourselves against people *not* like us and above all to gain advantage for our own children. Schooling is but an instrument for individual economic and political ends. The politics of community are surrendered to functionalism.

Against this background, radical criticisms of schooling develop quite naturally. These are unlike complaints which focus on economic success, meeting national policy needs and also unlike reforms which range from increasing "time on task" to more subtle notions like Theodore Sizer's "Coalition of Essential Schools."[26] These criticisms draw upon feminism and black studies, and from work on moral development. In common, they opt for a different pedagogy. Unlike progressivism—a label that they are likely to reject—they embed the sociability of learning in the actual diversities of cultures and times and places. To borrow from Carol Gilligan, they share the view that we must speak "in a different voice." Communities then can only emerge from an explicit acknowledgement of separated identities. They are, however, less sanguine than progressivism about the possibility for a widely shared community to emerge from an interplay of those differences. Indeed, the lively quarrel these days between separatists and interactionists is about whether such an interplay is either possible or desirable. In any event, they acknowledge the reality of a plurality of life-worlds.

Spurred by reflection on the civil rights movement, a fresh look at the "melting pot" raised questions about its moral legitimacy. Black nationalism—quickly joined by Latino and Native American nationalisms—challenged the hierarchical, linguistic, and conformist agendas that often hid behind Enlightenment cosmopolitanism. So, in a few short decades we have come instead to speak the language of diversity. The case was made for specific identities, for "roots," and for unique cultures. The effect was to separate. The school as community under this inspiration became a gathering place of separations.

In the name of community, the ideal of a shared community is even less likely today. Paradoxically, however, schooling in the practice of community increases. Myles Horton, founder of The Highlander Folk School and one of the pioneers of the critique of community, describes it,

> Since I chose to work with poor, oppressed people, I had to take into consideration that they'd never been allowed to value their own experience; that they'd been told it was dirt and that only teachers and experts knew what was good for them. I knew it was necessary to do things in the opposite way, to draw out of people their experience, and help them value group experiences and learn from them. . . . It also became clear that there had to be a place where people could learn how to make decisions by actually making real decisions. That's how you learn anything—by doing it. I believed then and still believe that you learn from your experience of doing something and from your analysis of that experience.[27]

The pale—and often Anglo-Saxon Protestant—homogeneities of a "melting pot" give way to rich, complex, detailed, and varied lifeworlds. A visit to a school assembly these days in or near any large city will reveal the presence of music and language and costume undreamt of a short while ago. A glance at student art work and a walk through the corridors confirms our variousness. Even near-homogeneous schools give evidence of a borrowed diversity in the language, music and costume of their students, although it is often superficial and faddist. The legitimation of ethnicities yields a double product: knowledge of and practice in doing the life of a community and the isolation of communities from each other.

If the villain of the ethnic critique of community is the melting pot, the villain of the feminist critique is masculinism. The feminist challenges the ways in which knowing and being are experienced and reported. More radical than the ethnic critique, feminism moves beyond questions of society and politics. In a revisionist metaphysics, as it were, it raises questions of being, that is, what it means to be a natural entity in a natural world. As Parker Palmer notes,

> I want to make it clear that these epistemologies [feminist, Black scholarship, Native American studies] do not aim at the overthrow of objectivity, analysis, and experimentation. Indeed, the feminist thinkers that I know use these very tools in their writing. But they want to put those tools within a context of affirming the communal nature of reality itself, the *relational* nature of reality. . . . For example, the mode of objectivity is held in creative tension with another way of knowing, the way of intimacy, the way of personally implicating yourself with the subject. Virtually every great scholar finds this way of appropriating knowledge, of living and

breathing it and bringing it so close to your heart that you and it are almost one. Objectivity and intimacy *can* go hand in hand; that's what the new epistemologies are calling for.[28]

Feminism and ethnicity come at the school from outside, so to speak. Within the school, the critique of community appears in different ways. One such criticism emerges from the concern with moral development. As Lawrence Kohlberg remarked,

> Essentially, however, it seemed to me that there were more fundamental limits to what we were doing before we could really have a viable kind of practice and on which a lot of research needed to be done. In the first place, of course, was the question of the relation of judgment to action. ... Research studies showed, empirically, certain relationships between judgment and action but we don't really know ... whether changes in moral judgment from educational programs would actually lead to changes in moral action ... the second thing is the concern for content as well as for structure.[29]

The move to action led Kohlberg and his associates to the notion of the "just community" and to its experimental implementation in a number of schools.[30] Along with the scientist's interest, there is the moralist's critique of the school's claim to be a democratic community. Kohlberg made no secret of his motives,

> as the present essay shows, I have relied on Dewey's idea of democratic community as the means of moral education. However, I have also been much influenced by another concept of community, one which is even more vivid than Dewey's though not as democratic. This is the concept of community once proposed by Durkheim, whose central ideas are that (a) the group, society, or community is a whole or collectivity greater than the sum of its individual parts, and (b) the experience of membership in the collective whole induces in the individual moral sentiments capable of generating moral actions.[31]

However, if the just community cannot integrate justice and caring it cannot be a community and fails as a criticism of practice. Fortunately, as Norman and Richard Sprinthall report,

> A major review of over eighty studies of the relation of moral behavior to reasoning has been done by Gus Blasi. ... [Mary] Braebeck's review reached the same conclusions ...
> To a major degree, then, the charge of sex bias has not been proven. ... It is true that the original sample was male, but there have been an enormous number of studies since that time (including cross-cultural replications) with both sexes. The results are highly consistent with the claim

of a universal sequence for both sexes. This does not mean, however, that there is nothing of substance to Gilligan's view. She has served as a valuable reminder that issues of caring and compassionate concern for others are important components of moral judgment. . . .

Kohlberg himself is certainly sensitive to Gilligan's position. . . . In his most recent writing, Kohlberg now describes the Golden Rule as having two elements: (1) Do unto others as you would have them do unto you, and (2) Love thy neighbor as thyself.[32]

Yet another criticism of school as community is found among the young themselves. Helped by some of the adults around them, they have moved schools toward connecting action and reflection, and toward the knowledge that morality and politics cannot be evaded in the name of a claimed academic neutrality and objectivity. Inheritors of the culture of relevance of the 1960s, the newer generation is less given to dramatization and more skilled in the uses of institutions. It is not, however, unfamiliar with the values of protest and of organized numbers. For example,

Earth Day is more than two decades old and many adults have felt their ardor for the environment cool off. Not teen-agers. . . . Hundreds of groups are cropping up around the country. . . . Just as the civil rights struggle and Vietnam shaped the baby-boom generation, global catastrophes like the Valdez oil spill or local crises like overflowing garbage dumps make their children brood darkly . . .

To fight the good fight, so-called green teens have turned to tactics their parents should recall from college days. According to a survey by Alexander W. Astin, a UCLA education professor, the percentage of college freshmen who have taken part in protests is higher than ever—surpassing even the late 1960s . . .

It's a reversal of the age-old generational war: now children are bullying their parents into changing their behavior.[33]

Less activist are other examples of the initiatives among the young. Among these are student-to-student projects like "peer mediation" and "peer counseling." The former is based on "conflict resolution" and has its roots in the labor movement and the Quaker tradition. In peer mediation, young people learn and use the skills and arts of negotiation.[34] Peer counseling is used effectively in dealing with adults with addictive behaviors, providing help in life-crisis moments, developing support groups around issues of single parenthood, sexual identity, aging. The move of peer counseling into the schools gets a mixed reception. My colleague, "Mal" Goodman of the Ethics Department at The Fieldston School, commented,

At the high school level, however, peer counseling programs seem much more controversial. The name "peer counseling" itself conjures up images of a squad of ill-trained amateur Freuds rushing through the corridors psychoanalyzing whomever they encounter. Understandably, this image is a source of alarm for teachers, administrators, and parents. . . . In reality, however, the literature indicates the use of peer counselors at the high school level is widespread and has met with considerable success.

. . . it is easy to overlook the degree to which peer counseling occurs naturally at all schools. When private school students were asked "to whom would you turn if you felt you needed advice?" students indicated they would most likely turn to another student in four of the most crucial areas: trouble in adjusting to school, personal problems, drugs, and relations with the opposite sex. Simply put, the closest contacts of students is with their peers.[35]

Student activism and peer-counseling lead us back to community service. More explicitly, they are a critique of the failures of community. Student activism challenges the self-interested politics of adults; peer-counseling points out the failures of our support for young people in trouble. In both, it is students who are not only doers but initiators. And, in both, the students reach from their existence as students to unknown others. While sharing the concern for community that shows up in feminism and ethnicity, the implication of the student effort is directly the encounter of strangers.

And that takes us finally to community service as a criticism of the school as community. Community service makes the claim—it would seem at first glance variously foolish, unrealistic, risky, dubious—that a shared community can be presumed in action. Unlike feminism and ethnicity which sustain communities at the cost of shared community, unlike progressivism and traditionalism which presumed a shared community and then debated its shape and content, community service is initiated by an awareness of the stranger but presumes the transformation of stranger into familiar even if only momentarily. When joined with schooling, this awareness and this transformation becomes a matter of deliberate choice and personal knowing. It is not surprising then that schooling finds the partnership with community service an uneasy one. The presumption in action which underlies community service intrudes upon our isolated habits of learning and being. It interrupts them. The relationship of schooling and democracy which was the rallying cry of the progressives returns, now, in a different way as a consequence of the experience of community service. In other words, the story of school as community remains unfinished until joined by the story of democracy as community.

NOTES

1. Howard Seeman, "Why the Resistance by Faculty," *Combining Service and Learning*, ed. Jane C. Kendall and Associates (Raleigh, N.C.: National Society for Internships and Experiential Education, 1990), vol. 2, p. 161.

2. Ormond Smythe, "Practical Experience and the Liberal Arts," ibid., Jane C. Kendall and Associates, vol. 1, pp. 299–300.

3. John Dewey struggled with the issue of "subjectivity" but he could not escape his scientific model nor could he foretell the radical diversity of modern experience. See, for example, *Experience and Nature* (New York: Norton, 1929) in which he developed the theme of experience as "precarious" and risky. See also *Art as Experience* (New York: Minton, Balch, 1934).

4. S. Kierkegaard, "Thoughts on Crucial Situations in Human Life," ed. T. C. Oden, (Princeton, N.J.: Princeton University Press, 1978), p. 38.

5. The *locus classicus* of the debate was, of course, John Dewey's philosophic reconstruction of the school. Typically, he wrote,

> much of present education fails because it neglects this fundamental principle of the school as a form of community life. It conceives the school as a place where certain information is to be given, where certain lessons are to be learned, or where certain habits are to be formed. The value of these is conceived as lying largely in the remote future. The child must do these things for the sake of something else he is to do; they are mere preparations. As a result they do not become a part of the life experience of the child and so are not truly educative.

John Dewey, "My Pedagogic Creed," reprinted in *The Philosophy of John Dewey*, ed. John J. McDermott, (Chicago: University of Chicago Press, 1981), p. 446.

6. This comment is by Donald Schon in *Educating the Reflective Practitioner*, (San Francisco: Jossey-Bass, 1987) and is cited in Steven K. Schulz, "Learning by Heart: The Role of Action in Civic Education," *op. cit.*, Jane C. Kendall and Associates, vol. 1, p. 217.

7. Parker J. Palmer, "Community Conflict and Ways of Knowing," *op. cit.*, Jane C. Kendall and Associates, vol. 1, pp. 107–108.

8. George Leonard, "The End of School," *The Atlantic* 269, 5 (May 1992), p. 24.

9. For my purposes, the specific forms and styles of connection between classroom and experience are not particularly important. What is important is the encounter of strangers. Obviously, some of the forms of "experiential education" are not germane. For example,

> Classroom-based experiential education in the form of simulations, games, programmed instruction, computerized learning packages, group process techniques, and library-based independent study;
>
> Career exposure and life-style planning programs, . . .
>
> Outward Bound programs and their counterparts using out-door and wilderness setting for growth and learning;
>
> Cooperative education, placing students primarily in "for profit" settings;
>
> Adult self-initiated learning exercises . . .
>
> Programs rooted in public need settings, including voluntary action programs, public service internships, academically based field practica, and some work-study programs.

Robert L. Sigmon, "Service-Learning: Three Principles," *op. cit.*, Jane C. Kendall and Associates, vol. 1, pp. 56–57.

10. Ernest L. Boyer, "For Education: National Strategy, Local Control," *New York Times*, September 26, 1989.

11. Peter W. Sipple, "Community Service Teaches Students to Think about Others," *The Morning Call* (Allentown, Pennsylvania), May 22, 1990, p. A7.

12. Robert A. Rutter and Fred M. Newmann, "The Potential of Community Service to Enhance Civic Responsibility," *Social Education* 52, 6 (October 1989), p. 373.

13. See Thomas S. Kuhn, *The Structure of Scientific Revolutions* (Chicago: University of Chicago Press, 1970).

14. See Howard B. Radest, *Can We Teach Ethics* (New York: Praeger, 1989), particularly Chapter 4, "Into the Classroom: Where Shall We Teach?," pp. 55–75.

15. The recommendation appears in Ernest L. Boyer, *High School, A Report on Secondary Education in America*, (New York: Harper and Row, 1983), pp. 306–307. Carnegie Units are standardized measures of the amount of course work a high school student should have for graduation.

16. Dan Conrad and Diane Hedin, "Youth Program Models," *op. cit.*, Jane C. Kendall and Associates, vol. 2, pp. 65–66.

17. There are numerous examples and the number grows every day. Among one of the earliest,

> In 1966, the beginnings of a service curriculum were introduced through the initiative of Radcliffe's President, Mary I. Bunting. The Harvard-Radcliffe service curriculum, Education for Action (EA) has all the necessary ingredients for providing educationally meaningful service opportunities for students . . .
>
> Significantly, EA carries academic credit for one of its seminars. Begun as a seminar on "Teaching in Urban Areas" last year, the course which requires field experience of the EA variety was translated into "educationese" and now appears in the official Harvard register as "Social Sciences 121. Studies in Education: The Changing Function of American Education in the City." There were 75 qualified applicants for 15 openings in the course last autumn.

Donald J. Eberly (1968), "Service Learning and Educational Growth," *op. cit.*, Jane C. Kendall and Associates, vol. 1, p. 176.

18. "Introduction," *op. cit.*, Jane C. Kendall and Associates, vol. 1, p. 21.

19. Alfie Kohn, "Caring Kids," *Phi Delta Kappan* 72, 7 (March 1991), p. 504.

20. Richard P. Feynman, *What Do You Care What Other People Think?* (New York: W.W. Norton, 1991), p. 11.

21. John G. Farr, "Motivated to Service: A Student Perspective and a Student-Led Seminar," *op. cit.*, Jane C. Kendall and Associates, vol. 2, p. 362.

22. For a discussion of the classroom as "dialogue," see Howard B. Radest, *Can We Teach Ethics*, (New York: Praeger, 1989), Chapter 7, "Character and Characters: Voices in the Classroom," pp. 121–144.

23. David Thornton Moore, "Experiential Education as Critical Discourse," *op. cit.*, Jane C. Kendall and Associates, vol. 1, p. 280–281.

24. Maxine Greene, "No Time to Lose," *Report of Centennial Educational Conference* (New York: The Ethical Culture Schools, 1979), p. 10.

25. No doubt, one of the more frustrating of John Dewey's notions was that the end of experience was the increase of experience. It was rooted in a Hegelianism without an ideal "end of history" and in Darwinian evolution.

26. Professor Sizer is chair of the Education Department at Brown University. The Coalition, founded nearly a decade ago, brings together high schools, public and private, that are willing to reconstruct school schedules, measure achievement by performances, portfolios and projects and not merely by standard tests, explore ways of developing a more coherent curriculum, etc. The founding of the Coalition was stimulated by Sizer's research on the American high school. See Theodore Sizer, *Horace's Compromise* (Boston: Houghton Mifflin, 1984).

27. Cited in a review by Steve Schulz of *The Long Haul*, Myles Horton with Judith and Herbert Kohl, (New York: Doubleday, 1990) in *Experiential Education* 16, 5 (December 1991), p. 10.

28. Parker J. Palmer, "Community Conflict and Ways of Knowing," *op. cit.*, Jane C. Kendall and Associates, vol. 1, p. 110.

29. Lawrence Kohlberg, "The Just Community Approach to Moral Education in Theory and in Practice," unpublished paper, International Conference on Moral Education, Fribourg, Switzerland, September 1982, pp. 5–6.

30. Experimental models were developed in Cambridge, Mass., Scarsdale, N.Y., and New York City. Reporting on these, Caesar Previdi, principal of Martin Luther King Jr. High School in New York City, noted,

> Although the program may have a different form, each model has a weekly meeting of all members during which the community issues are discussed and voted. It is during this community meeting that all 100 students and teacher members participate in discussion and through vote, take a stand on a norm of behavior proposed for the whole group. Each community member, teacher and student alike, has one vote. . . . The large community meeting is the heart of the program . . .
>
> Models operate differently in different schools. One Just Community model combines the program with lunch period. The Agenda and Fairness Committee meetings are scheduled on Monday, Core Groups on Tuesday and the large Community meeting on Wednesday. On Thursday and Friday, the students go to regular lunch while the staff are engaged in team meetings, planning the following week's curriculum and community activities.

"Administrative Practice and Moral Development; The Just Community: Teaching Students Prosocial Behavior," a paper presented at the American Educational Research Association, 1989 meeting, no page numbers.

31. Lawrence Kohlberg, "The Just Community Approach to High School Moral Education," unpublished and undated paper (probably sometime between 1984 and 1986). Kohlberg's reference is to *Moral Education: A Study in the Theory and Application of the Sociology of Education* (New York: Free Press, 1973). Kohlberg, citing Durkheim further on in that paper, responds to Carol Gilligan, writing, "Like Durkheim, and unlike Gilligan, our theory of the just community does not make a typological dichotomy between justice and care, or assume that both are not present in each sex (p. 10).

32. Norman and Richard C. Sprinthall, "Values and Moral Development," Easier Said Than Done, Winter 1988, p. 21. Reprint from *Educational Psychology, A Developmental Approach*, 4th ed. (New York: Random House, 1987), pp. 157–177.

33. Nancy Marx Better, "Green Teens," *New York Times Magazine*, March 8, 1992, p. 44.

34. In "Peer Mediation: When Students Agree not to Disagree," Debra Viadero writes,

> According to the National Association for Mediation in Education (NAME), at least 200 such programs are currently operating in elementary and secondary schools . . .
>
> the concept of using formal dispute resolution as a way to control potentially violent interpersonal situations had its origins in the 1960s and early 1970s but it did not take hold in the classroom until early this decade. . . .
>
> . . . the real catalyst for the school-based mediation movement . . . was the success of community-based mediation centers . . .
>
> "In the early 1980s," Ms. Gibson (Director of NAME) said, "they began to say, 'these are lifelong skills we're teaching adults and what if we began teaching these skills to children?' "

Education Week 7, 35 (May 25, 1988), p. 23.

35. Malcolm Goodman, "Peer Counseling at the High School Level," unpublished paper prepared while a Klingenstein Fellow at Teachers College, Columbia University, undated but probably 1980, pp. 2–3.

Chapter Nine

The Substance of Democracy

CONTRACT AND COMMUNITY

Democracy is a moral and political ideal that trusts in our capacity to rule ourselves and to judge and act fairly. As lived, however, democracy is a confusing and messy experience, a mix of self-determination and manipulation, of legal structures, informal arrangements, private desires and public policies. Freedom and limitation contend with each other. Meanwhile, several visions of democracy compete for the allegiance of the democrat and each has consequences for how we think about and do community service.

One of these visions is familiar to us as the "social contract" or a democracy of agreements. Human beings are imagined as separated, equal, rational, self-interested. They enter into agreements like business deals and other market activities. The public life is designed to protect the disparate privacies of the agreeing parties. We thus come upon the familiar picture of a limited democratic state—a government of "laws, not men" as we put it—made legitimate by the assent of a majority of its citizens and the implicit consent of the rest. The citizen in a democracy of agreements is jealous of his or her powers and cedes these to be state grudgingly and unwillingly. Such a state, in turn, is neutral as to ends and goods; it defends the "pursuit of happiness" but refuses to define happiness. So, the state is immoral if it prescribes the "good life" or even "the good lives" for its citizens. Such a state, then, is enacted by a government of forms and procedures. It deliberately denies content to itself. Its language is a language of rights and duties and its genius is the increase and protection of liberties.[1]

In a democracy of agreements, we are connected to each other by the agreements we make. We may freely choose to connect and disconnect with each other without moral fault as long as the conditions of agreement are met. We have, as we say, a "right" to privacy. We need not give reasons for our choices since our reasons are said to be our own. Of course, others may frown or raise an eyebrow but that, as we also say, is "not my affair." Naturally, we make and break agreements, quarrel over their terms, re-negotiate them, and so forth. In doing so, we are presumed to have equal powers or else agreements turn into tyrannies. Where such equalities are absent, we further agree to provide for them by balancing interests and establishing rules of fair play. The culture heroes of a democracy of agreements are the lawyer and the judge who are not merely "professionals" but keepers of the public morality. Not surprisingly, then, we freely mix morality and legality. Although we turn to lawyers and judges for interpretation and adjudication, however, we are presumed to be able to understand our interests and act on our understandings. Without this minimal rationality, agreements would merely be a dance of fools. Ultimately, of course, we cannot legitimately join together to stop that dance either since we may choose to be fools too and that is not the public's business. All in all, the democracy of agreements is pictured as a nearly ideal state of being since it is self-limiting, does only what we assign it to do and does not do what we do not assign it to do.

Finally, in a democracy of agreements, we have limited common obligations as well as those that flow from particular agreements between particular parties. In general, these common obligations—like military service, voting, serving on juries—are justified because they protect our chances to enter into particular agreements. Community service is then a form of public service and can be added to our common obligations as a matter of rational choice. It is interpreted as citizenship education, an education in the practices of common obligations. Since it is a contractual obligation, nothing in principle prevents us from demanding it, that is, making it mandatory as we do with military service or paying taxes or school attendance. If we decide to make it voluntary, we are making a psychological, pragmatic and pedagogical judgment, not a principled one; that is, it works better when it is chosen and not imposed. The places where community service is done are to be chosen from among those public locations that are legitimately accessible to the public. Thus, community service may address the improvement of common goods like lands and forests and city streets or it may address the abilities of other citizens to enter into agreements like literacy and tutoring.

Community service is, however, corrupted when it becomes interpersonal, that is, when it blurs the line between public duty and private life. On this view, then, it is both appropriate and right that the done-to should resent and resist the intrusions of the doer. The exchange appropriate in community service is a matter of procedural justice—a way of insuring conditions of fairness and of learning public skills. Or else it arises from an agreement, a contract. It is not a matter of caring.

The public life in a democracy of agreements is deliberately limited, neat, even austere. Obviously, life goes on in all its richness, complexity, and fascination but not in the public arena or at least not legitimately in the public arena. As it were, the instruction we give to workers, professionals, and others, to "do your job and leave your problems at home," is generalized. We are normally expected to live in two separate worlds, a society shared with others as citizens, and life-worlds shared with others as family members, friends, co-religionists. Of course, an implicit connection may exist between these worlds, for example, an inherited tradition or tribal line of descent or religious cosmology. But for a democracy of agreements this is not legitimately determinative of social practice. That it may be more powerful than acknowledged is also a fact, one which—as in the abortion debate—makes a democracy of agreements problematic.

In a democracy of agreements, community service is indeed an encounter of strangers but that is as it should be. It is, after all, the rule of all public encounters. The problems of that encounter may be practical—that is, we are not skilled enough to do the duties required of us—but they are more likely to be the result of confusing the private and public life. Talk of care, empathy, sympathy only confuses matters. In Kantian fashion, community service as public service is to be done as a duty and for the sake of duty. It follows from the nature of the public life.

Obviously, the realities of a democracy of agreements do not match its idealities. Society and life-world do not stay neatly separated, sympathy like other passions intrudes into the public life, habits of relationship on one side and curiosity—nosiness, gossip—on the other spill over from one place into the other. Memory cannot be erased. So a democracy of agreements is also the scene of conflict between public processes and traditional connections. The quarrel between "church" and "state" is a persistent reminder of that conflict. As serious is the evolution of the public life itself, its realization of the very virtues it proclaims. The logic of a public life of forms and processes is the perfection of functions and the skills needed to perform them. Austerity—as in the stoic's picture of duty—in the absence of other connections, turns citizenship into technique. The lost connection appears in a democracy of agreements as the isolation of functions and functionaries from each other.[2] The consequent rise of technicism and bureaucracy

was described by the sociologist, Max Weber—and by the institution-
alists who followed his lead—as a natural development of maturing
industrial societies, the move from *gemeinschaft* to *gesellschaft*.[3] Consequently, as Robert Bellah and his colleagues remark in their deservedly
classic study, *Habits of the Heart*,

> The most distinctive aspect of twentieth-century American society is the
> division of life into a number of separate functional sectors: home and
> workplace, work and leisure, white collar and blue collar, public and
> private. This division suited the needs of the bureaucratic industrial cor-
> porations that provided the model for our preferred means of organizing
> society by the balancing and linking of sectors as "departments" in a
> functional whole, as in a great business enterprise.[4]

Ironically, diversity run wild also appears in a democracy of agreements, but now it is also a diversity of functions and not just of life-
worlds. Efforts to reconnect are difficult here too since the languages
and practices of these functions just like those of life-worlds are radically
separated. I think here of the endless and growing number of special-
izations and sub-specializations in jobs and professions. Shared knowl-
edges and skills are hardly available. Public persons are scarcely
accessible to each other, talking neither with or to but past each other.

Community service as an effort of connection is frustrated in a democracy of agreements by the mysteriousness of the doing. In the absence of a community, what can the encounter mean? It is not surprising,
then, that it is most effective when restricted to more primitive activities
like digging ditches, teaching "ABCs" and to routine tasks like stuffing
envelopes; that is, to activities which wash away distinctions of personality, ancestry, and ethnicity. It is neither necessary nor desirable for
these activities to become more sophisticated as long as the intention is
induction into the practices of citizenship as a public obligation. In fact,
sophistication in the amateur and the volunteer is resented in a functional world, as those of us who have served in schools and social
agencies learn very quickly.

Another and earlier vision is the democracy of community. The state,
as Aristotle had it, is a natural outcome of the social nature of human
nature. Often, as in the argument between care and justice, a democracy
of community competes with a democracy of agreement. For example,
my concern for my family and friend may lead me to favor their needs,
to be unfair as it were, and so to behave in ways unjustified by the rules
of agreement. I am more likely to recommend my son or daughter or
neighbor for a job; more likely—at least in public—to find excuses for
his or her mistakes. However, since all persons are, by nature, embedded
in circles of family and friends, they are supposed to have similar re-

sources of concern available to them. Of course, some circles are "more equal than others" and this is an evident fact of a plurality of life-worlds. The situation of the "loner" in a democracy of community is both unnatural and disastrous. A "bond of sympathy" may partially remedy that situation as in acts of charity. A " bond of patriotism" provides a second line of defense against disaster for the loner as in a welfare "safety net." In a democracy of community, the person is understood to have many memberships with many different kinds of belongings and relationships and many different kinds of things to do like being a father, a friend, a worker, a citizen. The radical isolation of public and private worlds is replaced by intersecting "networks" of relationships.

The forms and practices of a democracy of community appear to be quite like those of a democracy of agreement but are not. Recourse to lawyers and law courts is the exception rather than the rule. They are likely to be asked to mediate rather than advocate. Agreements are informal and personal but no less binding. The language of a democracy of community is rich with family, historic and traditional references. Sustaining the democracy of community is a "narrative" that tells how community evolved from hierarchy to equality, from authority to consensus.

> Communities, in the sense we are using the term, have a history—in an important sense they are constituted by their past—and for this reason we can speak of a real community as a "community of memory," one that does not forget its past. In order not to forget that past, a community is involved in retelling its story, its constitutive narrative, and in so doing, it offers examples of the men and women who have embodied and exemplified the meaning of the community. These stories of collective history and exemplary individuals are an important part of the tradition that is so central to a community of memory.[5]

Finally, in a democracy of community, the virtue is patriotism and the end is a protection of memberships and identities.

Community service in a democracy of community is an initiation into the arts of wider relationship. Its model is the way we do things with and for each other in the family. Of course, we also want things done well but it is more important that they be done with love. Hence our suspicion of "experts." This underlies, too, our sense of the omni-competence of parents. They have nearly absolute authority in ethics and in law over their children and hence over the future. Only recently have we begun to take the "rights of children" seriously, a sign that a democracy of community is overwhelmed by a democracy of agreements. Doer and done-to are separated by differing life-stories since a democracy of community is built around the notion of a community of communities. Yet members of these communities are said to be partially accessible to each other because of the shared narrative. Kinships provide community service with its models—as we see in folk languages on all sides—and with familiar figures playing familiar roles of heroism, villainy and comedy. Paradoxically, while a democracy of agreement claims universality—as in the cosmopolitanism of Enlightenment democracies—and a democracy of community is rooted in particularity, persons find the latter more comfortable and the former more alien. In other words, I find it impossible to know a "person as such." But I recognize a person by name and association and history. I know when I have "come home" from a strange place even if that strange place is part of "my" society. But, it is also true that when I was in a strange place I could come to know the actors and could often arrive at sensible conclusions about what they were doing and what was expected of me. But, the shared narrative becomes shallow as life-worlds separate and lead us toward "our own kind."

Just like a democracy of agreements, so a democracy of community is corrupted by the "perfection" of its virtues. The strength and urgency of the narrative leads to its reification. It changes from a dramatic interpretation of experience which provides personal meanings into a theory of reality which claims objective truth. Creation stories turn into alternative biologies and geologies. The differing communities come to claim sole possession of their members. Otherness is not the occasion of a community of communities but of isolation. This corruption, which I have called diversity run wild, subverts the democracy of community, turns it into a mere treaty relationship between life-worlds, at best a nonagression pact between exclusive communities. But the exclusive claims do not work out since some kind of public life demands our attention—in order to earn a living, own property, use a public road. Ultimately, community itself becomes artificial and superficial as realities of job and school and nation come to play a more and more important part in living. Community is emptied of content. Finally, it becomes a fad.

Community service in a democracy of community is an attempt to restore the connection to others, to transform an encounter of strangers into a family relationship. The effort is an experience in frustration. So, community service is still an encounter of strangers but now the strangers have become aliens. The notion of diversity is an invitation to stay away and stay apart. Breaking into this pattern of isolation is not just difficult to do but difficult to understand given the shallowness of the common narrative. Symptomatically, as we say, we do not discuss matters of religion and politics since these are matters of private "taste." The doer is unclear about purposes; the done-to does not know how to receive the doer.

To be sure, the language of the common narrative persists—we continue to use words like "equality and freedom," the "founding fathers," the "stars and stripes," and so forth. But now they are interpreted in radically different ways from within the separate life-worlds. Blacks read the Constitution as the perpetuation of slavery which both astounds and offends whites. Feminists indict the "founding fathers" as insensitive and indifferent. Native Americans turn the "discovery" of America into a tale of violence and exploitation. In a democracy of community, disagreement and dissent were of course legitimate. The "village atheist," after all, was an accepted member of the cast of characters. As that democracy is corrupted, disagreements turn into causes of isolation, even of warfare.

A third option is a democracy of participation. It arises as a criticism of the aridity of contracts and the authoritarianism of communities. Traceable to classical Greek ideas of the *polis*, it also appeared in religion as the "priesthood of all believers." In Enlightenment democracy, this liberal line of development focussed on working out the unity of the revolutionary trinity, "liberty, equality, fraternity." Above all, as in the thinking of John Dewey, participation was conceived as a substantive and not just as a procedural ideal.

A democracy of participation is a theater of reciprocities. Government "by the people" is an offer of both universal citizenship and universal membership. In turn, this embeds developmental psychology in democratic politics by attributing to everyone the capacity to participate. Because this is learned, politics is wedded to schooling. Participation also implies that the world is accessible to the participant. A democracy of participation is not just a matter of contract as in a democracy of agreements or culture as in a democracy of community. Emersonian in its confidence in human abilities and Aristotelian in its re-introduction of the unity of ethics and politics, a democracy of participations give priority to the moral and political abilities of persons as such. Robert Westbrook sums it up,

> Dewey was the most important advocate of participatory democracy. . . . This ideal rested on a "faith in the capacity of human beings for intelligent judgment and action if proper conditions are furnished," a faith, Dewey argued, "so deeply embedded in the methods which are intrinsic to democracy that when a professed democrat denies the faith he convicts himself of treachery to his profession . . .
>
> "To say that democracy is only a form of government is like saying a home is a more or less geometrical arrangement of bricks and mortar; that a church is a building with pews, pulpit, and spire. It is true; they certainly are so much. But it is false; they are so infinitely more." The real importance of democracy lay in its larger ethical meaning . . . democracy was a way of life, "a form of moral and spiritual association."[6]

As with other visions of democracy, participation entails its own corruption. It can easily lead to doing for the sake of doing itself. Freed from a necessary connection to an authoritative tradition and committed to ideological pluralism, doing things in common becomes merely "pragmatic." The familiar picture of modern liberalism emerges: a politics of superficial alliances gathered around a collection of separate "causes."[7] Typically, then, the task of the theorists of participation is to find some way of depth—as in John Dewey's universalization of "scientific method" or as in his struggle to defend a "common faith."[8] A democracy of participation can, paradoxically, also result in passivity. To choose to do something presupposes the intelligibility and attractiveness of the thing chosen. If neither is the case, then it is permissible for the participant to withdraw, to refuse to participate. Indeed, it may even be morally necessary to withdraw as a "protest." The superficiality of alliances now exacts its price. The thing chosen—say, a political candidate who "speaks" to enough of the participants to get elected—simply doesn't seem worth the effort. We hear the complaint that there is no "real choice." Repeated over and over again, the experience of withdrawal itself becomes a social habit. Even theory falls into the trap.[9]

"Protest" can itself become a way of life as those of us who lived through the 1960s can recall. Finally, a democracy of participation presupposes that the participant can be an agent, that is, can do something intentionally. But in the confusing interplay of large numbers of participants, the thing done vanishes in a melange, a stew. Intention and action become unintelligible just when a democracy of participation seems to be working.

Community service in a democracy of participation is meant to be a schooling for democracy. Service is supposed to be mutual, cooperative and so the positions of doer and done-to are, in principle, temporary and interchangeable. Unfortunately, this does not in fact happen and so the position of the doer becomes privileged, an invitation to pride and egoism. Moreover, community service invites an activity which does not find content and purpose. So, for example, students commit to service only to find that their commitment is not reflected in the political and social realities they meet. The habit of activity established by community service is then broken as they realize the pointlessness of activity. Finally, community service settles for being a form of remedial education. It is under this umbrella of remediation that we hear the calls for rebuilding citizenship, or community, or mutuality or what have you.

ACTS OF CHOOSING

A traditional community simply expects the services of its members and an authoritarian society simply expects the services of its citizens. Obligations are imposed by history and role and placement. Service is simply a fact of life and it just makes no sense to think of it as a program, a project, or even a remediation for failures. Doer and done-to are already specified as are the things that pass between them. The choosing, if that word can even be used, is done elsewhere by history or tradition or God. But, as in Hegel's classic description of "master and slave," the alienation of imposed obligations under modern conditions opens the way for democracy.

> The master relates himself to the bondsman mediately through independent existence for that is precisely what keeps the bondsman in thrall; . . . and for that reason he proves himself to be dependent, to have his independence in the shape of thinghood. The master, however, is the power controlling this state of existence. . . . Since he is the power dominating existence . . . the master holds, in consequence, this other in subordination. In the same way the master relates himself to the thing mediately through the bondsman. The bondsman being a self-consciousness in the broad sense, also takes up a negative attitude to things and cancels them; but the thing is, at the same time, independent for him and in consequence, he cannot with all his negating get so far as to annihilate it outright and be done with it; that is to say, he merely works on it. To the master, on the other hand, . . . belongs the immediate relation, . . . in other words he gets the enjoyment.[10]

By contrast to the obligations of tribe and community, service acquires its value from the fact that it is chosen. In that sense, it is the paradigmatic act of a free person in a free society since it celebrates agency. Community service is an assertion of personal power—to give and to get— and a political act. In this context, both doer and done-to are making choices, shared choices. At the same time, the collective environment— secular society—encourages the interventions of the agent and is accessible to further intervention. The messy business of deliberate change becomes intelligible as a type of functional reciprocity.

However, centering of community service in a reciprocity of choosings is easily corrupted. The anxiety to get things done encourages the emergence of a leadership that acts as a surrogate for the choices of others. Social priorities appear as crises for which the stumbling efforts of free agents—especially young people, students—are said to be inadequate. In "serious" matters, there is neither time for nor wisdom in the efforts of ordinary persons. The traditional habits of authority of place and the contractual habits of authority of competence are reincarnated and are even invited by the fumbling efforts that inhere in democracy. Crisis, in other words, welcomes and legitimizes taking power. As John Dewey and James Tufts commented long ago in reflecting on the hidden agendas of reformers,

> the vice of the social leader, of the reformer, of the philanthropist and the specialist in every worthy cause of science, or art, or politics, is to seek

ends which promote the social welfare in ways which fail to engage the active interest and cooperation of others. The conception of conferring the good upon others, or at least of attaining it for them, which is our inheritance from the aristocratic civilization of the past, is so deeply embodied in religious, political, and charitable institutions and in moral teachings, that it dies hard. Many a man, feeling himself justified by the social character of his ultimate aim . . . is genuinely confused or exasperated by the increasing antagonism and resentment which he evokes because he has not enlisted in his pursuit of the "common" end the freely cooperative activities of others.[11]

Just as older habits of leadership re-assert themselves so the same justification—the messy, fumbling efforts of democracy—invite a dismay at politics. Community service now becomes a way of being active without being active. Doing for the sake of being a doer becomes a surrogate for agency. The "need to be needed" and the achievement of personal development emerge as the results of a corrupted freedom, the separation of community service from politics. The done-to are denied the capacity for reciprocating and are transformed into mere recipients. So, as Harry C. Boyte remarks,

Community service, widely touted as the cure of young people's political apathy, in fact teaches little about the arts of participation in public life. To reengage students in public affairs requires redefining *politics* to include, in addition to electoral activity, ongoing citizen involvement in solving public problems. It requires a conceptual framework that distinguishes between public life and private life. And it calls for a pedagogical strategy that puts the design and ownership of problem-solving projects into the hands of young people. . . .
. . . But service does little to connect students' everyday concerns with the political process. . . .
. . . young people find that their service meets their needs for personal relevance and a sense of membership in a community. Volunteers usually disavow concern with larger policy questions, seeing service as an *alternative* to politics.[12]

The record shows that community service is most often self-limiting and encapsulated. Those who enter community service are invited into a boundaried activity which is deliberately constructed to avoid a challenge to the powers-that-be and to the way things are. The typical project is developed under adult inspiration from a common sense agenda which calls for great energy but little critical power. Praiseworthy though it may be on other grounds, the record of most of the work of community service reveals that the good is in the serving and not in the questioning. In this context, the assignment of community service to the young may be read as a way of insuring that power and control will not be transferred to them. And, as young, they are neither expected to nor permitted to make social changes, only to practice for making changes later on.

Even where service is integrated with learning, the effort is easily distanced from the doer by a preparatory and even traditional view of schooling. The progressive's "learning by doing" is coopted by the "old education" which reinforces the world that is and continues a traditional politics. The moral impulse which moves the student toward community service is isolated from the political impulse. The connection between community service and democracy becomes a formality—for example, public relations rhetoric as we have seen—not only because leadership arrogates initiatives but because it amasses power. From the side of the adult, community service might even be interpreted as a restoration in a new form of assigned roles and obligations to "undisciplined" young people. Certainly, much of the talk about citizenship and civic duties which is heard in the languages of more conservative community service advocates explicitly announces that attempt at restoration.

I am, I think, getting closer to a key source of Rachel's dilemma. Community service seems to involve the young in choosing over and over again. But it is, most often, a choice of small matters. Typically, the doer asks, "Shall I do this or that, say this or that, report this or that." The done-to is involved in choices of accepting and refusing. In the choosing, paradoxically, community is both presumed and created. Yet, it is momentary, limited, artificial. Unexpected and unlooked-for relationships and outcomes, however, appear. But, it is the student who is left with matters that spill over the boundaries of the planned project and nobody seems ready to deal with them.

Choosing what to do with this spill-over is a hidden question of community service. For example, the encounter of strangers may promise friendship but the separation of life-worlds subverts that promise. With that, the connection of community service to democracy becomes problematic. Activists are restricted to brief encounters, miniature moral and practical lessons that form "character." Where community service is reduced to a classroom exercise, students treat the experience with the same superficiality with which it is presented. They "master" a unit of study and move on to the next subject. They satisfy a requirement. Similarly, where community service is reduced to acts of helping, to "volunteerism," the spill-over is again contained. The volunteer repeats the activity many times over until—as happens all too often with volunteers—he or she is "burned out."

The "spill-over" remains, however, in memory. The policy of containment is only partially effective. The connection between community service and democracy, despite its attenuation and subversion, persists. With it the questions, frustrations, angers, and unpredictabilities of the person who is touched by the experience persist too. There is, as it were, a fourth vision of democracy, a populist vision, latent in the experience of choosing. Community service here opens up experience in ways that its proponents may neither want nor expect. There is a wealth of anecdotal information if not formal evidence: the many stories of the social and political involvements of returned Peace Corps volunteers, the public service records of community service students after they have left school and college, the veterans of Vietnam-era activism now in the women's movement, the consumer rights movement and the environmental movement.

A democracy of choosing can be wildly unpredictable. But, as Harry Boyte reminds us,

> The theorists of change have tended to be educated professionals and cosmopolitans. So the theoretical issues they wrestle with are not really grounded in the everyday life experience of people—what it means for ordinary people to gain a sense of their own power and capacity and control over their environment. Theorists have focused on questions of justice and redistribution, not questions of power. Yet all the popular movements in the 19th century used the language of popular empowerment. The populists were the culmination of a series of movements— abolitionists, the Freedmen's Bureau, the women's movement, the late 19th century Knights of Labor—all created spaces where people experienced relational shared power as the launching pad for larger struggles.[13]

What this suggests is the possibility of yet another vision of democracy, a criticism of what has gone before.

A DEMOCRACY OF RELATIONSHIPS

Our visions of democracy are, so to speak, historically appropriate. Breaking loose from the world of princes and priests, the democracy of agreements centered on the free contracting agent. Establishing memberships where the isolations of geography and job had turned members into individualists and functionaries, the democracy of community centered in doing for and with each other as known persons. And searching out the needs of a society trapped in growing separations between "haves" and "have-nots," a democracy of participation re-asserted the social potency and good sense of the person. Each of these, however, carried its own deterioration with it: its failure was based on its actual response to the question of its moment. A vision of democracy cannot transcend its moment, cannot be established as a permanent political, economic or moral alternative. Nor is it possible to interpret these visions as orderly steps in a grand scheme of social evolution. Indeed, these visions reflect the conflicts of democracy with itself at least as much as the conflicts between democracy and its enemies.

The common feature of democracy is the assignment of political and moral power to persons. This confidence is celebrated—on the American scene and so in our "narrative"—by Emerson's call to each person to trust in his or her powers. For that reason, John Dewey justly called him the "philosopher of democracy."

> Against creed and system, convention and institution, Emerson stands for restoring to the common man that which in the name of religion, of philosophy, of art and of morality, has been embezzled from the common store and appropriated to sectarian and class use. Beyond any one we know of, Emerson has comprehended and declared how such malversation makes truth decline from its simplicity, and become partial and owned, become a puzzle of and trick for theologian, metaphysician and literateur— a puzzle of an imposed law, of an unwished for and refused goodness, of a romantic ideal gleaming only from afar, and a trick of manipular skill, of specialized performance.[14]

However, this Emersonian confidence remains only a worthy sentiment until it has a content. And it is a search for relevant content that is the point of the modern struggle for democracy. Community service is a tell-tale of this struggle. As Frances Lappe puts it,

> Most alarming is simply that we have no theory of democracy that is up to the challenges of the next century. We have what I would call the "liberal market model" of democracy: candidates are marketed to us like toothpaste or after-shave, and once they have been "sold" to us, we turn over the power to make decisions to them. Distant "experts" then become the people who control our lives. This results in a very passive view of the political process—one that fails to engage us actively in problem-solving. It also allows money to continue to play a disproportionate role in the political process since the political system and the market operate by the same metaphor.[15]

At the same time, a countermovement develops toward authoritarianism—neo-fascism, fundamentalism, nationalism. And—again at the same time—democracy is rejected and a dismay at democracy appears among the democrats themselves.[16] Meanwhile, and particularly in the "women's movement," an embryonic democracy of connections is evolving. Critical, on one side, of the dominations and powers of men, feminism affirms the urgency of restoring the lost connection but on new ground. No longer content to restrict connection to the household and to accept the duality of public and private worlds, intimacy becomes political and public.

Community service in this fifth vision of democracy is an exercise in care—not just caring for, but caring to and carefulness. As such, community service is variously an expression, a demonstration and an enactment. It is simultaneously private—in the sense that it is interpersonal and intimate—and public—in the sense that it exhibits morally acceptable relationships that wed love and power. Long before the appearance of modern feminism, however, Jane Addams caught this spirit of democracy as connection when she wrote,

> This paper is an attempt to analyze the motive which underlies a movement based, not only upon conviction, but upon genuine emotion, wherever educated young people are seeking an outlet for that sentiment of universal brotherhood which the best spirit of our times is forcing from an emotion into a motive.... These young people...have been shut off from the common labor by which they live which is a great source of moral and physical health. They feel a fatal want of harmony between their theory and their lives.... I think it is hard for us to realize how seriously many of them are taking to the notion of human brotherhood, how eagerly they long to give tangible expression to the democratic ideal. These young people, longing to socialize their democracy, are animated by certain hopes ... that is it difficult to see how the notion of a higher civic life can be fostered save through common intercourse ... that the good we secure for ourselves is precarious and uncertain, is floating in mid-air, until it is secured for all of us and incorporated into our common life.... There is something primordial about these motives.[17]

Community service is a way of teaching the ways of love and power for both doer and done-to. Both are learning the lessons of personal connections between strangers, that is, personal connections that become communal if only temporarily. Not the least of those lessons is the capacity to accept, to take and not merely to give. Of course, this can be paternalistic, passive, demeaning—neediness, as we saw earlier is its outcome. In a democracy of connection, however, it becomes an act of mutual recognition. Further, connection is not simply conveyed abstractly as a principle or rule or obligation. It is a performance. Finally, community service in a democracy of connections serves a critical role too. It adds flesh and blood to agreements, searches out avenues between separated life-worlds and rounds out participation by making it fully personal.

We can glimpse the possible corruptions of a democracy of connections too. Its feminist inspiration can—and in some instances does—lead to a different separation, not the dualism of public and private but of his and hers. Gender becoming politics generates still more life-worlds. More benign, perhaps, than other instances of biology as politics, it becomes a kind of racialism in another form, almost a mirror image of the very arrogation of power by men which motivates the feminist critique. The re-interpretation of the relationship of intimacy and power can also deteriorate into the projection of a merely interpersonal model onto the public life. Politics at that point becomes a form of psychology and a form of sentimentality. The political life deteriorates into a practice of small actions in small places leaving the larger issues of power—business life, international relations, the military—to the unscrupulous.

A democracy of connections can be corrupted by the ways in which it uses our energies. Invited to turn inward—for that is the habit of intimacy—we can be deluded into thinking this turn can simply be converted into a usable social form. Consequently, the very strength of a democracy of connections becomes its weakness as we exhaust ourselves in coming to know and to respond to everyone, to turn every stranger into a familiar. Community service re-takes the form of tribal obligation; at the same time, it becomes a frenzied effort to be everywhere at once since tribe and family have, in principle, lost their traditional boundaries. Consider, by way of example, the following report about one of the people interviewed for *Habits of the Heart*,

> Ruth Levy, whom we heard above speaking of people in terms of their history, understands that more than cost accounting is involved. She believes a central therapeutic goal is "reconnecting people with families" and, given the conventional family's fragility, it follows that "it doesn't always have to be blood relations." Yet, she sees that isolated families on their own will not be enough. People can "generate families on their own" and nurture them only by drawing on the larger community and its many subcultural worlds more self-consciously than in the past. Thinking of her own renewed commitment to the local synagogue, Ruth notes that "two people aren't enough" to care for children or even for each other. "You need to put into the pot. You need to be there if something needs to be done. To make courtesy calls and sympathy calls and to deliver food. But the other part is that you are also a beneficiary and when you are stuck and need to have someone for your kid to play with or when disasters strike, you have support. On the joyous occasions of a bris (circumcision) or a wedding, you have people to share those with as well. The event itself is wonderful. It's magnified when you have other people who are as happy as you and you can share in other people's happy occasions." In this passage, we hear the familiar language of exchange and support, but we also hear something else—that meaning is "magnified" when it is shared with others.[18]

Community service as a method for the democracy of connection is corrupted in other ways as well. The fact of strangeness is simply denied in the "discovery" that "they (or he or she) are just like us." The painful, frustrating, and always partially successful efforts to encounter the stranger are dissolved. A rhetoric of familiarity is used, but it is not believable. The stranger no matter how amicable remains a stranger for all our efforts, insists on and has a right to his or her own life-world and tells a life-story that is only partially recognizable. A democracy of connections, lacking a sense of tragedy, thus invites its own frustrations—and angers and hostilities—precisely because of its commitment to caring, to loving. Overwhelmed, in Stephen Toulmin's useful phrase, is the troubling but necessary possibility of an "ethics of strangers,"

> In dealing with our children, friends, and immediate colleagues, we both expect to—and are expected to—make allowances for their individual personalities and tastes . . . our perception of their current moods and plans. In dealing with bus driver, the sales clerk in a department store, the hotel barber, and other such casual contacts, there may be no basis for making these allowances. . . . In these transient encounters, our moral obligations are limited and chiefly negative—for example to avoid acting offensively or violently. So, in the ethics of strangers, respect for rules is all, and the opportunities for discretion are few. In the ethics of intimacy, discretion is all and the relevance of strict rules is minimal.[19]

The special and puzzling place of doer and done-to is blurred in a democracy of connections. The relationship does not fit neatly into the categories of intimacy. Neither master nor servant nor functionary, the relationship does not fit neatly into inherited categories of authority either. As it were, the democratic credentials of community service reveal the compound quality of both doer and done-to in the relationship. The terms of description that flow from our visions of democracy—citizen, member, participant, chooser, intimate—both capture and miss the act of community service. That, along with the ambiguities of need and the puzzles of development generates Rachel's dilemma. Where then in a world of lost connections shall we take community service and where will it take us?

NOTES

1. This is not the place for a discussion of "consent" and "liberty." Suffice to say, the connection between the two is abundant in the literature of "social contract" ranging from John Locke's *An Essay Concerning the True Original, Extent, and End of Civil Government* (1690) to John Rawl's *A Theory of Justice* (Cambridge, Mass.: Harvard University Press, 1971). Government is an artifact, a human contrivance and convenience—hence Gary Will's notion of "inventing America," in his discussion of Thomas Jefferson. See Gary Wills, *Inventing America: Jefferson's Declaration of Independence* (Garden City, N.Y.: Doubleday, 1978).

2. In thinking about a democracy of agreements I have benefited from Robert Bellah's work on "civil religion" and, more recently on "habits of the heart." On the theme of lost connections, Bellah and his associates write,

> Though urban Americans still get involved in an astounding variety of voluntary associations, the associational life of the modern metropolis does not generate the

kinds of second languages of social responsibility and practices of commitment to the public good that we saw in the associational life of the "strong and independent township." The metropolitan world is one in which the demands of work, family, and community are sharply separated and often contradictory, a world of diverse, often hostile groups, interdependent in ways too complex for any individual to comprehend. Unlike the town father, the metropolitan's work is carried on in large private corporations that produce commodities for a national or international market or in large government bureaucracies that deliver a range of services in response to the pressures generated by conflicting interest groups. The urbanite's family and community relations are carried on in homogeneous circles of individuals with whom he feels a personal affinity because they share similar beliefs, values, and styles of life. The separation between the worlds of work and of family and community is often expressed and realized by a daily commute between factory and office and residential neighborhood.

Robert N. Bellah et al., *Habits of the Heart* (New York: Harper and Row, 1985), pp. 177–178.

3. See *From Max Weber: Essays in Sociology*, trans. and ed. H. H. Gerth and C. Wright Mills (New York: Oxford University Press, 1946), particularly pp. 196–244.

4. Robert N. Bellah et al., *op. cit.*, p. 43.

5. Ibid., p. 153.

6. Robert B. Westbrook, *John Dewey and American Democracy* (Ithaca, N.Y.: Cornell University Press, 1991), pp. xv, 41.

7. For a discussion of this theme in a related context, see Howard B. Radest, "Doing Good: The Liberal Temptation," Chapter 6 in *The Devil and Secular Humanism* (New York: Praeger, 1990), pp. 81–97.

8. Both themes recur in Dewey's work. For example, see *Logic, The Theory of Inquiry* (New York: Henry Holt and Company, 1938) and *A Common Faith* (New Haven: Yale University Press, 1934).

9. For example,

In Hegel's view, the owl of Minerva—philosophy—spreads her wings only at dusk; only when an action has already been completed or a way of life grown old is it possible to grasp it fully in thought. This conception of philosophy as a "looking backwards" holds, with some qualification, for Rawls's theory as well. That is just as Marx criticized Hegel for failing to recognize at the beginning of the nineteenth century in Germany, the movement toward democracy in the political domain, so I believe Rawls's theory has not taken seriously the call for democracy in the economic domain in this century. Certainly the radical implications of the women's movement have yet to capture his attention. And I believe in both cases the reason is the same: Similar to the political employment of Hegel's dialectic, reflective equilibrium starts from the data of our philosophic tradition and "public political culture." . . . examining our philosophical tradition and public political culture, although necessary and important, cannot be sufficient; the realm until recently has been composed entirely of males. This suggests that for a far more "adequate" account of the well-ordered society, reflective equilibrium must be "radicalized" and extended into new (in particular, into the so-called private) domains.

Sibyl A. Schwarzenbach, "Rawls, Hegel, and Communitarianism," *Political Theory* 19, 4 (November 1991), p. 563.

10. G.W.F. Hegel, *The Phenomenology of Mind*, trans. J. B. Baillie (New York: Harper and Row, 1967), p. 235.

11. John Dewey and James H. Tufts, *Ethics* (New York: Henry Holt and Company, 1909), pp. 303–304.

12. Harry C. Boyte, "Community Service and Civic Education," *Phi Delta Kappan* 72, 10 (June 1991), pp. 765, 766.

13. Jo Calhoun, "Public Life and Public Service," an interview of Harry Boyte, *Experiential Education* 15, 4 (September-October 1990), p. 18.

14. John Dewey (1903), "Ralph Waldo Emerson," in *The Philosophy of John Dewey*, ed. John J. McDermott (Chicago: University of Chicago Press, 1981), pp. 29–30. It is worth noting that "In the last few years we have witnessed a major revival in Emerson scholarship. Since 1977, twenty books have been published on Emerson, including two major biographies." Jack Miller, "Ralph Waldo Emerson," *Ethics In Education* 4, 2 (November 1984), p. 3.

15. Steven Schultz, "The Active Practice of Citizenship," an interview of Frances Moore Lappe, *Experiential Education* 15, 2 (April 1990), p. 1.

16. Symptomatic of this loss of democratic content are "post-modernist" philosophies and, among other things, the revival of interest in the work of Nietzsche. I had not been to a formal philosophic conference in some years when, this January (1992) I finally attended one again. I was astounded at the number of papers on Nietzsche that were included in the brief—two-day—program. Consider, too, these comments from a colleague in England,

> One feels compelled to ask why Nietzsche is undergoing a revival at the moment (though "revival" does not capture the intensity at which secondary work on Nietzsche is being produced; perhaps "fever" is a better description). This revival is largely a product of the growth of post modernism. . . .
>
> Where this started is difficult to ascertain, but the current explosion seems to be a product of deeper rumblings that began with French philosophy in the late 1960s, in particular with the work of Foucault. . . .
>
> The most important influence Nietzsche has had on Foucault has been in Foucault's conceptualization of power and his dissolution of the subject. . . .
>
> Where does all this leave Foucault? The honest answer would seem to be: nowhere. As a left-liberal radical intellectual, who rejects the concentration of power in the state, he is left considering the possibility of only minor resistances to the capillary forms of power such as prisons, asylums, schools, etc. Yet, at other times, he criticizes those who try to reform such institutions and explicitly denies that this is where his project leads. . . . At best then, he seems to be left in a sort of nihilism.

Mark Neocleous, "Nietzsche and Postmodernism," *The Ethical Record* 97, 3 (April 1992), pp. 12–13.

17. Jane Addams, "The Subjective Necessity for Social Settlements," *Twenty Years at Hull House* (New York: MacMillan, 1910), pp. 115–117.

18. Robert N. Bellah et al., *op. cit.*, p. 137.

19. Stephen Toulmin, "The Tyranny of Principles," *The Hastings Center Report* 11, 6 (December 1981), p. 35. Nel Noddings is particularly careful to delimit the range of an "ethics of caring" although I think she has not paid enough attention to the relevance of care to a social ethics and a public morality. See *Caring, A Feminine Approach to Ethics and Moral Education* (Berkeley, Calif.: University of California Press, 1984).

Chapter Ten

Mutuality, Solidarity and Diversity

ON BEING IN NEED

I hope that I have shown that "community service" is not one but many and that this is a matter of differences of idea and not just a fact of practice. As promised, I am still an advocate of it but, to be worth supporting, community service must meet the conditions of moral democracy—mutuality, solidarity and diversity[1]—or else it is only the benevolent activism that generated Rachel's dilemma.

Community service has been a response to actual or perceived crisis—a wave of new immigrants, a war, a depression, more and more homeless people on the streets, welfare dependency, single parent families, a drug "culture," or what have you. It is no accident, then, that William James is a common reference for talk about community service. He appeals to our affinity for crisis when he calls for a "moral equivalent to war." And he appeals to our moral sensibilities when he urges the normalization of the transformation of our behavior under threat. Interest in community service, however, continues to follow on the dramatic event. Recall that recent legislation mobilized support around the conviction that having lived through a "decade of greed," we had raised up a generation that cared for neither country nor community. The young were the crisis. But, scarcely two years later, our interest has diminished and community service programs are modestly funded at best.

Absent crisis, we comfort ourselves with the notion that "doing our thing" is really the best way to serve the commonwealth. A democracy of agreements—which is our inheritance from the "founding fathers"—elevates self-interest to a moral ideal. Its outcome, in what John Dewey called the "old individualism,"[2] invites us to invest our idealism in the workings of a perfected private life. The "old individualism" assumed that an "invisible hand" would keep collective things going well and that common cultural values would provide us with good sense. Neither assumption is defensible under conditions of a corporate economy and of lost connections.

Usually, we look for James' "moral equivalent" after the crisis has passed. We look backward, attracted by the hope of perpetuating the experience of adventure and self-sacrifice. We recall, with a certain fondness, the good feelings and the sense of accomplishment when patriotism dominated our lives. Like military veterans we tell "war stories" that grow in the telling as our distance from the event increases. Thus even the "great depression" takes on a romantic glow in the recollection. Of course, when a crisis persists, we become numb and blind. We walk past a homeless man or woman without paying attention and pretty soon, we are able to walk past without realizing that he or she is there at all.[3]

Typically, when we reflect on our indifference—when it is called to our attention—we accuse ourselves of moral insensitivity. Guilt becomes a convenient, even self-serving, reaction. But I think we are wrong to try to perpetuate our responses to danger in permanent form. We forget, all too conveniently, that emergency responses are not unalloyed goods. In our anxiety for a "moral equivalent," we ignore those other behaviors and attitudes that are also part of how we deal with danger. In war, we invent an enemy who is entirely evil, restrict freedom in the name of defense, and mislead ourselves into calling aggression defense, and so on. We enjoy our virtue too much. In short, we should be grateful we have not found a "moral equivalent" or we might have found ourselves condemned to live under "Spartan" conditions, conditions of permanent mobilization. It is not incidental, although foreign to James' intent, that such an incarnation of community service exists quite comfortably under totalitarianism.

Crisis is also a point of view. So, we democrats feel ourselves in crisis when radical inequality appears between doer and done-to. Puzzled, we work out variations on the theme of neediness ranging from paternalism to indifference. And, as we have seen, neediness tends finally to serve our egos as in the "need to be needed." By demeaning the other as a receiver of services, we confirm our alienation from him or her, reinforce our sense of power and our state of privilege. Crisis leads then to the subversion of the democrat. Nothing much changes which confirms us in our pessimism. Sooner or later, pessimism is transformed into a belief in the inadequacies of our fellow human beings. The democrat becomes a realist and crisis vanishes.

Crisis distorts. It may lead us to reject community service as wasteful, a kind of moral busy work. Denied a politics, we fail to attend to much less resolve the problems that gave rise to community service in the first place. And, when we try to use crisis as a strategy of continuing mobilization—community service as public service—we soon find out that the necessary energies are not available. Hence, we settle for lesser deeds or for no deeds at all. Community service becomes a temporary amelioration of a permanent condition and is reduced to "helping out" or volunteering. The "realist" smiles and condescends—community service, after all, can do no harm and it keeps the "do-gooders" busy. Alternatively, community service becomes one among many strategies of submission to authority as in the assignment of community service to the young in the name of institutional convenience and citizenship training. On other occasions, community service is delegated to the poor in the guise of a form of employment. And on still other occasions community service is used as a punishment.

Crisis is attractive. I think that is why we have been misled by William James' romanticism. In fact, a "moral equivalent" is the very last thing we need. The "good" things we associate with community service—helping others to be free, learning the arts of citizenship, working out relationships between idea and practice—become luxuries under conditions of mobilization. Where crisis is only a point of view, however, it serves the needs of power. Community service talk becomes self-deluding, as in a "kinder, gentler nation" that is able to tolerate the increase of homelessness, ineffective health care, deteriorating housing, and all the rest. And community service works against itself by celebrating the deeds of the doer—medals are for heroes, not victims—and by failing to listen to the done-to.

Community service would appear differently if it was conceived under conditions of ordinariness. We would simply be "of service" to each other, be for each other and not require the inducement of danger. But, crisis itself has become ordinary in a world so given to inequalities, to gaps between what is and what is desirable, to failures of response, to blindness and deafness not only to others but to one's self. It has become our expected diet, so much so that we ignore its function as a point of view. But that is to convert a point of view into a description, to move from perspective to ontology. Ordinariness, then, is really a utopian idea.

I am trying to avoid the delusions of crisis become routine. Yet, this routine is precisely what the bounded and momentary nature of community service programs acknowledges. This is, finally, the source of Rachel's dilemma. In a sense, the doer knows that he or she is doing *something* and yet, that really *doing* something—bridging the gulf between doer and done-to—is not on the agenda. The done-to is only the object of an exercise. The action simply goes on because it feels like a good thing to do or because we are told that it is a good thing to do or even because, in isolation from other events, it is a good thing to do.

"Ordinariness" as a utopian idea, suggests the following question: suppose there were no crisis, for example, no gulf between haves and have-nots, would community service be needed at all? The idea of ordinariness is, thus, directive rather than descriptive—utopia has always had this critical and heuristic function. Plato's *Republic* projected the ideal state in order to understand the human being. Bellamy's *Looking Backward* extended the logic of science in order to criticize the industrialism of entrepreneurs and exploited. More recently, it is the use of imagination that Richard Rorty calls upon,

> To keep this notion [of human solidarity] while granting Nietzsche his point about the contingently historical character of our sense of moral obligation, we need to realize that a *focus imaginarius* is none the worse for being an invention rather than [as Kant thought] a built-in feature of the human mind. The right way to take the slogan, "We have obligations to human beings simply as such" is as a means of reminding ourselves to keep trying to expand our sense of "us" as far as we can. . . . The right way to construe the slogan is as urging us to *create* a more expansive sense of solidarity than we presently have. The wrong way is to think of it as urging us to recognize such a solidarity as something that exists antecedently to our recognition of it.[4]

Ordinarily, I am in need and I am able to respond to need. I am vulnerable except as I find protections and associations in the company of others. I know that there is no way that I can meet my needs by myself. Of course, I may refuse to act upon my knowledge, may deny it, may distort it. Yet, I am in need of another, incomplete without another.[5] At the same time, I can respond, be present for and answer to the needs of another. And this is so independently of my condition as rich or poor, healthy or ailing. Accustomed to crisis, we are forced to discover the rarity of the unremarkable: the strengths and loyalties of mothers and children in the world of the poor; the support of the dying in a hospice; the risks of the rescuers in occupied Europe. Yet, these relationships should be unexceptional precisely because they are models of what human beings ordinarily are, that is, interdependent, simultaneously powerful, and needy. What is indeed worth a remark is that acts like mothering or fathering or friendliness have to become discoveries for us.

Ordinariness need not necessarily be benign. Need and response can appear in pathological, horrifying and destructive ways too—as in the sado-masochist, the street gang, the fascist state. Here too being in need and being able to respond to need are modeled for us but now it is a different model. Otherness is made external to me and I am engulfed to the point of a loss of identity in some transcending identity. Human being is, as it were, a double-edged sword. To say, "that's human" is not to say anything morally definitive.

In any case, I am both doer and done-to. I have a capacity for self-consciousness and for otherness. As Nel Noddings describes it,

> Caring involves, for the one caring, a "feeling with" the other. We might want to call this relationship "empathy," but we should think about what we mean by this term. The *Oxford Universal Dictionary* defines *empathy* as "The power of projecting one's personality into, and so fully understanding, the object of contemplation." This is, perhaps, a peculiarly rational, western, masculine way of looking at "feeling with." The notion of "feeling with" that I have outlined does not involve projection but reception. I have called it "engrossment." I do not "put myself into the other's shoes" so to speak, by analyzing his reality as objective data and then asking, "How would I feel in such a situation?" On the contrary, I set aside my temptation to analyze and to plan. I do not project; I receive the other into myself and I see and feel with the other. I become a duality. . . . The seeing and feeling are mine, but only partly and temporarily mine, as a loan to me.[6]

Community service introduces us tangibly to the reciprocities of doer and done-to. On the positive side, community service is a particular way of learning my human "being" precisely because it is an encounter of strangers with whom I am nevertheless connected by the possibility of a reciprocal interchange of positions. I can be doer; I can be done-to. On the critical side, community service is a way of challenging those relationships that separate human beings into the near-permanent haves of power and near-permanent have-nots of powerlessness. When viewed from the point of view of ordinariness, crisis may be redefined, then, as the loss of human being precisely because situations like poverty, war, lack of shelter, starvation invite misperceptions of myself and others and separations of myself from others. Under conditions of crisis the directive is clear: meet the need now and ask questions later. But as ordinary, community service is not a transference of what is mine, my surplus of wealth, power, energy, to another as in acts of charity or acts of leadership but rather a restoration of what is mine and what is yours as human beings which actual situations have subverted or even destroyed.

Approached from the perspective of ordinariness, community service is not a cyclic interest—a fad—but a continuing and comprehensive methodology. It is also an expressive activity and so serves the arts by breaking into their isolation as in a museum from other life-activities.

In the encounter of strangers, expressive activity is a likely mode of meeting, a bridge between life-worlds. Even where common cognitions and values are nearly absent, doer and done-to exchange meanings in the act—of feeding, of helping, of building, of tutoring—by acting. I learn that expression is a language.

In the doing, community service also models a vocation and criticizes the mere job. This connects community service to a religious ideal, to the monastic "laborare est orare," and to Martin Luther's idea of "the calling." And this is quite other than charity which can too quickly fall into the trap of the powerful doer and the passive done-to. But religion has no monopoly here. The decay of human productivity was, after all, the point of the Marxist criticism of the reduction of work to alienated labor.[7] From the point of view of ordinariness then, community service announces that human beings are mutual beings. Only derivatively— as a way of providing content to form, of exhibiting expressiveness— does community service become a matter of good deeds. Our habit of associating community service with a reaction to crisis has masked this affiliation with aesthetics and productivity.

It is not difficult to re-interpret the present outcomes of community service. Needing to be needed is a pale reflection of the reciprocal capacity to express and to respond—that is, under conditions of ordinariness, I understand that human beings need to be needed and also need to accept themselves as being in need. Intergenerational projects and programs that cross the lines between life-worlds are attempts to restate the ability in practice, to be for others in order to be for oneself. Under conditions of mutuality, this is as true of the resident in a nursing home as of the young visitor to it. To be a doer in the presence of the done-to is to mirror the other in myself; to be the done-to in the presence of the doer is to respond to the other in myself. Both of us are active; neither is passive. For example, it is not unusual to hear an older person report that a young partner made him or her "feel and act" young. It is also not unusual to hear the young partner report that the older person taught him or her perspective and history. Both, typically, express surprise at what has happened.

Mutuality should not be confused with similarity. It is precisely because the other remains the other and because I remain myself that community service works out. The persistence of otherness provides community service with a permanent tension that generates its interest and our energy. I do not need the stimulus of crisis to move me to action once I learn that I and the other continue to be different and, at the same time, that we can rely upon each other precisely because we are and remain different. Our needs will not echo each other and where I am in need some other is able to respond. Like art and vocation, the activity of strangers never becomes merely familiar, merely routine. The persistent otherness of the other person will surprise me. And since that otherness does persist, community service does not disappear when we dispense with the point of view of crisis.

FROM MUTUALITY TO SOLIDARITY

By itself, mutuality tempts us to universalize the interpersonal. In the encounter with strangers, it relies on the knowledge that an exchange of positions between doer and done-to is always in order. In the exchange, I remain myself and yet the other becomes an actual person for me. But, any attempt to turn this exchange of positions into an exchange with "everyone" as if they were an "each-one" turns out, to be impossible. I suspect, here, that the quarrel between "justice" and "caring" arises from this attempt, that is, to universalize caring, to personalize justice. I know that Kohlberg was aware of this problem. Typical of his writing and conversation toward the end of his life, he noted,

> Recently, Gilligan has criticized my moral theory as ignoring altruism, care, or "response." Like Durkheim, and unlike Gilligan, our theory of the just community does not make a typological dichotomy between justice and care, or assume that both are not present in each sex. For Durkheim, the collectivity was both the authority behind "the right" of rules and obligations and the object of altruistic aspiration toward "the good." Durkheim's double-aspect theory of morality is even clearer in our just community theory. Through participatory justice and democracy, a sense of the group as valuable and united, the source of altruism and solidarity, is enhanced. Through collective acts of care and responsibility for the welfare of the group and each of its members, the sense of justice is enhanced.[8]

The failure to universalize mutuality sets us up for doubt about our moral credentials. In what looks like a counsel of moral sanity, we limit ourselves to relationships of reciprocity with a known number of others like family members and a small circle of friends.[9] Too many relationships are governed by abstract rules—of procedure, of ethics—and are resigned to the functional like office friendships and contracted services. We generalize the habits of using each other and these habits replace the exchange of positions between doer and done-to. As user and used, we demean each other on the one hand and resent each other on the other. A strong sense of the dignity of the other must be imposed—by self-discipline, by powerful public rules of conduct—so that a contracted service does not deteriorate into the relationship of master and servant. This need to impose, however, invites the deterioration of democracy in whose name it was imposed.

Ironically, under conditions of the lost connection—the crisis of community is one way we speak about it—a boundaried mutuality is converted into an ideal. Expressed as the radical isolation of ethnicities and other life-worlds from each other, boundaried mutuality appears as a resurrection of tribalism. But, because real tribes are just about gone, boundaried mutuality is only arbitrary. In a world of artificially resurrected tribalisms made ordinary, community service is simply unnecessary. On one hand, people living in the public world of a democracy of agreements are told to help themselves in a competition for goods. On the other, in a reminder of nineteenth-century mutual-aid societies, people are advised to turn for service to self-help groups, to "people like us." We sing the praises of the support Korean and Chinese families provide for each other. They—or at least the ones that make the headlines—don't "go on welfare" and above all they become market-economy success stories. Jewish liberals recollect the powers of community support they heard about from their parents and grandparents. And, in the recollection find a convenient instrument for condemning others who do not or cannot engage in self-help and for dealing with the guilt of deserting their liberalism. By implication, those that do not have this possibility of insider help are simply unworthy of support.

If community service is undertaken at all, it is for functional reasons like citizenship education or getting those "other" people "off welfare." Community service is kept narrow and superficial. Symptomatically, the total enrollment of publicly supported service programs—despite the rhetoric of a short time ago—is well under a million. Religiously inspired community service might seem an exception. Yet, most of it is embedded in a missionary spirit and, as such, denies the possibility of an expanded mutuality. It is theologically impossible to imagine an exchange of positions, say between saved and damned or believer and pagan. Alternatively, religiously sponsored community service down-plays the religious commitment for the sake of social acceptance and fund raising.

The duality of us and them which characterizes boundaried mutuality neglects a middle range that can exist somewhere between tribe and society. Once upon a time, it appeared in the rich associational life of our country. Along the way, people discovered more enduring relationships and achieved implicit ends unrelated to the announced interest. Not least of all, they learned the habits of association itself. It is this learning that Robert Bellah describes as the politics of the middle range,

> In ways that Jefferson would have understood, Tocqueville argues that a variety of active civic organizations are the key to American democracy. Through active involvement in common concerns, the citizen can overcome the sense of relative isolation and powerlessness that results from the insecurity of life in an increasingly commercial society. Associations along with decentralized local administration mediate between the indi-

vidual and the centralized state, providing forms in which opinion can be publicly and intelligently shaped and the subtle habits of public initiative and responsibility learned and passed on. Associational life, in Tocqueville's thinking, is the best bulwark against the condition he feared most: the mass society of mutuality antagonistic individuals, easy prey to despotism.[10]

But associational life is tainted by compulsive ethnicity and by functionalism. Not as profound as the intimacy of lovers but deeper than the superficialities of utility, this middle range is exposed as a possibility when doer and done-to spill over the boundaries of a community service project. What begins as the intention to help an unknown other turns into an exchange of positions and into the blurring of boundaries. An "illiterate" that I meet in a "literacy project" exhibits an imaginative use of symbolism or shares a rich and fascinating biography with me. He or she becomes a proper name and not an adjective. Then I learn that it is possible for others to be known under conditions of reciprocity. Of course, they remain others and do not linger with me for very long—only now they are recognized. We have passed each other by—that is our normal and ongoing condition—but we do not forget; we come to know each other personally but not permanently. Community service without intending it is thus a move toward an experimental mutuality of the middle range in an environment that is unfriendly to it. But as mutual it is still interpersonal.

Mutuality can only take us so far. It is still a personal event. Thus, I come upon the second condition of community service, solidarity. Mutuality, after all, neglects my relationship with the stranger whom I do not encounter, neglects the idea of my readiness for encounters. Solidarity is the name of my relationship to the stranger who remains unknown—only a person in an abstract sense—but who is, like me, a human being.[11] Solidarity is then a preparation for the future and at the same time a grounding in the present. As Deborah Shogan puts it,

> Proximity to another in a family makes it possible to be aware of another's problems as well as how this person might flourish. It is far more likely that benevolent desires directed at a family member will include a desire that this person flourish as well as a desire that he or she not suffer. Benevolent desires for strangers are limited to desires that they not suffer because, without knowledge, it is not possible to desire, in more than a general way, that a stranger flourishes. With this knowledge, someone is no longer a stranger. This difference creates a barrier which separates us from strangers. Strangers are often seen as objects among other objects. Breaking down barriers between oneself and a stranger is more easily done if we are in a state of what Gabriel Marcel calls *disponibilité*—a state of availability or receptiveness. If I am not available to a stranger, there will

not be an opportunity for an opening to appear in the barrier which separates us. Being available means that acts of communion are possible with strangers even if, to use Buber's example, they are as fleeting as the glance between two people in an air-raid shelter or between two people in a concert hall.[12]

In a sense, Defoe's *Robinson Crusoe* can be understood as a commentary on solidarity. Before Friday appears on the scene, Crusoe is ready; he may be said to have a relationship of solidarity with the (any) unknown stranger. Even if Friday had never appeared, that relationship would exist. But, when he does appear, mutuality is added to solidarity; the potential has become actual in at least one event. Both are learned relationships, however. Had Crusoe been raised by wolves—to use another favorite theme of poets and story-tellers—then mutuality between Crusoe and Friday might well have occurred but Crusoe's capacity for solidarity would have developed with a different content.

Solidarity is an act of imagination in the absence of an actual encounter. As Rorty comments, "It is to be achieved not by inquiry but by imagination, the imaginative ability to see strange people as fellow sufferers."[13] With solidarity, acknowledgments of relationships I could have, and in particular, relationships of being needed and being in need, become part of my awareness of myself. But, solidarity is no less actual. It is, in Dewey's sense, a "habit" of character, a consistent readiness to act, to respond in the presence of an encountered other. By contrast, we often confuse solidarity with our relationship to an abstraction like "humankind." That, of course, doesn't work—is neither a relationship nor a readiness for it—as reflected in the mocking sentence, "I love humankind but can't stand human beings." The same error is reflected in the socialist idea of the "solidarity" of the working class, a solidarity which was betrayed over and over again. As Carey McWilliams remarks,

> The creed of universal fraternity derives much of its appeal from these dangers and deficiencies of the romantic dyad. My relation to mankind is, of all the relations and kindred of men, that which demands the least psychological risk; it is most automatic, the most stable, the longest-lasting. If I must grieve whenever the bell tolls, I am never bereft: some of my kinsmen will remain. Indeed, I need not grieve much—even, lest I suggest some preference among my brethren, should not grieve much—for each loss is small compared to what remains. The "love of humanity" too, reduces any fear that I will be injured by access to myself which I have given to another, for I will have given no individual much, if anything. It is possible to love everyone equally only if one loves nothing in particular.[14]

Repairing the neglect of solidarity is a more likely reconstruction of the lost connection than the nostalgia for communities that cannot be revived. Community service is a method for learning to be ready for that reconstruction. It thus carries the burden of mutuality, the actual encounter of strangers, and is at the same time preparation for future encounters. In that act of preparation, the relationship with the encounter-that-does-not-happen is already prefigured. As it were, community service models relationships in the world of events that might not happen but could. This is not, of course, only a fact of feeling and sensitivity, although it is certainly that. Solidarity entails cognitive readiness too. In that sense, it gives a certain "spin" to the notion of transcultural literacy. Basic to that cognition is recognition, the capacity to know when an encounter is at hand and with whom. In this way, solidarity connects to schooling, justifies schooling—for example, in world history, comparative anthropology, languages—as other than, the learning of utilitarian skills or of academic ends-in-themselves. Above all, solidarity calls for a certain generosity of perception, the will to find the other unthreatening in his or her otherness and to acknowledge the legitimacy of the call of the other upon me.

In the context of solidarity, altruism, then, is not a saintly virtue. It is the perfected ability to exchange the positions of doer and done-to. Obviously, this doesn't just happen. It is as schooled as its opposite. Finally, mutuality and solidarity lead to the third condition for community service under a democratic inspiration. Both rely on a notion of otherness and so point to diversity as a basic form of democratic sociability.

OTHERNESS

Obviously, we find others in many different ways. They are, variously, friendly and threatening, familiar and alien, attractive and fearsome. Above all, our experience teaches that otherness is not simply a feature of the distant but of the nearby. My neighbor, my friend, my brother or sister, will force me to encounter otherness in my actual relationships.

> Friendship, (Emerson) said, was man's ultimate ideal, but because it is, men are tempted to romanticize—to believe that the other is "tantamount" to the self and not separate, or to "idolatrize" the other to the detriment of vision. The "ultimate friend" is a "dream and fable," Emerson counseled; men are always separate and imperfect, though the ideal remains valid. Actual friends must be honored, not resented, for their independence. Anticipating Nietzsche, Emerson insisted that a friend must be a "beautiful enemy" and not merely a "trivial convenience."[15]

I will encounter otherness in more extreme forms. And this will appear both as fact and as fiction, in reports of travelers and in the inventions of story-tellers. Finally, I will meet myself as other, surprising myself for better or worse, a puzzle to myself. Otherness is, in all of these senses, ordinary. It is, at the same time, a point of view. By contrast, were I to adopt a cosmopolitan point of view, as in the Enlightenment, each is like everyone and otherness vanishes.

Of course, my response to otherness is various too. I can welcome or reject it, make it an occasion of getting interested or of becoming defensive. My welcome can be patronizing or genuine. My defense can take form as a doctrine of similarities—as the sentimentalist says, "we're really all alike." Denial can also appear as exclusion, a mark of radical separation. Otherness appears not simply as differing individual identities but in collectivities: in families, tribes, nations but also in clubs, groups, careers. Indeed, I find out that much of what counts as individual identity arises within recognizable collectivities—which I have also called life-worlds. So, for example, some others tend to be more like each other than any of them are like me. And I find out too, that identities can reflect the intersections of more than one collectivity as in hyphenated names like Afro-American or Polish Catholic. Some of these collectivities are more important than others although it is not possible to tell, in advance of the fact, which of these will have priority for any given person at any given time. It is not possible to establish an objective hierarchy of collectivities, say nation before ethnicity or religion before political party or what have you.

Otherness is a confusion of inheritances and influences. Looking backward, Bellah identifies otherness with what he and his associates call "communities of memory."

> People growing up in communities of memory not only hear the stories that tell how the community came to be, what its hopes and fears are, and how its ideals are exemplified in outstanding men and women; they also participate in the practices—ritual, aesthetic, ethical—that define the community as a way of life. We call these "practices of commitment" for they define the patterns of loyalty and obligation that keep the community alive. And if the language of the self-reliant individual is the first language of American moral life, the languages of tradition and commitment in communities of memory are "second languages" that most Americans know as well and which they use when the language of the radically separate self does not seem adequate.[16]

But memory fades and otherness, under modern democratic conditions, is a matter of choosings and not just of inheritings. Indeed, these choosings now extend to matters once thought inherited like family and faith. Separation from the tribe today is usual—we are, as we say, a mobile society—and religious experiment is usual too. Unlike Abraham, we do not need to "break the idols"of the tribe in order to find our way from faith to faith to faith. The domination of functionalism is, in this context, a defense against this confusion and so against otherness. The virtues of function are standardization, routine, regularity, dependability. Above all, there can be no surprises. Otherness as the opposite of these is both exciting and frightening.

The encounter between confusion and dependability makes a cause out of otherness to which we give the name, "diversity." The issue of diversity, however, is not simply one of race or class or caste and the resolution of the issue is not simply one of inclusion, toleration and appreciation. Once the possibility of otherness opens up in as radical a form as it has now taken—diversity run wild or the normalization of differing "life-styles" and "life-worlds"—then, in a sense, human need and human response acquire novel content more and more rapidly. Added to the usual concerns of need—the typical issues of having and not having that stir the reformer—the encounter with strangers moves onto a new territory. Community service in meeting the conditions of diversity initiates us into the organized practice of otherness. Above all, like art and like vocation, it denies the temptation to "remain at home." As an encounter with strangers, it forces us to be travelers. So, community service, like art and vocation, becomes even more urgent under an ordinary, that is, utopian, point of view. From the point of view of crisis, community service is only a good and useful project. As an encounter with strangers becomes, as it were, itself an over-arching way of living, community service along with art and vocation becomes part of a race-pedagogy. "Being at home" has already been radically redefined and we are not ready.

To be sure, we are growing accustomed to the language of diversity. At the same time, our resistance does not disappear. Nostalgia is one form resistance takes; functionalism is another. There is something comforting—if aesthetically impoverished—in the fact that wherever we go we seem not to have left familiar places behind. Goods for sale, houses and public buildings, airports and shops and roads are homogeneously present and presented. National—and now international—TV and radio build a common but restrictive language for us. This homogeneity as a defense against leaving home exacts the price of superficiality. The encounter with strangers can all too easily turn into an encounter with "people like us" or, more likely, into the illusion that it is an encounter with "people like us," people who only look like strangers but really aren't. When this happens, community service fails to contribute to a discourse of diversity. As Fred Newmann writes,

> A persisting problem, however, is how to nurture in schools a culture of conversation in which students can talk honestly and seriously about personal dimensions of civic participation. Authentic discourse is usually

suppressed by the belief that the purpose of teaching is to transmit fixed knowledge to students so that they can reproduce it in identical form for the teacher, by rewarding students for playing the game of telling teachers what they want to hear rather than asking and answering questions which students consider important, and by enormous efforts to keep order and control over masses of students. In pursuing the agenda for reflection [on the experience of community service or service learning] outlined here, we must work constantly on the problem of building authentic discourse.[17]

Schools and the community service they teach are still inadequate to the task of "traveling" away from home. They are scenes of unresolved controversy over "multi-cultural" curricula and bi-lingual education to take two examples of the problems attendant on "leaving home." At the same time school people on all sides of the debate know the growing presence of a varied population of students, families, and teachers. The modern democratic state meets diversity too, although not without pain as in affirmative action, the struggle to "recognize" the social presence and the rights of homosexuals, the continuing struggle against racism and sexism to name but a few. Under conditions of otherness, however, the easier habits of diversity that are already being formed will come under attack—not only from those who want to restore things as they were but from those whose form of otherness is not yet within the discourse of diversity. Again, as with mutuality and solidarity, community service does not need to be justified only in the condition of crisis. Otherness demands it.

PRACTICE AND DISCOURSE

Community service introduces concreteness into a "conversation" that would otherwise deal in merely symbolic encounters. Indeed, without it—and work and art—we would, as it were, be looking at the travelogue but not doing the traveling, and for ethics and politics, this is a particularly serious indictment. At the same time, the appeal to practice is dangerous, particularly in an environment that invites us to be spectators, to operate "by the numbers" and to pay for surrogates. We are easily misled into confusing doing with secondary activities like fundraising, going to meetings, signing petitions and the like. Doing itself can easily deteriorate into a standard function, an abstraction. However, the call to "do something"—even to "do anything"—comes to us as a relief, even a pleasure. It reaches to our sense that something is awry when our reality reaches us by abstraction. Of course, we are taught to behave as if we should not want to "get our hands dirty" and so we value the maneuver of symbols, particularly symbols of hierarchy and power, above the handling of things. But at the same time, we are not entirely won over by the lesson. Community service, then, is welcomed as action is welcomed. Indeed, just because it is a relief from the burdens of passivity—for example, the passivity of a schooling trapped in academicism, a politics trapped in expertise, and a vocation trapped in administration—it becomes a "good" whose credentials are not carefully reviewed. It is, in short, good to be doing good—just that, and nothing more. To raise questions—beyond questions of improving our practices—is even resented.

As a practice, community service is shaped by its setting which puts boundaries around what is to be introduced and how and by whom. Practices, however, are available to manipulation in alternative and even contradictory ways. Under authoritarian conditions, practice is set by the reinforcement of a particular loyalty against the competing and often threatening loyalties of alien others. Patriotism, for example, becomes exclusionary. Civic obligation in this environment would sharply isolate us and them and sharply delineate doer and done-to.

Crisis is a partner of authoritarianism. The temptation, of course, is to name a crisis where none exists or to perpetuate authority after its reason has vanished. Authority becomes our habit like released prisoners who continue to pace a six-foot cell. In an emergency, response needs to be direct, swift, unquestioned. There are those who know and those who do. It follows, then, that community service set in the perspective of crisis is vulnerable to authoritarianism. A look back at the CCC and the decision to assign its operation to the military is instructive. The struggle of Camp William James for civilian and participatory control and its failure is equally instructive. In an interview, Robert Coles identifies that danger in a different way when he comments,

> I would hate to see community service limited to minority students, for instance, to work out their own sensitivity to their own experience. I would hate to see legislation written in such a way that only the poor students are being prompted into doing the service because it offers financial benefit. Some of the students who need community service the most, I think, come from well-to-do backgrounds, students who are so geared to competitiveness and greedy self-assertion that we really are in serious moral jeopardy. Community service is a means for us, perhaps, to get some kind of moral assistance.[18]

"Learning by doing," the appeal of community service to the progressive, is a truncated slogan. As such, it is misleading advice until we specify what and who the doers are, what and who the done-to are, and what their relationships to each other are and are expected to become. We may, in other words, learn precisely the wrong lessons from community service if we forget that practice as such can serve alternative ends and values.

We speak as if community service carried its moral credentials within itself. But that is not the case. In the choosing, practice—which is the genius of community service—must meet the conditions of mutuality, solidarity and otherness. Mutuality announces the actual meeting of strangers in a particular way, the reciprocal encounters of doer and done-to, the capacity to be active, to accept, to move between, and to sustain self respect in the exchange. Solidarity prepares us for the encounter-not-yet. And otherness insures that the stranger we encounter is indeed a stranger and not simply a misperception. So, a discourse of diversity involves us in the deliberate interchange of positions and not only of ideas and symbols. Above all, it presumes that this interchange is available to all and is not the possession of a privileged few.

Having cautioned against sentimentality and crisis, I end as an advocate of community service. It arms us against the pressures of passivity and abstractness that invade the ways in which we know and do under modern conditions. It puts us in position to do for ourselves and to be done-to for ourselves. In that, it is a radical instrument for stripping away the veil of indirectness that, all too often, is our social reality. Much like the prisoners in Plato's cave, we confuse shadows with what is, particularly as names and labels and categories multiply. We are too easily distanced from each other and the instruments for bridging that distance like the media and tourism only increase it. So, community which once entailed connection becomes the compulsive self-chosen and boundaried life-style association in a diversity run wild. As against this, community service can re-connect doer and done-to.

Because community service is worth advocating only as it becomes a critical instrument of personal and social conduct, it is likely that its popularity will fade just as it is doing its work. After all, the passion and the knowledge that are aroused in the exchange of doer and done-to can be very troubling to a *status quo*, even a democratic *status quo*. As Carey McWilliams points out,

> All intimate relationships are dangerous. A man bares his soul, revealing his affection and admiration for another; he thereby subjects himself to the risk that his fellow will prove false and will use these acknowledged weaknesses against him. Too, a sincere but weak fidelity may be undermined by conflicting loyalties. These perils, characteristic of all intense relations, will seem greater to those trained to play the traditional masculine role with its emphasis on independence and the corresponding fear of acknowledging the "feminine" side of man's nature. . . . That anxiety, moreover, is only one of the problems which beset those who would enter a fraternal covenant.[19]

Questions will be asked—as Blacks and Latinos asked them, as Peace Corps veterans asked them, and as Rachel asked them. And the routine answers will be inadequate. But, taking experience seriously—as community service expects us to do—makes us vulnerable. As John Dewey remarked,

> Let us admit the case of the conservative: if we once start thinking, no one can guarantee where we shall come out, except that many objects, ends, and institutions are doomed. Every thinker puts some portion of an apparently stable world in peril and no one can wholly predict what will emerge in its place.[20]

Ironically, the community service that emerged from the consensus around the 1990 legislation, and that emerges as schools and colleges adopt a "community service requirement," will turn out to be unexpectedly subversive of its proponents' intentions. They see it as peaceable, unthreatening and polite. It is offered as controlled activism—an activism without politics. However, a community service worth doing must lose its consensus and its innocence. At that point it becomes worthy of our support.

NOTES

1. In working on this theme, I am particularly indebted to the thought of Richard Rorty although, as is obvious, I do not share his radical pluralism.

2. See John Dewey, *Individualism Old and New* (New York: Capricorn, 1962).

3. The phenomenon of the "invisible poor" was brilliantly documented by Michael Harrington in his book, *The Other America* (New York: MacMillan, 1962).

4. Richard Rorty, *Contingency, Irony, and Solidarity* (New York: Cambridge University Press, 1989), p. 196.

5. On reading Plato's Symposium, I used to pass by Aristophanes' description of the origins of love in the search of two separated halves of persons seeking the restoration of their original union. Seeming a comic intervention in a serious discussion of love, I now think this notion of union, of completion, is an acute rendering of the experience of the reciprocity of need and response. See "Symposium," *The Dialogues of Plato*, trans. Benjamin Jowett (New York: Random House, 1937), vol. 1, p. 317.

6. Nel Noddings, *Caring* (Berkeley: University of California Press, 1984), p. 30.

7. For discussion of this theme, see Erich Fromm, *Marx's Concept of Man* (New York: Ungar, 1961).

8. Lawrence Kohlberg, "The Just Community Approach to High School Moral Education," unpublished paper, undated but probably mid–1980s, p. 10.

9. While I have found Nel Noddings' work on "caring" most valuable to my thinking—as should be obvious—on this point her ideas trouble me. She writes

> Although I understand why several writers have chosen to speak of special kinds of caring appropriate to particular relationships, I shall claim that these efforts obscure the fundamental truth. At bottom, all caring involves engrossment. The

> engrossment need not be intense nor need it be pervasive in the life of the one-caring, but it must occur. This requirement does not force caring into the model of romantic love, as some critics fear, for our engrossment may be latent for long periods. We may say of caring as Martin Buber says of love, "it endures, but only in the alternations of actuality and latency." The difference that this approach makes is significant. Whatever roles I assume in life, I may be described in constant terms as one-caring. Formal constraints may be added to the fundamental requirement, but they do not replace or weaken it.

She seems to universalize this single view of relationships and so caring stops short of a genuine social ethics. Nel Noddings, *op. cit.*, p. 17; see also "Construction of the Ideal," pp. 104–131.

10. Robert N. Bellah et al., *Habits of the Heart* (New York: Harper and Row, 1985), p. 38.

11. I have, on occasion, speculated on the relationship to other beings under the heading of "companionship." That, however, would take me much too far afield for the present essay. See Howard B. Radest, "A Humanist's Companions: Democracy Reconstructed," *The Devil and Secular Humanism* (New York: Praeger, 1990), Chapter 8, pp. 119–141.

12. Debra Shogan, *Care and Moral Motivation* (Toronto, Canada: OISE Press, 1988), pp. 73–74.

13. Richard Rorty, *op. cit.*, p. xvi.

14. Wilson Carey McWilliams, *The Idea of Fraternity in America* (Berkeley: University of California Press, 1973), p. 48.

15. Wilson Carey McWilliams, *op. cit.*, p. 16.

16. Robert N. Bellah et al., *op. cit.*, p. 154.

17. Fred M. Newman, "Reflective Civic Participation," *Combining Service and Learning*, Jane C. Kendall and Associates, eds. (Raleigh, N.C.: National Society for Internships and Experiential Education, 1990), vol. 1, p. 82.

18. Arthur Levine (1989), "Learning by Doing Through Public Service: For Students and Faculty Alike," an interview with Robert Coles, *op. cit.*, Jane C. Kendall and Associates, vol. 2, pp. 166–167.

19. Wilson Carey McWilliams, *op. cit.*, p. 18.

20. *Intelligence in the Modern World*, ed. Joseph Ratner (New York: Modern Library, 1939), p. v.

Bibliography

Addams, Jane. *Twenty Years at Hull House*. New York: MacMillan, 1910.

Belenky, Mary Field, and others. *Women's Ways of Knowing*. New York: Basic Books, 1986.

Bellah, Robert N., and others. *The Good Society*. New York: Alfred A. Knopf, 1991.

————. *Habits of the Heart*. New York: Harper and Row, 1985.

Black, Algernon D. *The Young Citizens*. New York: Ungar, 1962.

Boyer, Ernest. *High School: A Report on Secondary Education in America*. New York: Harper and Row, 1983.

Boyer, Ernest, and Fred Hechinger. *Higher Learning in the Nation's Service*. Washington, D.C.: Carnegie Foundation for the Advancement of Teaching, 1981.

Buckley, William F. *Gratitude*. New York: Random House, 1990.

Coit, Stanton. *Neighborhood Guilds*. London: Swan Sonnenschein, 1892.

Conrad, Dan, and Diane Hedin. *High School Community Service: A Review of Research and Programs*. Madison, Wis.: National Center on Effective Secondary Schools, 1989.

Cremin, Lawrence A. *American Education, The Metropolitan Experience 1876–1980*. New York: Harper and Row, 1988.

Damon, William. *The Moral Child*. New York: Free Press, 1988.

Danzig, Richard, and Peter Szanton. *National Service: What Would It Mean?* Lexington, Ken.: Lexington Books, 1986.

Delve, Cecilia I., Suzanne D. Mintz, and Greig M. Stewart, eds. *Community Service as Values Education*. New Directions for Student Services, Number 50 (Summer 1990). San Francisco: Jossey-Bass, 1990.

194 Bibliography

De Tocqueville, Alexis. *Democracy in America*. Edited by Andrew Hacker. New York: Washington Square Press, 1976.

Dewey, John. *Democracy and Education*. New York, Free Press, 1966.

———. *Individualism Old and New*. New York: Capricorn, 1962.

———. *Intelligence in the Modern World*. Edited by Joseph Ratner. New York: Modern Library, 1939.

Drucker, Peter F. *Managing the Nonprofit Organization*. New York: Harper Collins, 1990.

Durkheim, Emil. *Moral Education. A Study in the Theory and Application of the Sociology of Education*. New York: Free Press, 1973.

Eisenberg, Nancy. *Altruistic Emotion, Cognition and Behavior*. Hillsdale, N.J.: Erlbaum Associates, 1986.

Ellis, Susan J., and Katherine H. Noyes. *By the People*. San Francisco: Jossey-Bass, Revised Edition, 1990.

Engels, Frederick. *The Condition of the Working Class in England* (1892). London: Panther Books, 1969.

Friere, Paolo. *Pedagogy of the Oppressed*. New York: Continuum Publishing, 1970.

Fromm, Erich. *Marx's Concept of Man*. New York: Ungar, 1961.

Gilligan, Carol. *In a Different Voice*. Cambridge, Mass.: Harvard University Press, 1982.

Gilligan, Carol, and Edith B. Phelps. *Seeking Conversation: New Insights and Questions for Teachers*. Cambridge, Mass.: Harvard Graduate School of Education, 1988.

Goldman, Eric F. *Rendezvous with Destiny*. New York: Vintage Books, 1955.

Goodlad, John. *A Place Called School*. New York: McGraw Hill, 1984.

Greenleaf, Robert K. *Servant Leadership*. New York: Paulist Press, 1977.

Habermas, Jurgen. *Communication and the Evolution of Society*. Boston: Beacon, 1979.

Harrington, Michael. *The Other America*. New York: MacMillan, 1962.

Harrison, Charles H. *Student Service: The New Carnegie Unit*. Princeton, N.J.: The Carnegie Foundation for the Advancement of Teaching, 1987.

Himmelfarb, Gertrude. *Poverty and Compassion*. New York: Knopf, 1991.

Hofstadter, Richard. *The Age of Reform*. New York: Vintage Books, 1955.

Hunt, Morton. *The Compassionate Beast (The Scientific Inquiry Into Human Altruism)*. New York: Anchor Books, 1991.

Kendall, Jane C. and Associates. *Combining Service and Learning*, Two Vols. Raleigh, N.C.: National Society for Internships and Experiential Education, 1990.

Kohlberg, Lawrence. *Essays on Moral Development*, Vol. 1, *The Philosophy of Moral Development*. San Francisco: Harper and Row, 1981.

Kuhmerker, Lisa, ed. *The Kohlberg Legacy for the Helping Professions*. Birmingham, Ala.: R.E.P. Books, 1991.

Jagger, Alison M. *Feminist Politics and Human Nature*. Totowa, N.J.: Rowman and Allanheld, 1983.

James, William. *The Moral Equivalent of War and Other Essays*. New York: Harper and Row, 1971.

Janowitz, Morris. *The Reconstruction of Patriotism: Education for Civic Consciousness*. Chicago: University of Chicago Press, 1983.

Levison, Lee. *Community Service Programs in Independent Schools*. Boston: The National Association of Independent Schools, 1986.

Lewis, Anne C. *Facts and Faith: A Status Report on Youth Service*. Washington, D.C.: William T. Grant Foundation Commission on Youth and America's Future, 1988.

Luce, Janet, ed. *Service-Learning: An Annotated Bibliography*. Raleigh, N.C.: National Society for Internships and Experiential Learning, 1988.

McWilliams, Wilson Carey. *The Idea of Fraternity in America*. Berkeley, Calif.: University of California Press, 1973.

Maslow, Abraham. *Religions, Values and Peak Experiences*. New York: Viking, 1970.

Moskos, Charles C. *A Call to Civic Service*. New York: Free Press, 1988.

Newmann, Fred, and R. Rutter. *The Effect of High School Community Projects on Students' Social Development*. Washington, D.C.: National Institute of Education, 1983.

Noddings, Nel. *Caring, A Feminine Approach to Ethics and Moral Education*. Berkeley, Calif.: University of California Press, 1984.

Oliner, Samuel P., and M. Pearl. *The Altruistic Personality*. New York: Free Press, 1988.

Perry, William G., Jr. *Forms of Intellectual and Ethical Development in the College Years: A Scheme*. New York: Holt, Rhinehard and Winston, 1970.

Preiss, Jack J. *Camp William James*. Norwich, Vt.: Argo Press, 1978.

Rachels, James. *Created from Animals (The Moral Implications of Darwinism)*. Oxford, England: Oxford University Press, 1991.

Radest, Howard B. *Can We Teach Ethics*. New York: Praeger, 1989.

———. *Toward Common Ground*. New York: Ungar, 1969.

Riis, Jacob A. *The Making of an American*. New York: MacMillan, 1901.

Rolzinski, Catherine A. *The Adventure of Adolescence: Middle School Students and Community Service*. Washington, D.C.: Youth Service America, 1990.

Rorty, Richard. *Contingency, Irony and Solidarity*. Cambridge, England: Cambridge University Press, 1989.

Salmond, John A. *The Civilian Conservation Corps, 1933–1942: A New Deal Case Study*. Durham, N.C.: Duke University Press, 1967.

Schwartz, Karen. *What You Can Do for Your Country*. New York: William Morrow and Company, 1991.

Scott, Anne Firor. *Natural Allies, Women's Associations in American History*. Urbana, Ill.: University of Illinois Press, 1992.

Shogan, Debra. *Care and Moral Motivation*. Toronto, Canada: OISE Press, 1988.

Sizer, Theodore. *Horace's Compromise*. Boston: Houghton Mifflin, 1984.

Stoskopf, Alan L., and Margot Stern Strom. *Choosing to Participate*. Brookline, Mass.: Facing History and Ourselves National Foundation, 1990.

Textor, Robert B., ed. *Cultural Frontiers of the Peace Corps*. Cambridge, Mass.: MIT Press, 1976.

Thomsen, Moritz. *A Peace Corps Chronicle*. Seattle: University of Washington Press, 1970.

Westbrook, Robert B. *John Dewey and American Democracy*. Ithaca: Cornell University Press, 1991.

Wigginton, Eliot. *Sometimes a Shining Moment: The Foxfire Experience*. Garden City, N.Y.: Doubleday, 1985.

Wills, Garry. *Democracy's Next Generation, A Study of Youth and Teachers*. Washington, D.C.: People for the American Way, 1989.

———. *The Forgotten Half: Pathways to Success for America's Youth and Young Families*. Washington, D.C.: William T. Grant Foundation Commission on Work, Family and Citizenship, 1988.

———. *Inventing America: Jefferson's Declaration of Independence*. Garden City, N.Y.: Doubleday, 1978.

Index

About the Author

HOWARD B. RADEST is the retired Director of Ethical Culture-Fieldston Schools in New York City and an Adjunct Professor of Philosophy at the University of South Carolina-Beaufort. He is the author of several books including *Toward Common Ground* (1969), *Can We Teach Ethics?* (Praeger, 1989), and *The Devil and Secular Humanism* (Praeger, 1990).